When Broken Glass Floats

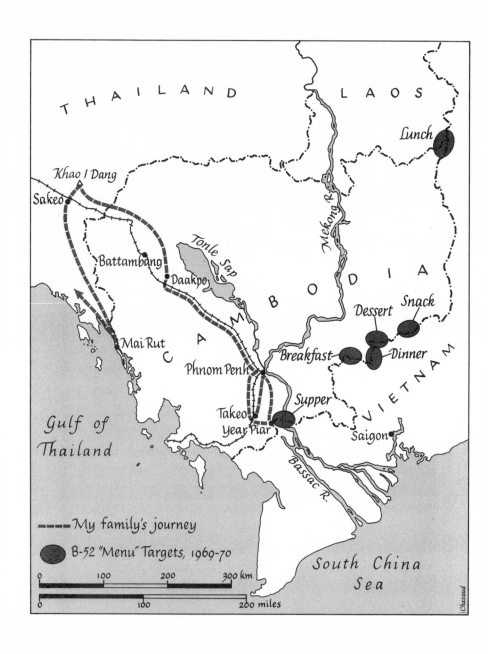

THAILAND

LAOS

Lunch

Khao I Dang

Sakeo

Battambang

Tonle Sap

Daakpo

C A M B O D I A

Mekong R.

Dessert   Snack

Mai Rut

Breakfast   Dinner

Phnom Penh

Supper

Takeo
Year Piar

V I E T N A M

Saigon

Gulf of
Thailand

Bassac R.

▬ ▬ ▬ ▬ My family's journey

🔴 B-52 "Menu" Targets, 1969-70

| 0 | 100 | 200 | 300 km |

| 0 | 100 | 200 miles |

South China
Sea

Chazaud

WHEN
BROKEN
GLASS
FLOATS

Growing Up under the Khmer Rouge

A MEMOIR

Chanrithy Him

W. W. NORTON & COMPANY
New York • London

AUTHOR'S NOTE:
Although I have photographic memories of what happened
in my childhood as early as when I was three, some of the
events in this book were recounted to me as I grew up
and filled in by my relatives. To protect some people,
I have changed their names in the book.

For information about permission to reproduce selections from this
book, write to Permissions, W. W. Norton & Company, Inc.,
500 Fifth Avenue, New York, NY 10110

The text of this book is composed in Centaur with the display set in
Lilith Light and Nuptual Script. Composition by Matrix Publishing
Services. Manufacturing by Courier Companies Inc.
Book design by Charlotte Staub

Library of Congress Cataloging-in-Publication Data

Him, Chanrithy, 1965–
When broken glass floats : growing up under the Khmer Rouge /
Chanrithy Him.
p.   cm.
ISBN 0-393-04863-2
1. Him, Chanrithy, 1965–   2. Cambodia—Politics and
government—1975–1979.   3. Political atrocities—Cambodia.
4. Political refugees—Cambodia—Biography.   5. Political
refugees—United States—Biography.   I. Title.
DS554.83.H56 A3 2000
959.604'2'092—dc21
[B]   99-058417

W. W. Norton & Company, Inc., 500 Fifth Avenue, New York, N.Y. 10110
www.wwnorton.com

W. W. Norton & Company Ltd., 10 Coptic Street, London WC1A 1PU

2 3 4 5 6 7 8 9 0

In dedication to

Pa and *Mak*,
I honor you.

Chea,
my idol,
who enriched my life.

Tha, Avy, Vin, and Bosaba,
who will live forever
in my memory,
I love and miss you dearly.

For Cheng,
who helped me escape
the death camp.

Please Give Us Voice

When broken glass floats, a nation drowns,
Descending to the abyss.

From mass graves in the once-gentle land,
Their blood seeps into mother earth.

Their suffering spirits whisper to her,
"Why has this happened?"

Their voice resounds in the spirit world,
Shouts through the souls of survivors,
Determined to connect, begging the world:
Please remember us.
Please speak for us.
Please bring us justice.

C. H.

CONTENTS

Acknowledgments

I remember a little girl's wish for the world to learn the bitter chill of her grief, and of the tragic death of her family. Her wish is mine and it is realized. I must thank those individuals who've helped the dream come true: Ryan Hinke, my dear, loving friend, who provides a home with precious solitude that allowed me to write this memoir.

I am grateful to Uncle Seng for bringing us to America.

I am indebted to Amy Cherry, a sensitive, shrewd, godsent editor.

Meredith Bernstein, my agent, I thank you for believing in my story. Your kind words gave me courage.

My sister Channary, who cheers me on in my journey.

I thank the Literary Arts, Inc., and those who have helped Cambodia and her people in the Khmer diaspora.

Family Tree

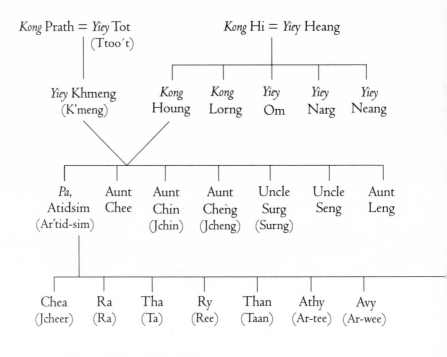

Kong Prath = *Yiey* Tot
(Ttoo′t)

Kong Hi = *Yiey* Heang

Yiey Khmeng
(K′meng)

Kong
Houng

Kong
Lorng

Yiey
Om

Yiey
Narg

Yiey
Neang

Pa,
Atidsim
(Ar′tid-sim)

Aunt
Chee

Aunt
Chin
(Jchin)

Aunt
Cheng
(Jcheng)

Uncle
Surg
(Surng)

Uncle
Seng

Aunt
Leng

Chea
(Jcheer)

Ra
(Ra)

Tha
(Ta)

Ry
(Ree)

Than
(Taan)

Athy
(Ar-tee)

Avy
(Ar-wee)

Aunt Cheng m. Uncle Sorn
(Sornne)

Uncle Surg = Aunt Heak
(Surng)

Ateek
(Ar-tteh)

Infant son

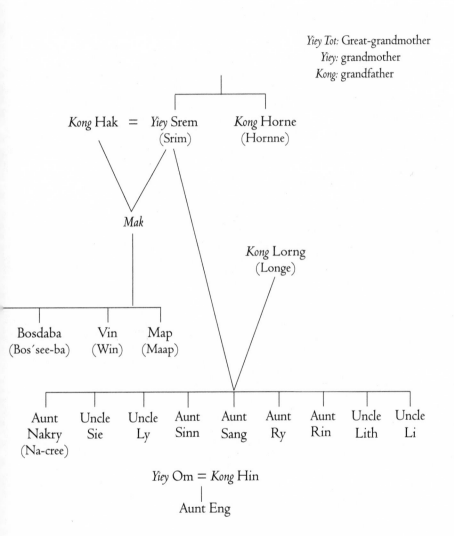

Yiey Tot: Great-grandmother
Yiey: grandmother
Kong: grandfather

Kong Hak   =   *Yiey* Srem   *Kong* Horne
                 (Srim)   (Hornne)

Mak

Kong Lorng
(Longe)

Bosdaba   Vin   Map
(Bos´see-ba)   (Win)   (Maap)

Aunt   Uncle   Uncle   Aunt   Aunt   Aunt   Aunt   Uncle   Uncle
Nakry   Sie   Ly   Sinn   Sang   Ry   Rin   Lith   Li
(Na-cree)

Yiey Om = *Kong* Hin
Aunt Eng

PREFACE

ᗩ Seed of Survival

To every thing there is a season, and a time to every purpose
under the heaven.   —ECCLESIASTES 3:1

I wake, confused. *It's still dark.* My past has haunted me again.
Memory has taken me back in my dreams, a hapless passenger, even
though I'm no longer in Cambodia. In my nightmares I am trying
to keep a childhood promise that I made to the spirit of my mother,
who came to me in my sleep twenty years ago. A promise made in
another dream which I must honor.

In this dream, I am crying out to God to help me find Map, my
three-year-old brother. Enemies are infiltrating the United States. I
hear a voice cry out. I can't distinguish words, only human fear.
*America is being invaded? This can't be happening. I fled to America to escape
war. Now where do I go?* My questions are shattered by the familiar
sound of gunfire, a hollow boom, the distant chatter of artillery that
still sends terror pulsing through my veins. The sounds are of Cambodia, but the landscape is of the Pacific Northwest. The guns speak
from somewhere I can't see, beyond a grove of pine trees in the
shadow of a mountain. The world has become a landscape of light
and shadow. Around me, a human river flows crazily out of control. People are running everywhere. A sobbing woman carries a
bundle of clothes and a child, slowed by the weight of her own ter-

ror. I am stiff in fear and shock. In the blur of faces around me, there are no Americans, only Cambodians.

I am carried along by the crowd, and yet I'm alone, without my family. *Where is Map, my baby brother?* My heart races and my head moves like a windshield wiper, looking for him. I can't find him. The sound of gunfire obliterates the human noise around me. It's getting closer and louder. My sobs accelerate, and I begin to gasp for air. My lungs are screaming, my insides crying out in unison with my mind. I can no longer run and drop to the ground. I scream with all my might: *No, my promise! I can't lose another brother! God, help me.*

It has been twelve years since I came to America. From here, I look back upon a childhood consumed by war. I could recognize the sounds of war at the age of four, when the spillover from the Vietnam conflict forced my family from the home my parents had spent their life savings to build in the affluent Takeo province in southern Cambodia. By the age of ten, I was forced to work in child labor camps, among thousands of children separated from parents and siblings by a system of social slavery instituted by the Khmer Rouge in their bizarre quest to create a utopian society.

Family ties were suddenly a thing of suspicion. Control was everything. Social ties, even casual conversations, were a threat. *Angka*, the organization, suddenly became your mother, your father, your God. But *Angka* was a tyrannical master. To question anything—whom you could greet, whom you could marry, what words you could use to address relatives, what work you did—meant that you were an enemy to your new "parent." That was *Angka*'s rule. To disobey meant the *kang prawattasas*, the wheel of history,* would run over

---

* The wheel of time or change. The Khmer Rouge often used such terms to threaten us, to force us to follow their rules, their revolution. If we didn't follow their rules, the wheel of history would run over us. This could mean punishment or death.

you. That's what they told us as we cast our eyes downward under the weight of their threats.

Unlike so many of the children I worked with in muddy rice fields and irrigation canals, unlike many in my own family, I outran the wheel of history. I survived starvation, disease, forced labor, and refugee camps. I survived a world of violence and despair.

I survived.

Since 1981 my new home has been mostly in Oregon, as verdant as the land I left, but different. The coconut and papaya groves, the mango trees that grew in front of my childhood home, have been replaced by mountains dense with pine and fir, timber-flanked valleys, and cold, clear streams. From dramatic coastal cliffs to lacy spigots of waterfalls that feed the Columbia River Gorge, the sites, scenes, and sounds of this place have become my image of America. Now, strangely, it has also become the landscape of my nightmares.

In Cambodia the term for childbirth is *chhlong tonlé*. Literally translated, it means "to cross a large river," to weather the storm. Looking back, I have crossed the river on my own, without my mother. I have started a new life in a new country. I have learned a new language and lived in a new culture. I have been reincarnated with a new body, but with an old soul. It lives symbiotically inside me.

In many ways I occupy a world of blurred boundaries. Since the fall of 1989, I have been involved as a researcher on the Khmer Adolescent Project, a federally funded study of post-traumatic stress disorder (PTSD) among 240 Cambodian youths who endured four years of war in Cambodia.

The need for this research was initially prompted by the observations made by Dan Dickason, an ESL (English as a second language) teacher at Cleveland High School in Portland, Oregon. In the early 1980s, Cleveland High School had experienced an influx of young immigrant Cambodians. In these students Dickason saw something unfamiliar. Once, on a trip to a high school teacher's home, a young Cambodian girl was digging in the ground and unearthed a bone. She began to unravel, screaming and running about. Slowly other Cambodian students began to share their stories. One shared stories about cannibalism. Another described how the Khmer Rouge had cut people open to eat their livers. At the time, little was known about the horrors of Cambodia. Dickason himself was in denial until he saw footage on the CBS News in May 1983 showing a mountain of human skulls in Cambodia. Then he began to pay attention. The next day he called Dr. David Kinzie, director of the Indochinese Psychiatric Program at Oregon Health Sciences University.

I was one of the Cambodian students at Cleveland High School. When three psychiatrists, Dr. William Sack, Dr. David Kinzie, and Dr. Richard Angell, came to our school to interview us, I asked them why they were so interested, what was their goal? What did they know about Cambodia that I didn't? I told my cousin and a friend of my fear of talking to them, my fear that I could not be strong about the past. That I would cry in front of strangers. Even in our relocated Cambodian communities, the past was something we had tried to leave on the road behind us.

Most of our scars were well hidden, set aside in our battle for academic success. Out of forty students at Cleveland High School who had lived under Pol Pot, half were diagnosed with PTSD, and half suffered from some form of depression. It seemed curious. Many were motivated students and some were on the honor roll. At the time, it all sounded abstract to me.

Four years later, Dr. William Sack received a grant for over $1 million from the National Institute of Mental Health to expand the research. I was approached at that time to help interpret and to interview subjects. In two weeks I suddenly had to master a brand-new vocabulary including terms like "schizophrenia," "cyclothymia," and "dysthymia." Harder still, I had to learn to ask questions that triggered memories. At twenty-four, I had no idea what I was getting into. Like soldiers going into battle, I didn't know what outcome to expect. Maybe it was better that way.

My first hint came at the end of our training. The staff had gathered to watch documentary films about Cambodia, including part of the Academy Award-winning film *The Killing Fields*. After a few minutes, I stormed out. I remember taking refuge in the women's rest room, leaning against the wall and weeping. For the first time in years, I had allowed myself to feel the pain of the past that was buried in my soul.

How familiar everything was: the fields of broken flesh; legs, arms gushing blood; corpses covered with buzzing flies; and the sweet stench of decaying flesh. I didn't need to watch this to have a better understanding of what Cambodian subjects had endured. I had lived through it myself. All I needed to do was to close my eyes and the memories came back.

And so began my dual life. As a researcher, my job was to be a cultural voyeur. I was to use my knowledge of Cambodian customs, culture, and my own wartime experiences to establish a common ground with other refugees. In theory, they would be more comfortable talking to someone who knew what they had endured. It was a strange role for me. In conducting psychiatric interviews, I was both the insider, who knew their trauma, and the outsider, the dispassionate, clinical researcher. There I sat, efficiently recording details that jogged so many of my own harsh memories. Unlike during my training experience, I couldn't run away and take sanctuary in a rest room. I couldn't stop listening when subjects' and their parents' or guardians' distressing stories awakened my emotions. My job was to listen, to record answers, and continue to ask questions, pressing until some of these people broke down as they confronted things that had been successfully repressed.

A memory of this time returns to me. Sitting in Room C in Gaines Hall, I am interviewing a woman, the mother of a subject. In the interest of reliability, I interview her about her daughter's experience as well as her own. The woman weeps when asked about her family's separation. She studies the tabletop as if the answers were projected there like a movie. While sitting only a few feet across from me, she is distant. For her, as for many subjects and their parents, this was the first time since leaving Cambodia that she could turn and face the brutality she had left behind.

Were you ever tortured by Khmer Rouge soldiers? Did you ever witness others being killed during this time? Did you ever see corpses during this time? Did you ever lose your mother or father during the Pol Pot time? Did you lose any siblings during this time? Did you ever witness the executions of family members? Did you suffer from not having enough to eat so you looked thin, had swollen legs, or a puffy stomach? Were you ever forced to do things by the Khmer Rouge soldiers against your will? . . .

These questions are sharp triggers. As soon as they leave my mouth, I too search for answers. I watch as suffering is released through the ragged sounds of sobbing. It is all I can do to offer Kleenex while I fight back my own tears. There is recognition. The woman's red, flooded eyes look briefly into mine—a directness unusual in Cambodia. She apologizes for interrupting the interview, a mark of Cambodian courtesy that survived the years of brutality. I am always amazed that some bit of humanity outlived *Angka* and is more powerful than the wheel of history.

Often the subjects meet with me in medical offices, but sometimes I am invited into their homes. I am braced for their reactions when I call them to arrange for interviews or when I'm about to interview them. Sometimes they're angry or paranoid. I try to fight it with familiarity. "Oh, I'm Sam's cousin," I tell them. "You know Sam?" Sometimes they are open, surprised that I'm interested enough to ask, referring me to other families, unwilling to let our conversation end. Sometimes they are suspicious. In 1990 Cambodia still remains home to political unrest. Pockets of the Khmer Rouge still fight. And we refugees were well aware of their deceptions. Orwell's words aptly describe the Khmer Rouge: "Big Brother is watching you." Even on the streets of Portland I look over my shoulder. And here I am on these survivors' doorstep, asking them to reveal difficult memories. The Khmer Rouge are a continent away, and yet they are not. Psychologically, they are parasites, like tapeworms that slumber within you, living passively until something stirs them to life. I was asking these subjects to wake those parasites.

The woman is crying so hard that the interview stops. In the past she had made up stories when her daughter asked "Where's *Pa?*" She could never bring herself to say that the child's father had been executed by the Khmer Rouge. "He went away, he'll be back soon," she would say. All that was left of her husband was pain, which was only compounded by the questions posed by her daughter and, now, me. I assure her that in the long run, talking about it will help. Pain was simply reality.

I am reminded of the Buddhist doctrine *Mean ruup mean tok*, which means "With a body comes suffering." I heard a monk say these words once and immediately thought them overly grim. But to survive Pol Pot is to accept this doctrine as readily as you might accept the change of the seasons, the death of winter and the rebirth of spring.

After a few hours of interviews, I am exhausted. My fingers work, recording hellish images in exquisite detail. *The memory of crude executions—seeing a pregnant woman beaten to death with a metal spade. Makeshift hospitals filled with feces; flies and rats hungry for food, human corpses, anything—everything. The memory of bodies swollen with edema. Cheeks and temples sunken with starvation.* As I note it all, my body and soul are drained. Inside these four walls I am flung back to Cambodia. A door separates me from safety. I step out into the sunshine, the rolling green campus of the Oregon Health Sciences University. I squint to get my bearings. I have escaped from Cambodia again.

Another day, another interview, another horrific reality. This time it's an account of the massacre of Cambodian refugees pushed over a mountain precipice. Thai soldiers gathered up hundreds of Cambodian refugees in 1979 and told them that they would be taken to a camp and given aid. Yet the Thai were devils in disguise. At gunpoint, they forced refugees to run down the precipice facing Cambodia. Run they did. There before their eyes rolled their children, wives, husbands, and the elderly. A carpet of bodies tumbled down the precipice as they ran, like pebbles in a rock slide. They had been shot, the subject recounts. The story paralleled a Cambodian parable: "In water one faces a crocodile, and when on land, one faces a tiger." People were caught between two devils: the Khmer Rouge and the Thai soldiers.

I dutifully record the carnage, yet my mind doesn't want to accept it. But this same inhumanity was also documented by a journalist in the *Washington Post*. I had never heard of it. How strange, I thought, to find a history lesson about my own homeland here in America. Stranger still to realize what might have been in my own life.

In the end, I know only that war is inevitable in the world as long as leaders such as Pol Pot are empowered by their kind—and as long as those who can make a difference by doing good deeds choose to look the other way. Under those conditions, more human lives will be lost, and many more children will be parentless. The cost of war is a lifelong legacy borne by children.

And I know this: As a survivor, I want to be worthy of the suffering that I endured as a child. I don't want to let that pain count for nothing, nor do I want others to endure it. This may be our greatest test: to recognize the weight of war on children. If thousands upon thousands of children will suffer and are suffering right now in the world, we must be prepared to help them. But it's folly to look at the future without an eye to the past.

The little girl within me often cries out to the adult to help and make a difference. I feel obligated to help my boss, Dr. Sack, and our colleagues understand the Cambodian children who have suffered war trauma. It's my hope that our research will make significant contributions to knowledge about the clinical and social needs of Cambodian refugees and perhaps the needs of other refugees who have suffered or will suffer a similar fate.

I also like to think that telling my story and assisting the PTSD studies are my way of avenging the Khmer Rouge. It is also my way of opposing governments that have inflicted pain and suffering on innocent children, whose trust has been exploited time and time again throughout history: during the Khmer Rouge era, the Nazi era, the Chinese Cultural Revolution, and, more recently, amid the ethnic aggression and bloodshed in Bosnia and Rwanda.

Throughout a childhood dominated by war, I learned to survive. In a country faced with drastic changes, the core of my soul was determined to never let the horrific situations take away the better part of me. I mentally resisted forces I could only recognize as evil by being a human recorder, quietly observing my surroundings, making mental notes of the things around me. There would come a day to share them, giving my voice to children who can't speak for themselves. Giving voice, as well, to my deceased parents, sisters, brothers, and extended family members, and to those whose remains are in unmarked mass graves scattered throughout Cambodia, the once-gentle land.

As a child, I believed in the power of magic. I remember sitting enthralled in our living room watching a Cambodian movie set in the Himalayas. The hero was journeying to find a wise, bearded man who knew an incantation that could save the innocents from the murderous villains of the jungle. Simple, powerful words would make robbers disappear, abolish evil forces. Palms pressed together and raised in front of the chest with eyes closed, the characters murmured in soft recitation. Immediately things were set right. *So easy,* I thought. *I just have to make it to the Himalayas.* It was obviously a place where magic dwelled.

My father knew magic. I was convinced of this. I felt him work his magic when the heavy fingers of asthma clutched my lungs. I would sit up and gasp for air, but everything was stuck. Quickly my father would open his drawer of French medicine, grab a vial and a syringe. Then the magic worked, as it always did. It was as amazing to me as the wise man of the Himalayas—one minute I was taking my last breath, the next minute I was running off to play.

Sitting before my computer, I feel the long-ago magic of my childhood, now memory's shadow. The war crushed my innocent belief in magic as neatly and efficiently as you might smash a cricket beneath your heel. At first I tried to hide inside the magic. It was a refuge against the surreal realities of war. My friends and I would pretend we had the power to raise the dead. I would talk to imaginary friends in the orchard behind our house. The guava, katot, and teap barang trees and the pond behind my home became the jungle I would have to pass through to get to the Himalayas.

For a time I thought the growing fears of the Viet Cong invasion into Cambodia in the late sixties were an abstraction, an illusion.

Time would tell me otherwise.

Time would take away the magic. And time would give it back.

Tonight the light from my computer screen reflects dull blue on my face. I feel my body and soul recovering from stress, from weeks of intense studies leading up to the MCAT, the all-day Medical College Admissions Test. Yet I feel a gnawing need to resume my writing. At first I felt it was my responsibility as a survivor. But now writing has also become my trek to the Himalayas, my search to recapture the long-lost magic in my life. This time I'm trying to use the power of words to caution the world, and in the process to heal myself. And even with an intellectual hangover from the toughest academic test I've ever taken, I'm searching for the words, the incantation, to make things right in my soul.

My heart keeps me writing despite the hour. Pushing hard has become my addiction. At first it was a lesson of necessity, my only means of surviving the Khmer Rouge regime, of outrunning the wheel of history. Being raised by educated and open-minded parents, I had advantages. I was never forced to live up to the sexist expectations of traditional Cambodian culture—a fact that would become important to my survival.

As a child trying to endure the Khmer Rouge regime, I had many questions about the strange world that had overtaken my homeland. At twelve years of age, during the Khmer Rouge regime, I asked my oldest sister, Chea, a question in the hope of understanding our pain and the loss of those I loved. Her answer became the seed of my survival, planted by a sister whom I idolized.

"Chea, how come good doesn't win over evil? Why did the Khmer Rouge win if they are bad people?"

Chea answered: " ចាញ់បានជាព្រះ ឈ្នះបានជាមារ—*jchan baan chea preah chnae baan chea mea*," which means "Loss will be God's, victory will be the devil's." When good appears to lose, it is an opportunity for one to be patient, and become like God. "But not very long, *p'yoon srey* [younger sister]," she explained, and referred to a Cambodian proverb about what happens when good and evil are thrown together into the river of life. Good is symbolized by *klok*, a type of squash, and evil by *armbaeg*, shards of broken glass. "The good will win over the evil. Now, *klok* sinks, and broken glass floats. But *armbaeg* will not float long. Soon *klok* will float instead, and then the good will prevail." Chea's eyes pierced me with an expression that reinforced her words. *"P'yoon, wait and see. It will happen."*

At age twenty-two, in 1978, Chea died of a prolonged fever and deprivation, three months before the Vietnamese incursion into Cambodia that drove the Khmer Rouge to the border. At thirteen, unable to help save her, I was angry at myself for not having *Pa's* medical knowledge, for not having learned from him. As if talking to Chea's spirit—as her wrapped-up body was being carried away to be buried in the woods—I said in my mind: *Chea, if I survive I will study medicine. I want to help people because I couldn't help you. If I die, I will learn medicine in my next life.* That vow helped me cope with my own helplessness and pain, but I never knew how it would later affect my own life in America.

In 1982, when I began high school in Portland, Oregon, my desire to study medicine was rekindled. After finishing my undergraduate studies at the University of Oregon in 1991, I was determined to become a medical doctor. It has been thirteen years since Chea's death, and I wanted to fulfill my promise to her spirit and to take up where *Pa* had left off.

In preparing for the MCAT, I had tried to shelve my memories, deliberately shoving them aside to make room for chemistry and physiology. Yet they had a way of sneaking back. Studying how the body uses carbohydrates, fat, and protein for energy would remind me of the edema that was rampant in wartime villages. The lack of salt in our diets became lethal, robbing our bodies of the ability to produce energy. In Cambodia we had a term for vitamin A deficiencies—a condition we called "blind chicken." At night, my eyes wouldn't work. With no real medicine available, the cure was a folk remedy: catch water in a banana leaf or lotus leaf and throw it into the eyes of the afflicted. Listening in the classroom and looking back, these weren't abstract lessons.

The sight of someone dressed entirely in black would also trigger a memory—the uniforms of the Khmer Rouge. And for a moment it could paralyze me as if I was under a spell. Watching a documentary on Ethiopia showing children lining up for rations would jolt me back to the muddy fields, to a time when I was as frail and exhausted as those African waifs, existing only for food. Memories seep back to me in ways I hadn't imagined. A stay in Hawaii stirred a sensory memory—moist, green smells, blossoming mango trees, dangling clusters of coconuts, the dance of palm trees at the airport, the humid breeze. The senses awakened the long-forgotten.

There are times when I've denied my own memories, when I've neglected the little girl in me. There would always be time to grieve, I told myself. I pushed down memories in pursuit of important things. Education. Medical school. I wanted to make a difference in the world, to do good deeds, fulfill a child's wish. There would be a time for memories, but I never anticipated it, never sought it out. There would be a time.

As I sit in the eerie glow of my computer screen summoning up the past, I know that it is time. I invite the memories back in, apprehensive but hungry for them. In trying to understand my drive to tell others what was scorched in my mind, I recognize my fortitude and ambition, which are rooted in the people who gave me life—my parents.

1
A Heavenly Comet Foreshadows War

The New York Times
Phnom Penh, Cambodia—March 28, 1969

(AGENCE FRANCE PRESS)

The head of state, Prince Norodom Sihanouk, charged today that "Vietnamese Communists were increasingly infiltrating into Cambodia." The prince showed newsmen here a detailed map drawn up by his general staff showing Communist implantation in Cambodia.

*M*y parents' future marriage had already been decided when they were children. Both their parents told them that someday they would marry each other. Both came from well-to-do families, which caused wide speculation about the marriage. Some thought that they were paired up because the brothers *Kong* Houng and *Kong* Lorng didn't want their wealth dispersed. This way, the family wealth was centralized. And in Cambodian culture, it's common for cousins to marry.

Fortunately, my father's feelings were in harmony with the ideas of his elders. When *Pa* turned seventeen, he fell in love with *Mak*. She was a bright girl, and strong in her ideas. As a child, she would sneak away to the Buddhist temple to learn to read and write in Khmer, and to read Pali, the language of the Cambodian bible. In time, she picked up French as well, a skill that was forbidden for women. Parents didn't want a daughter to have education for fear that she would write love letters before they had had a chance to arrange a suitable marriage. Denying education was but one way to cloister her. In many ways, *Mak* defied that, secretly studying on her own.

This was the girl *Pa* fell in love with—a bright, headstrong young woman who spoke her mind. Hardly the demure, traditional Cambodian bride. But *Pa*, too, knew his own mind. He waited patiently for his parents to fulfill their promise, to make the arrangements for him to marry *Mak*. Tradition required them to approach *Mak*'s family for a formal engagement. Investigations would follow, including interviews with others about the class and behavior of the groom and his family. But they took too long. *Pa* couldn't wait. He went to his favorite aunt, *Yiey* Om, in Srey Va village. He begged her to serve as his guardian, to ask *Yiey* Srem and *Kong* Lorng for *Mak*'s hand. Understanding the depth of both her nephew's love and his fear—that any man could come at any time to claim *Mak*'s hand—she took a boat to Prey Ronn village. She was an unlikely messenger of love, but effective.

Mak's parents agreed to speed up the marriage. But Cambodian tradition still must be followed. His parents, *Kong* Houng and *Yiey* Khmeng, were required to formally seek the approval of *Mak*'s parents. Permission was granted. At seventeen, *Pa* finally got his wish, marrying *Mak*, a slightly confused fourteen-year-old bride.

Pa brought her to Year Piar to live with his parents. Either from fear or simply because she was too young to adjust to married life, *Mak* immediately ran away, scurrying back to her parents. To her surprise, her mother shipped her right back. Later, *Mak* laughed about it. But she remembered, too, the heavy expectations of her new mother-in-law.

Yiey Khmeng must have expected a lot of *Mak*, forgetting that she was so young. In Cambodian custom, the scalps of newborn babies were traditionally marked with a mashed root called *paley*, the saffron color of turmeric. This denoted the baby's "soft spot," and the root was thought to help harden the skull. You knew an infant was maturing when the powder fell away. When *Mak* married, you might say her *paley* had not yet fallen away. But it made little difference. High expectations were common among many mothers-in-law, whose words ruled. A woman isn't just married to her husband, but to his whole family. But *Pa* didn't see it that way; he was a man who had the courage to turn away from cultural expectations with which he disagreed. In time, they had two children, both of whom died. Their third child was a skinny, sickly baby. They held little hope for her survival, but she surprised them, earning the nickname Chea, which means "heal." With a frail new baby, *Pa* and *Mak* left Year Piar.

They embarked on a journey, abandoning the financial security of their families to seek their own way, to make a life on their own. They went to Phnom Penh. Bitter about his parent's unyielding expectations, *Pa* and *Mak* made a vow on the Preah Monivong Bridge: If they didn't succeed in life, they would never return to Year Piar to see his parents. They would kill themselves first, jumping into the deep, flowing waters that ran beneath them.

Now in their early twenties, they were no longer troubled by this vow. Together they built a home in Takeo. *Pa* was a good husband and father. At twenty-five, he was successfully supporting a growing family. In truth, my father and mother surprised not only his parents but also *Mak*'s. A home was a status symbol, a measure of making it. Even their parents wondered, Where did they get the money to build a house this big?

They didn't know of the vow that burned deeply in *Pa* and *Mak*. The home was the temple of their vow. A trophy *Pa* won for *Mak*, his bride.

It was in this home that I first heard the word "war." The year was 1968, and I was three years old. It was a clear night and the sky was adorned with stars. *Mak* came into our living room and asked my siblings and me if we wanted to see a comet. *Mak* said it had a long, bright tail.

I remember our excitement. I hurried along with five of my brothers and sisters. They were Chea, eleven, whose intelligence and thoughtfulness earned her the respect an oldest child demands; Ra, ten, my shy sister who liked to help *Mak* cook and clean—her tidy, domestic ways pleased our mother. At nine, Tha was my oldest brother. He was good in math and mischievous. Tha's way of finding out if the corn was sweet was to take a bite out of every cob on the platter. Ry, seven, was my easily amused sister, who liked to baby-sit me and Avy, our one-year-old sister. Than, five, was the second-oldest brother, whose tree-climbing sense of adventure often invited my own curiosity. He was my rival.

As we followed our mother, we scurried close behind her like six chicks following a hen. *Mak* lifted me up and I saw the heavenly body with a starlike nucleus and a long, luminous tail. Its radiance was intensified by the dark sky and the surrounding stars. We were all in awe, crowded near our mother, leaning against the railing.

A moment later my mother's joy seemed to fade—even a child could feel it. She told us of an old folk superstition: When the tail of the comet pointed to a particular place, Cambodia would be drawn into war with that country. The word "war" diluted the aura of excitement, even with me, a child who didn't have the slightest idea what the word meant. I sensed the fear in my mother and older siblings. I wondered what the word "country" meant, and what country the tail of the comet was pointing to.

In 1969 war comes, and I am only four.

Loud rumbling noises wake me. I fumble in the dark, trying to open the mosquito netting around my bed. I run in the dark toward the living room, searching for my mother and father. "*Mak! Pa!*" I scream with all my might, trying to compete with the raucous sounds.

From the living room, I hear my oldest sister, twelve-year-old Chea, screaming: "*Mak! Pa! Yeakong chol srok Khmer! Yeakong chol srok*

Khmer!" The Viet Cong are invading Cambodia! Her voice is itself a blast of terror.

Chea's hysterical warning makes me realize that the raging noise outside could be related to the word I had been wondering about: *war*. More than anything, I want to see my parents. Suddenly the light flips on, revealing my frightened sisters and brothers running around frantically, randomly—as disoriented as ants whose hill has been plowed under.

I see my mother clutching my baby sister, Avy, and my father standing at the wall where he has just turned on the light. I run to stand beside *Mak*. My father reaches out to hold Chea's shoulders. He looks into her eyes and carefully says: "Achea, *koon*, take your brothers and sisters with you and hide in the bunker by the pond. Hunch and walk low, so you won't get hit by bullets. Hurry, *koon Pa* [father's child]!"

My brothers and sisters rush out the doorway, a small, traumatized herd of cattle. I clench my mother's hand, and my body rattles with each echo of gunfire. Carrying Avy and holding on to me, *Mak* hurries toward the door. She can't move quickly, for she is six months pregnant. Artillery explodes outside, and I scream and burst into tears. *Mak* shakes off my hand, then grabs onto it tightly.

"*Pa vea!*"* She shouts to my father, who is running from one window to the next, sticking his head out and listening. "What are you doing? You'll get shot! Why aren't you careful? Help me with the children!" *Mak* is scared, and her tone frightens me even more than the artillery roaring in the night air.

Pa shouts back, "I just want to know where the gunfire is coming from."

---

* The familiar address of a wife to her husband, a term of endearment which means "father of the children."

Mak bends toward me. Her words come as hard and fast as an auctioneer's: "Athy,* *koon*, wait for your father here. *Mak* takes Avy downstairs." My heart races when I see that she is scared for my father. After she hurries out, I cry, jumping up and down, anxious for *Pa* to take me to the bunker.

Pa runs over to comfort me, snatches me down from the peak of my hysteria. He carries me to the open bunker, a hole in the sticky clay soil ringed with sandbags. Safe at the bunker, he can't rest. He needs to go back to the house for *Yiey Tot*, his grandmother, who is blind and frail. He takes Chea and Tha with him to help carry her. Above the noise I can hear my great-grandmother's groans.

"Hunch, *koon!*" I hear *Pa* cry. "Don't you hear the flying bullets? Don't worry, *Yiey*, we won't drop you."

I'm relieved when everyone in my family, including Aunt Cheng, *Pa*'s younger sister, finally hides by the pond. Lying beside my mother in the cold night, I wonder if everyone is as scared as I am as the bullets whiz over us—a fierce hiss and invisible whisper, so quick you wonder if you really heard it. Flares erupt like lightning, illuminating the dark sky.

So this is war. Will it ever stop?

Finally the gunfire belches its last round. Silence and relief. *Now we can go back home*, I think to myself, ready to be freed from worries about war. I look forward to the morning. I want to forget the adult world that pulled me from my dreams and into a nightmare.

What I don't know is that there is a world outside Cambodia— a world that will affect me, my family, and Cambodia as a nation. I do not know who owned the guns that night—only that they were aimed at me. It will be years before I begin to understand the causes

---

* Thy (Tee) is my nickname; the prefix *A* is an added endearment used by an older person addressing a younger one, especially a girl—relative age is very important in defining Cambodian relationships, and is reflected in the language, as are gender roles.

and effects of war, the political gamesmanship. But by then my family will have become flotsam caught in the heave and thrust of its tide.

I look back now as a survivor educated in America. I've sought out answers to questions I raised as a little girl. Trying to make sense of what happened. Trying to understand the players in the Vietnam conflict and those who took advantage of the situation, pulling Cambodia—the pawn, they called it—into the whirlpool of destruction.

The heavenly comet that we saw so long ago had more than one tail. My mother, my siblings, and I could only see the long, bright one—the one that pointed to Vietnam. The other tiny tails were blurred by the glare of the night sky. One of them invisibly pointed to the United States.

On April 20, 1970—in an attempt to incapacitate the Viet Cong troops operating in the border sanctuaries of Cambodia—forces from the United States and South Vietnam launched a massive drive into Cambodia, making Cambodia a stage for war. Early on, U.S. leaders denied involvement, until finally the American public demanded the truth. This Vietnamese conflict violated Cambodia's borders, disregarding the precarious neutrality Cambodian Prince Norodom Sihanouk had sought to preserve for years. On March 18, 1970, Prince Sihanouk was ousted by his premier, Lon Nol, and his cousin, Prince Sisowath Serik Matak, in a bloodless coup backed by the United States. China welcomed Sihanouk with open arms, eager to help save Cambodia from "American imperialists." Later, Chinese leaders encouraged him to form a government in exile consisting primarily of his enemies, the Khmer Rouge, a band of guerrillas who had exploited the upheaval of the Vietnamese conflict. Thus, another invisible tail of the comet emerged. This one pointed to China, which had helped create the Khmer Rouge—a lethal virus that would years later destroy most of its former host, Cambodia, and so many of its own people.

When gunfire breaks out, my family only senses a dangerous presence, and I wish for things to return to normal. The next morning things seem quiet. We are hostages of our own thoughts, especially my father. While eating breakfast, *Pa* turns on the radio. A man's voice tells something about the Viet Cong coming into Cambodia. People died, houses burned, and the Viet Cong came close to Takeo City, he says, talking rapidly. I hear a reference to *rotcross* (tanks) entering Takeo City. *Pa* says that the Viet Cong have invaded *srok* Khmer (Cambodia).

At school I have seen posters of the Viet Cong posted on tree trunks in the school yard and on the school fence.* Pointing to the posters, a teacher told us that the men wearing black shirts and pants with black sandals were called *yeakong. Yeakong* had big teeth and scary smiles and carried long guns on their shoulders. Behind them was a large pot called *tae ong* (metal pots that resemble the shape of a bell) sitting on top of human heads with tongues of flame coming between them. The heads, the teacher said, were the Cambodians' heads, used as cooking stones. When we are caught by the *yeakong*, she said, they will do that to us.

Pa decides to go to the office. He works for the government in Phnom Penh, overseeing import/export violations, but he also owns a number of pedicarts, which people rent from him monthly. My father is different from my uncles. He helps my mother around the house, washing diapers and even the bloodied bedsheets after she's had a baby. Although culturally women are the preparers of food, I often watch Father work in the kitchen. He finds pleasure in small things, helping us clean and trim our fingernails, pouring water over us in our shower—things women do. I can feel my father's ambition, and also his desire to escape tradition. An entrepreneur at heart, he imports televisions via Vietnam and rents out two bedrooms downstairs. He dreams of filling our home with children.

---

* Because I was an articulate, curious child, *Pa* had tried to place me in first grade at age three, but didn't succeed until I turned four.

It's only been about eight hours since I first encountered war, but already I am beginning to worry like an adult. I am so afraid that our family might be separated from my father if fighting breaks out again. Oh, how much I want to tell *Pa* that I'm scared, but I'm even too scared to tell him this. I've learned from grown-ups that you don't think about or say terrible things or else they will come true.

They come true anyway, and *Pa* isn't home yet. We shiver as the gunfire rumbles in the distance. At least it's not close to our home, as it was the night before. We stay inside. I wish for the war noise to stay where it is. I'm too tired to stay awake. The next thing I feel is my body shaking, Chea waking me up.

The morning is cloudy and chilly as I stand outside the gate near our packed suitcases. I've been asked by *Mak* to watch for a bus to pick us up for Phnom Penh. I look at my home: the pine trees, three on each side, stand before our big two-story stucco house, almost as tall as the house itself. Along the front cement fence, a cool, shady row of mango, papaya, and coconut trees overlooks swings—a playground I already begin to miss almost as much as I miss my father.

Mostly, I feel relieved: *We won't be captured by the Viet Cong after all. We're going to be with Pa.*

A faded blue bus packed with people stops in front of the house. Everyone, it seems, has the same idea. On top of the bus rises a growing tower of suitcases and bags. Through the open gate, I run to tell *Mak*. As I begin to climb the cement stairs, my family is coming down. My mother holds Avy on her hip with one hand and a bundle in the other. Her black hair is combed neatly, framing her face and curving against her neck below her earlobes. She wears a colorful sleeveless blouse with a flowery long sarong, similar to that worn by Hawaiians. As always she is composed.

I ask *Mak*, "What about *Pa*? *Pa*'s coming home tonight, and we are not going to be here. Will he be scared when he doesn't know where we are?"

"Your father will know. He'll find us. Go on now. Go to the bus, *koon Mak!*"*

As the bus starts to leave, I look at my home, one last snapshot, click. With my eyes, I caress all that I see—the pine trees, the swings by the shaded mango trees near the fence, the balcony with hanging houseplants cascading from the ceiling. I remember how we used to come out and sit on the balcony and enjoy warm evening breezes together. I would chase fireflies hovering near the house-plants.

Everyone on the bus is quiet, even little kids. We glance at each other and see silent worry, especially on the adults' faces. Some people hide it—they look out the bus windows, staring at trees and passing landscapes.

Pa somehow finds us in Phnom Penh. We find shelter at Bantiey Sheichaak, a military garrison of sorts. We enter a world of curfews. At II A.M. we can't leave the house. For hours Cambodian surveillance planes circle overhead in search of Viet Cong infiltration. If they detect any movement, you could be shot. Whenever I hear the whine of engines above, I am afraid to breathe, to play, even to pee.

For two months this is our life. Then *Pa* says we're going home to Takeo. "It's safe now," he announces. But it is not the same. Our home has been bombed.

Surprisingly, Akie, a collie, has survived these months alone, unlike our guard dog, Aka Hom, who is gone. Akie endured the war, waiting loyally outside the charred remains of our decimated home. When *Pa* arrives, Akie runs up to him, licking him again and again. In Cambodia, it is rare to see public displays of affection between adults. But with pets, we feel free to lavish our affections. *Pa* has always enjoyed pampering Akie, shampooing him, feeding him prime table scraps.

* A term of endearment meaning "mother's child."

Instead of staying at our home, we go to the house of *Kong**
Horne, my mother's uncle. His family has abandoned it and has not
returned. But he is one of the lucky ones, whose house is untouched
by war. His two-story stucco home overlooks the Bassac River, located near the heart of Takeo City.

Sitting on the scooter, *Pa* tells Than to go with him to see our
home, but I ask to go along too. He looks at me, hesitant, but then
says I can come.

Along the streets lie clothes and debris. I look for people, but
there's no one. When *Pa* says we're here, I look at our house, but
the top part is gone. It looks broken, shorter than before. The gate
is broken. The mango, coconut, and papaya trees look dry, burned.
The tops of two pine trees have broken off, withered, and turned
brown, and now are dangling.

Pa holds my hand as we climb the stairs. When we get to the
top, there is no door. Metal spikes stick out of what used to be the
walls of the bedrooms and the balcony. The floor of the living room
is partially gone, exposing the downstairs room. *Pa* holds me back
from moving any further. The sofa, the glass cases holding crystal
and engraved silver chalices, the pictures, and everything else in our
house are reduced to ashes. Where the television set, radio, and
record player once stood there is nothing but charred debris.

When *Pa* takes us to the backyard, the pond is dried up, its beautiful water lilies and green lotus and *trey pra*, the catfish we used to
feed, are dead. The trees once bowed with the weight of fruit are wilted
and brown. Our house is dead, and I ask my father to take me away.

---

* Meaning "grandfather of Chinese descent," though *Kong* Horne is really my mother's
uncle. In Cambodian forms of address, age sometimes takes precedence over actual
family relationship; hence this uncle, who was the brother of my mother's mother,
was called "Grandpa" Horne. Similarly, a man or woman of one's parents' age might
be called "uncle" or "aunt" as a sign of respect, even if he or she was biologically
unrelated.

2

B-cinquante-deux

The New York Times
July 18, 1973
"Secret Raids on Cambodia Before '70 Totaled 3,500"

BY SEYMOUR M. HERSH

Washington, July 17—United States B-52 bombers made at least 3,500 secret bombing raids over Cambodia in a 14-month period beginning in March, 1969, Defense Department sources disclosed today. . . . Military sources did confirm, however, that information about the Cambodian raids was directly provided to President Nixon and his top national security advisers, including Henry A. Kissinger.

There is a story about the life of Buddha in which a mother carries her dead son to him draped in her arms. The woman has heard that he is a holy man who can restore life. Weeping, she appeals for mercy. Gently, Buddha tells her that he can help save her son's life, but that first she has to bring him a mustard seed secured from a family that has never experienced death. Desperately she searches home after home. Many want to help, but everyone has already experienced a loss—a sister, a husband, a child. Finally the woman returns to Buddha. "What have you found?" he asks. "Where is your mustard seed and where is your son? You are not carrying him."

"I buried him," she replies.

As a young child, I had never known loss. I never envisioned my family without our home. But the Vietnamese invasion changes that. My brother Tha becomes ill. The mischievous boy who climbs trees like a monkey has come down with a fever. My mother sits up with him at night, dabbing his face with cool, damp cloths. But he is not getting better.

Pa gives Tha some medicine, but nothing changes. Tha can't move or pee and just lies in bed, breathing slowly. He sleeps a lot and his face has turned white. When *Mak* and *Pa* try to talk to him, he squeezes his eyes open, eyelids fluttering, but he can't talk.

Mak is desperate. At one point she seeks a spiritual adviser. The answer is simple: at some point, Tha has peed on someone's grave. That is why he cannot pee or speak. The angry spirit steals his spirit as retribution. Without an apology, Tha surely will die. My mother racks her brain trying to think of where the offended grave might have been—perhaps in Phnom Penh, during our brief stay there. By now she grasps at any explanation, any thin hope.

With the city abandoned, there is no medical help available. *Pa* has to get a doctor from far away to help Tha. The doctor gives Tha shots and removes a catheter and hose from his medical bag. *Pa* motions with his hand, telling me to stand away from Tha's bed while the doctor tries to get his pee out. Tha groans. *Pa* and *Mak* are twin mirrors of distress.

After the doctor finishes, he and *Pa* go outside and I walk over to *Mak*, who sits by the bed. *Mak* feels Tha's stomach and gazes into his eyes. *Mak* strokes his hair. I want to touch his hand to comfort him. Then I hear a click sound, and suddenly Tha's lips slowly widen into a smile. "*Mak*, Tha is smiling!" Than exclaims happily, standing at the foot of Tha's bed. We all smile.

Mak says gently, "Than, *koon*, let your older brother hold your toy gun for a second," and he does.

Tha does not recover, however. He shuts down, taking nothing in, giving nothing out. He only breathes. *Mak* and *Pa* are always by his side.

My parents haven't prepared us for the idea of death. It is never discussed. When Tha dies, our mother cries very hard. Her ragged sobs scare me and yet pull me to her. *Pa's* eyes are red, wet with tears. He covers his face and leaves the house. I am saddened by the death of my older brother, who once let me hold a baby crow, warm and wriggling, with its tiny feet scratching for a perch in the palm of my hand. But in a way, my parents' distress and helplessness bother me even more.

Increasingly, our lives are spinning out of control.

We have been squatters in the house of *Kong* Horne, *Mak's* uncle, for a month when he returns with his wife and children. The house is filling up. People gradually return to Takeo, and life slowly begins to seep back into the vacant streets.

With a growing household, our family moves into the second floor of the home—a place with an eerie history. Years before I was born, a Vietnamese woman broke into my uncle's home intent on stealing jewelry, gold, and silver ingots that were hidden in a stack of firewood—a crude but practical safe-deposit box for many Cambodians fearful of inflation and the shifting value of paper money. The intruder somehow lured my seven-year-old aunt upstairs. No one knows what happened. Perhaps she was trying to scare her into revealing where the gold and jewelry was. Maybe she was silencing a witness. In the end, the woman hanged my aunt by her neck, suspending her small body by a rope from a ceiling beam. The murderer was later found hiding under a bed upstairs not far from the body. She never did find the gold.

For years the entire second story of the house was closed off. Cords of wood and thick wooden poles were stacked against it to counterbalance the evil. Whenever we get scared, my great-grandmother rattles off her spiritual defense, a rapid string of Pali words that come out as a chant, asking Buddha to ward off the bad spirits, to set up an invisible boundary so that ghosts can't enter. In Cambodian culture you can also ward off ghosts in a single gesture: a defiantly uplifted middle finger.

At night my mother swears she can hear someone pouring tea. Some nights when she rises to get water, she spies a dark shadow sitting on the hammock. One night I call out to my father. Someone is running a finger down my arms, as light as a spider's touch. "*Pa*, ghosts!" At first he pretends to misunderstand. "What? Ant?" he teases, deliberately confusing two words that are phonetically similar. By my third cry, he comes running.

Amid this place of death and ghosts, there is more destruction.

Something drops down loudly. The house shakes. I open my eyes. It drops again and again as if a big fist were pounding on the ground. Ry runs out of the mosquito netting. I follow behind her. It's dark. When Ry and I reach the hallway, *Pa, Mak*, Aunt Cheng, Than, Chea, and Ra are already crowded by the front window.

"*Putho* [Mercy]!" *Mak* cries out, wincing with each strike.

I want to see what they're looking at, and squeeze through them to reach the window. Gigantic tongues of fire and smoke lick the black sky, lighting up the landscape in the distance, somewhere on the other side of the Bassac River. Silhouettes of planes loop in the darkness with sequins of light pouring from them. The sequins dissipate in the brushy shadow of distant trees, then erupt in enormous explosions, bright fire on the earth. We see it before we hear it, the explosion arriving as a delayed echo. Each burst concludes with a huge mushroom of smoke.

"*Pa?*" I squeeze my father's hand, looking up at the shadow of his face. He doesn't say anything, but keeps on looking at the burning sky, trembling. I stand there with *Pa* watching it after everyone else has gone back to their beds.

Never before have I seen men cry, so much, like *Pa* tonight.

A few days later, news circulates. *Pa* and other adults talk about casualties reported in different villages outside Takeo province. He says that *B-cinquante-deux* (B-52s) bombed those areas, and many

Cambodian civilians were killed in villages where his aunts live, near Srey Va village. Some were killed by direct hits, others perished in the intense heat created by the bombs. *Pa*'s young sisters' families have had to leave their homes since the bombs dropped near their villages. Like other families, they seek refuge in Takeo City, staying in a house close to us. I don't understand that these are planes from across an ocean. I don't understand they are in pursuit of escaping Viet Cong soldiers, who have infested Cambodian border provinces like stubborn cockroaches, refusing to leave.

After this destruction and death comes a new life.

My baby brother, Bosaba, is born in June, two months after the bombing. He is named after the month of February, the rice-ripening season, when the land is lush and the rice heads golden and heavy and ready for harvest. *Mak* caresses the dark, fuzzy head of her eighth child. "We lost the older one, and now we have a little one," she tells us. *Mak* gazes at Bosaba's closed eyes and his tiny mouth, which moves as if he is nibbling. His small pink fingers open and close, and I insert my index finger into one of his fists. A snug, perfect fit.

I am glad that Bosaba is born because it makes *Mak* and *Pa* happy, but my youngest brother is only a brief gift. Perhaps he was born prematurely, his health compromised by the trauma my mother endured during the pregnancy. He falls ill and cries constantly. No one can console him. *Pa* can't help him, and neither can the doctor.

Medical help is becoming so scarce that many people fall back on traditional folk ways. *Pa* begins suffering sharp pain in his abdomen. He says he is suffering from appendicitis. A friend of his, or perhaps a doctor, cautions him, "If you don't get medical intervention to break the "turtle neck"—the inflamed appendix—you will surely die." But the hospitals are not manned. Only time and fate can help him. Somehow, *Pa* lives. But life has become so ten-

uous. Real medicine is increasingly out of our reach, and the con-
sequences are frustrating and deadly.

After a few weeks, my new brother Bosaba dies.

More displaced villagers and refugees are pouring into the city,
including *Mak*'s mother and six brothers and sisters. Her father remains in Prey Ronn village to take care of his farming business.
Our second-story home is becoming crowded. We have to share it
with *Mak*'s mother and siblings. Signs of war have already begun
to trickle into the city. One day I am playing marbles along a street
with cousins and neighborhood children. We glance up to see a
cluster of grown-ups. Our game is abandoned as we run to discover what has captured their attention, fighting our way to the
front of the crowd. There on the street sit the decapitated heads
of two men. The blood on their necks is encrusted with dirt and
hay. Their faces are puffy and purple, their eyelids bruised. "Here,
see, Khmer Rouge heads," a man fiercely declares. "We captured
them. Look at them."

My first reaction is to reel backward, my spine slapping into the
circle of adults standing around me. I am baffled. Rouge is "red."
Khmer means "Cambodian." I do not understand what I am hearing. These lifeless faces before me could be those of anyone in the
crowd. Quickly, other adults begin to herd us away from the gory
spectacle, chastising those who rolled the heads before us like mel-
ons at a market. "Don't you know better?" they bark at them.

Pa says that there has been more bombing along the Cambodian
border, and more people are fleeing their homes to Takeo. In these
strange times, after returning my brothers, sisters, and me to school
for a year, my parents consider relocating. They decide to buy a
house in Phnom Penh that had been owned by a Vietnamese family. *Pa* says many Vietnamese families have been involuntarily repa-
triated, and their homes in Phnom Penh are being sold in a hurry
and at good prices.

For *Pa* these have been months of frustration entangled in brutal lessons. He has lost two sons, children not touched by bombs but who might have survived if there had been access to hospitals and advanced medical care. *Pa* has become silent, but out of his silence comes a burning desire. A desire to fight back, not with guns but with the mind—a desire to learn.

In ways I can never imagine, his desire will come to affect us all.

3

A Grain of Rice on a Dog's Tail

*P*hnom Penh is a city designed for the senses. Everywhere there is activity, sound, and tantalizing smells. Here, people don't seem to feel the shadow of war creeping up on them. Now it's the summer of 1972. We delight in the sudden normalcy of human activities. People stroll through the city. Others crowd around the carts of food vendors, jostling for their right to fried noodles, sour yellow fingers of pickled green mangoes served on a stick with a touch of red chili and salt, or crispy, golden fried bananas, battered with flour and sesame seeds. My personal favorite is the pâté sandwich— thick baguette rolls stuffed with three kinds of sliced meat, wafers of cucumber, and green onion or cilantro.

Phnom Penh truly is a capital city. Everywhere we see markets, pharmacies, restaurants, schools—the normal bustle of urban living. Even though the bus has taken us only seventy miles north of Takeo, following winds up from the Gulf of Thailand, it is a different world.

Soon after our arrival, we welcome another person into our family. *Mak* gives birth to a healthy baby boy, whom she and *Pa* name

Putheathavin, who has beautiful, long eyelashes, longer than those of anyone in our family, and velvety tan skin like *Pa*'s. We call him Vin, using the last sound of his first name. Similarly, my name is Chanrithy, and everyone calls me Thy or Athy. Ra is Chantara, and we call her Ra, but *Pa* and *Mak* call her Ara because they're older and they can use *A* before her name. Ry is Channary, Than is Chanthan, and Avy is Putheatavy, but Chea is Chea because this is her special nickname, which means "heal," but at school her friends call Chanchhaya. Now *Pa* and *Mak* have seven children, more than the neighboring families.

Our neighbors on the right are two Chinese families, quiet and polite people. On our left is a nice Cambodian family, pure and cultured Cambodians, *Mak* said, with dark skin and large eyes. Across from us lives another Cambodian family, an aunt with her family and a niece who is single and works as a policewoman. Her name is Veth and I am in awe of her.

Sala Santeu Mook (elementary school) is my school and also Than's. Colorful flowers in planters stand sentry before each building and around the flagpole, where we uniformly line up to salute the flag every morning and sing the national anthem:

> We the people of Cambodia are well known in the world. We succeed in building monuments. Our glorious civilization and religion, our ancestors' heritage, have been kept on this earth. Cambodians, stand up, stand up, fight, defend the republic. When enemies attack, we defend, we fight.

Two years after Vin was born, *Mak* has another healthy baby. He is adorable with dark brown eyes and light skin like *Mak*, but his face resembles *Pa*'s. After his birth, a nurse told *Mak* that the placenta had been wrapped around his body. This means he will be a teacher when he grows up and will be smart and compassionate. That makes *Mak* smile, her eyes gazing at his pink face. His name is Phalkunarith, but sometimes *Pa* calls him Map (chubby) because his cheeks are plump.

Now I'm eight, forgetting the past with its enemies and bombs. I've learned new things in school, among them Cambodian history, which I have to memorize. Sometimes I find it boring because it is filled with wars, battles with neighboring countries, and dead Cambodian kings with names as long as my first and last name combined. It seems Cambodia has never been a country fully at peace. Chea says it's important to learn Khmer history. But right now I'd rather learn math or, better yet, I'd like to know more about the magical power of the medicines tucked in the drawers of *Pa*'s desk.

When no one is around, I gently, ever so gently, slide open one of *Pa*'s medicine drawers. Before me lie boxes of powdered medicine in vials, and clear liquid medicine in small glass cylinders blown into different shapes. There are tiny metallic seesaw blades, which *Pa* uses to saw into the cylindrical glasses, and alcohol papers wrapped in little packages. I am spellbound by the array of glittering, magical treasures. Finally my eyes come to rest on two things: the medicine for the injections *Pa* gives me in my butt and the liquid he shoots into the veins of my arms.

There is a kind of magic in my home: medicine. I'm not sure where or how my father has learned medicine, but he does so hoping never to be as helpless as he was during Tha's and Bosaba's illnesses. This is very much like *Pa*. To him, life is a series of problems waiting to be solved.

Pa is a good father and, now, a good doctor. When I am sick with asthma, he always takes care of me. When my breathing is labored, he puts his ear against my chest and back to listen for wheezing. Sometimes he takes me to a hospital for X rays and blood tests. Then he knows what medicine to give. Somehow, with seven children to treat, he readily makes room for other patients. No appointments necessary. As he helps my ailing cousins and the neighbors' children, I look on with adoration. I hold *Pa*'s hand and say to him, "*Pa*, when I'm big I want to be like you. I want to give people shots. Make them better."

Beside *Pa*, Chea is my number two idol. She's very smart. She often receives presents and awards for being at the top of her class. *Mak* and *Pa* are proud of her. I want to be like her—to do math in a thick spiral notebook and have lots of good friends. Chea teaches me how to sing French and English songs. Often I ask her to teach me how to count to ten "in American." Noticing my fascination with the language, she promises me she will talk to *Pa* about enrolling me in a private English school called Engloria when I turn ten.

There's no doubt *Pa* will let me. He and *Mak* are pleased when my brothers, sisters, and I study. It makes me think of a poem Chea once recited to me:

"Knowledge cannot be destroyed by termites. . . . One can spend it and never run out of it."

Our household shifts once again. *Pa* helps arrange Aunt Cheng's marriage, then takes her and her husband under his wing. They stay with us until they can find their own place. It's nice to have Aunt Cheng around. It feels strange to see her married to someone she doesn't know. And I miss her, the aunt I knew before she married.

Eventually Aunt Cheng moves, but Uncle Seng, *Pa*'s youngest brother, who has lived with us since we bought the house, stays. He's my favorite uncle who likes to tickle me on my stomach. Uncle Seng is single and good-looking, especially when he wears aviator sunglasses and his pilot's uniform. *Pa* once told friends of his who came to our house for dinner that Uncle Seng flew reconnaissance missions for the Cambodian air force. He looks for *khmang*, enemies, *Pa* explained softly. I know he means the Khmer Rouge.

I have taken an interest in the world and the ways of adults. Often I sit quietly on the red couch watching the news on television with *Pa* or listen to the radio. I don't understand many things, but

I know it's important. There is news about fighting with the Khmer Rouge, about Prince Sihanouk, the "god-king" whom many Cambodian elders believe to have the divine touch, who has somehow lost power and joined the Khmer Rouge. It is his voice, *Pa* says, that now calls out on the radio, in Peking, China, beseeching Cambodian people to join the Khmer Rouge in the jungles. Pleading for us to join the "king-father" and fight against people supporting the "American imperialists." The broadcaster reports the mounting casualties among soldiers and civilians and pinpoints outlying provinces where skirmishes have taken place. It is news that still seems very far away.

Although I make time for adult news, I also turn my back on it, drawn to my childhood duty in life—to have fun. When Than and his friends are about to play kick-the-can, I dash out and open the gate. I hope they haven't divided into two groups yet. I make my way into the circle of boys. "Hey, can I play?"

Than says, "Wait! Athy, come here!" He waves me away from his friends.

"What?"

"Don't play with boys—you're a girl. Go play with your own friends! Go!"

"But I want to play kick-the-can. You can play with them, why can't I play with them?"

"But they're my friends! If you play, I'll tell *Mak*. *Mak* will hit you for playing with boys." He glares at me as he makes his way back to his friends.

Right behind him, I say, "Well, your friends don't say I can't play!"

I couldn't care less about the culture or what *Mak* will do or say to me. Besides, Than's friends don't seem to mind that I play with them. During the game, I run as fast as any of them. I have fun and forget all about Than's warning.

Than runs home. I race with him. I pass *Mak* sitting on the red couch and *Pa* sitting at his medicine desk with his glasses on, inspecting something.

"Athy, where did you come from, all sweaty?" asks *Mak*.

"Play."

"*Mak*, she played with boys! I told her not to, but she's stubborn."

"Why is that, Athy?"

I walk back to the living room to defend myself.

"*Koon*, they didn't want you to play with them, why didn't you listen?"

"Why couldn't I play? His friends didn't say I couldn't play. Only Than told me not to play!" I reply.

"But she was the only girl, *Mak*!"

"But my friends weren't playing tonight. Why couldn't I play kick-the-can with your friends? Selfish!" I retort. "Want to have fun by yourself."

Mak laughs as if amused by what just transpired. She turns to *Pa*, sitting at the desk, then says: "*Pa vea* [Father of the children], listen to your children!"

I look at *Pa*, bracing for what he will say. I wonder if he will have me kneel on his desk again as my punishment, as he did when I sneaked out to watch TV at my friend's house after he had told me not to watch ours. By now *Pa* should know that this sort of discipline will never work with me. Crying as hard as I possibly could, I had slowly climbed up the chair onto the desk. My shrieky cry was more difficult for *Pa* to handle than having me kneel on his desk. So now I wonder what *Pa* will do as he slowly looks up. He turns to *Mak* and gazes above his glasses, which hang on the tip of his nose. To my relief, he grins.

The verdict is clear. I'm exonerated again.

Strangely, without my knowledge, the same thing that has been going on in our childhood game of kick-the-can has been escalating throughout the country, on a grand, and dangerous, political scale. Just as my friends and I challenge each other to sneak in and kick a tin can over to the winning side, so government and grassroots armies have been challenging each other, jostling for a win. Just as neighborhood children size up their teams, picking the strongest players, so the Khmer Rouge has been sizing up their allies. *Who to pick? Who can run the fastest? Communist China? Russia? Certainly it cannot be France or the United States.* In the midst of all of this, Cambodia has become the coveted tin can. We begin to feel the reverberations of a game growing out of hand.

Fighting around the country is escalating. As the Khmer Rouge begin to seize outlying provinces, thousands upon thousands of families flee their homes, seeking refuge in Phnom Penh. In a matter of months, the population has more than tripled from about 600,000 to almost 2 million.

With so many people now living here, prices are sky-high. And so is the corruption among government officials. When my aunt's husband, an officer in the Cambodian army, is arrested for secretly selling weapons to the Khmer Rouge, my father is devastated.

"How stupid, greedy. He has sold the country," *Pa* murmurs, unable to comprehend the pressure to betray. My aunt weeps, telling *Mak* and *Pa* about the sentencing, the bail. Somehow, my uncle is released.

To make things worse, terrorist activity is seeping into the city. Plastic explosives have now been planted in public places, such as movie theaters and markets. We hear warnings on the radio, which prompt *Mak* to remind Than to be careful, "*Koon*, Than, do you hear that?" The newspapers also say the Khmer Rouge are terrorizing the nation, especially Lon Nol's government.

At night *Pa* updates *Mak* on what has happened at work or the news he reads. He talks about fleeing families. There are more beggars in the city and, now, homeless families. Children sneak into restaurants and ask customers for leftovers. Proprietors tell them to leave. They vanish for a moment, but appear again.

That evening he tells me a Cambodian saying. *Pa* says to me, "There comes a time when a grain of rice sticks on a dog's tail, and everyone will fight for it." He looks at me gravely, and so does my mother, awaiting my reaction. It makes no sense to me.

"Don't be picky, *koon*," *Mak* adds. "Eat what we have."

"*Koon*, there's a lot of hungry people out there," says *Pa*.

In his eyes I see his concern. Only then do I begin to realize how much my parents love me, how much they want to teach me, to prepare me for the changing world surrounding us. To prepare me for the Year of the Rabbit, for the unknown it will bring.

Already it is the Time of New Angels. The Cambodian New Year is around the corner, April 13. That's when families throughout the country begin to celebrate the festivities that traditionally stretch until the fifteenth. On the radio we hear music that tells of old angels who will be sent back to heaven, replaced by new angels who will take care of mortals. Usually, my family goes to Wat Phnom, a beautiful temple perched on a hilltop in Phnom Penh, or the Independent Monument, a parklike national memorial. At home we offer food and drink before the shrines of Buddha to welcome the angels—rice, candles, incense, and fruits.

But in this year, 1975, there's no New Year spirit. Fear, not angels, is in the air. The Khmer Rouge have grown big and dangerous. They have seized most of the outer provinces. Inch by inch, they close in on Phnom Penh. They shell the city. The bombing hasn't touched our lives, but sometimes we hear the shrill whizzing of artillery overhead. Families dig up the earth, create makeshift bunkers and bomb shelters in their yards, using whatever space they can find. Schools close pending further notice. My own school has become a field hospital, a ragtag home for hundreds of soldiers, many of whom are wounded. We must stay close to home, no bike-riding to market. In the meantime, we pray for the safety of loved ones.

Even though I am only nine, my mind constantly chants the Buddhist wish, something only adults usually do. But I've watched, listened to them, and learned. While the crowded population of Phnom Penh braces for the impact of artillery, I chant the wish again and again:

សត្រូវមកពីមុខឲ្យវាលង សត្រូវមកពីក្រោយឲ្យរលាយ —*Sadtrow mok pe mook ay romlong. Sadtrow mok pe croay ay rarliey.* "If the enemy comes before you, make it pass over. If it comes behind, make it vanish."

4

When Broken Glass Begins to Float

The New York Times
May 6, 1975
"Victors Emptying Cambodia Cities, U.S. Now Believes"

Washington, May 5—State Department officials said today they believed the Cambodian Communists had forcibly evacuated virtually the entire population of Phnom Penh soon after they took power in the capital early last month.

*T*wo days after the New Year, April 15, 1975, Uncle Seng comes home, brusquely shoving the gate open. Without a word he scurries into the house. He rushes to his bedroom, dropping a camouflage bag onto his bed, and crams clothes inside it. I dash to the kitchen, where *Mak* is.

"*Mak*, *Poo** Seng is acting strange. Just came in and shoved his clothes in his bag. *Mak*, go and look at him."

Mak frowns. She pauses, then bends toward me and says, "Go tell your father. Go, *koon!*"

I tell *Pa* exactly what I told *Mak*, except this time I speak at a rate twice the speed of my pulse. *Pa* gets up quickly and strides through the house to see Uncle Seng. He's already on his way out. *Pa* and I intercept him near the gate.

"Seng! Where are you going?" *Pa* demands.

"I'm leaving Cambodia," Uncle Seng replies. He avoids *Pa*'s eyes, and stares at the ground as if there's no need for discussion.

* Uncle.

"Aren't you going to see *Yom?*"* *Pa* sputters, indignant that he would leave without consulting an elder.

Uncle Seng sadly replies, "*Lok bang!*† The Khmer Rouge are my first enemy. I won't stay to see their faces." His words tumble out like flat stones. He speaks decisively. "I'll fly to Kampong Chhnarng and meet my friends, then fly with them to Thailand. *Lok bang*, I'm going."

Uncle Seng walks out. *Pa* is speechless. He looks at me, and in his eyes I see tears. It is hard for the oldest brother to lose control, and yet in the face of war he has none.

Like many families whose houses are built close together, we don't have any space for a bomb shelter. We count on Aunt Nakry, *Mak*'s younger sister, who has a bomb shelter about two houses down. In the stark moment after bombs have fallen elsewhere in the city, children, men, and women run outside their homes, craning their necks to watch the danger. We do the same, including my siblings, my parents, and Uncle Surg, *Pa*'s younger brother (who is older than Uncle Seng), whose family has been staying with us for a few months. Where is the danger? Our eyes survey the surroundings. Little is said. Glancing at our neighbors, we wonder where the bombs will hit. Will there be more? Which part of the city will the Khmer Rouge bomb? No one knows. For now, I'm relieved that the bombs have missed us.

The next morning, April 16, 1975, *Pa* goes to his office. It is a desperate bid to be normal. Although he doesn't think many of his subordinates will come to work, and there will be no ships coming to the port, he feels compelled to oversee the facility. While *Pa*'s at work, everyone else stays home. There's been no school for a month now.

---

* Father—a term used by a son who has been a Buddhist monk.
† A respectful term for an older brother or a man who is older than oneself.

When night shadows stretch between the houses and spill onto the streets, *Pa* still isn't home. Then it's completely dark, and still he's not home. Suddenly a hollow boom explodes behind our home. A chatter of artillery shakes the foundation of our home, sending shrapnel almost simultaneously onto the roof, as if rocks are showering down on us like rain. *Mak* comes running from the kitchen with my baby brothers, "*Koon*, hide somewhere! Hide! Under your uncle's bed. Take your brothers!" *Mak* screams to Ry and Than.

We hide under Uncle Seng's mattresses, sliding under it swiftly. Another boom and I bump my head, jerking against the bedsprings. Then another, and it sends me into a cramped huddle with Ry, Than, Avy, Vin, and Map. The sounds are deafeningly loud. I am too scared to pray even the Buddhist wish.

The shelling stops. A while later *Mak* tells us it's okay to come out. I'm relieved and feel I can breathe normally again. *Mak*, Chea, and Ra peek in at us, and reach out their hands to help us unfold our stiff bodies, which are clenched into tight little balls.

The next morning, April 17, 1975, I awake to a voice. The radio blasts. My legs involuntarily slap against the mattress. For a second I feel as if I'm awakening from death, for my body has never felt this exhausted before.

An unusual male voice comes on the air. It doesn't speak, it shouts. "*Surrender! Phnom Penh has been taken over!*" I leap out of bed to find everyone. *Mak*, Chea, Ra, Ry, and Than are crowding onto the couch listening to the radio. Threatening words shoot from the radio: "*If you don't give up your weapons and display a white flag, our comrades will consider this an act of rebellion against us,*" the voice intones.

"Chea, all of you, Ra *koon*, make a flag! Hurry!"

Chea, Ra, and Ry disperse as soon as *Mak*'s words leave her mouth. Ra looks in one closet and Chea runs to another with Ry. For a second I panic, burning with the need to do something. But then I see Ra fumbling through the closet. *Mak* dashes into her bedroom. Than runs out the door, and I follow. Than unlashes the gate and I zip through it to the road.

The morning is overcast as I make my way up the road. I don't see any flags, but I notice some women running to other neighbors. They seem as frantic as my mother. With shrill voices, they alert people to put up white flags, warn each other to listen to the news on the radio.

More people are out of their houses, and the road fills with them. Men and women ask about others, wondering what will happen next. No one knows how this sudden change will affect them. Thankfully, I spot *Pa* approaching on his light blue scooter. He stops abruptly in the middle of the road, planting his feet on the ground to secure the scooter near a few men. *Pa* says something while keeping his grip on the scooter's handles. One of the men says something back, and *Pa* nods his head. As quickly as they've come together, they scatter, scurrying. As *Pa* is about to take off, more people approach him, anxious for news.

"*Pa!*" I keep running, overjoyed that he's all right.

When I reach the crowd surrounding him, I call out again. *Pa* stops his conversation. He turns and is surprised to see me. *Pa* quickly says, "Athy, why aren't you at home? Go back home, *koon*. Go."

I obey. I can't help noticing how weary and rumpled *Pa* looks. His eyes are bloodshot, cloudy with a web of pink little veins, and more sunken than usual. I realize that he's not wearing his inspector's uniform. Instead, he wears an ivory-colored shirt and dark brown slacks.

As I'm running home, I hear *Pa*'s voice shout: "Put a white flag in front of the house! They won, and we lost."

A woman shouts from her balcony, "*Lok!** We don't have a white flag. Where can we get a white flag?"

* Sir.

Pa diverts his attention from the crowd. He looks up. "It doesn't have to be a nice white flag. A white pillowcase or a white piece of bedsheet will work. Anything white will show them we surrender!"

I'm anxious to let *Mak* know that *Pa* is coming. Through the open gate I fly, shouting: "*Mak!* *Pa's* coming home. I saw *Pa* tell people to put out white flags. *Pa's* almost home."

Everybody anxiously rushes out of the house. We swarm around *Pa* like bees around honey as soon as he walks inside the gate. After a deep breath, he exclaims, "The Khmer Rouge got the country. We're in trouble."

A powerful admission for everyone. *Pa* shakes his head and slowly walks into the house. Everyone is anxious to hear what he has to say about the Khmer Rouge. He sits on the couch and sighs. Without a word, we take our places.

Pa speaks, choosing each word with precision: "*Srok* Khmer [Cambodia] has fallen into the hands of the Khmer Rouge. Our lives will not be the same. They have ordered Lon Nol's soldiers to put down weapons and surrender. If people refuse to give up their weapons, they will be shot."

Pa sighs deeply, his face pale. He continues, "They caught Lon Non* and his relatives. I don't think they will let these people live. They have no mercy for civilians. They threaten people who still hide in bomb shelters. They shout a few times for them to come out. They don't give those scared people a chance to get out. Then they throw hand grenades into those bomb shelters. No one can survive that, not even an ant."

"Why didn't you come home last night?" asks *Mak*. "I thought something terrible had happened to you. Our children were frightened and kept asking for you."

---

* Lon Nol's brother. Lon Nol was the prime minister, commander in chief, and head of state of the Khmer Republic from 1970 to 1975. He fled to Hawaii on April 1, 1975.

"I wanted to come home as soon as our bureau realized the Khmer Rouge were just across the river from Phnom Penh, but we were not allowed to leave. The Khmer Rouge shelled everywhere in the city. We were absolutely forbidden to leave." He jerks back to the moment. "Did we put a white flag in front of the house?"

"Not yet, *Pa*," Chea replies. "I ran out to see you and didn't get to finish making the flag." She looks apologetic—a strange expression for my bold big sister. But the bad news tames everyone.

"It doesn't have to be nice, *koon*. Get a white pillowcase, hang it up somewhere where it can be seen. Hurry! It's important to show the Khmer Rouge our cooperation."

Pa gets up from the couch, and so does everyone else, almost in unison. He turns to *Mak*. "I'll go see if our neighbors have put up their flags. If we don't help each other out, the Khmer Rouge will think we don't want to surrender. They'll harm us all. I'll be back."

I run behind my father. I call out, "*Pa*, I want to go, too." I reach out and cling to his right hand.

He stops and says, "Athy, stay home with your mother! I'll be back."

"But I want to go with you!" I look at the ground.

"All right, come!" He holds on to my hand.

I'm relieved, feeling secure simply by being in his presence. *Pa* and I stop at houses that post no flag. He stresses its importance. I feel proud that my father takes the initiative to care for strangers as if they're family.

The next morning I leave my home right after breakfast. Now that *Pa* is all right, school has been on my mind. I run to my friend Thavy's house, about seven houses down. I'm anxious to find out if our school was destroyed since the Khmer Rouge bombed around it several times.

Thavy brings her six-year-old brother along as if we're going to the grocery store to buy candy or gum. As we walk, each of us holds her brother's hands. We share frightening experiences of the bombing night. It's like telling ghost stories. Before we know it, we're on the sidewalk of our school, or what is left of it.

We freeze. Like small statues, we go chalky in shock. Our eyes are drawn to the raw, gaping crater formed by one of the bombs, where the left side of the fence had been. We slowly begin to walk through the torn fence. Pieces of broken fence and tree branches are littered in crazy disarray. A breeze fans my face, and with it comes a potent, reeky smell. "Something stinks," I announce.

The destruction of something so familiar draws us closer. We dash toward the crumbled buildings, and the stench grows stronger. On the ground along the way, we see a soldier's camouflage hat and burnt pieces of wood from the classrooms. As we move even closer, the smell gets stronger and buzzing flies swarm.

Before our eyes lie piles of dead soldiers in destroyed bomb shelters that had been constructed in rectangular spaces where flower beds used to bloom, between the steps to each classroom. Big flies with greenish heads and eyes swarm the gaping wounds in the soldiers' decaying bodies. One blown-away leg lies beside the step to the first classroom, lonely and morbidly out of place. One soldier's crooked body lies on top of other soldiers', his mouth frozen open in excruciating pain.

I am nine years old.

Never have I seen so much death. For a moment I am hypnotized, spellbound by the ways these soldiers have been killed. I'm oblivious to Thavy or her brother's hand, which is still caught in my ever-tightening grip. I cover my mouth and stare at the heap: piles of blood-encrusted, decaying body parts, and green swarms of hungry flies gorging on open wounds. My stomach begins to move. The breakfast I ate makes its way up my throat, followed by dizziness. Only then do I get hold of myself and feel the repeated tug, the persistent pull of Thavy's brother's hand.

"Thy, let's go," Thavy cries out, a voice that seems to drone on like a slow echo. When the words reach my ears, it is as if they reach me from some place dense and distant. They snap me out of my trance.

We run toward the hole in the fence where we entered. I run, then behind me I hear a boy crying in a sudden burst at the top of his lungs—Thavy's brother trips and falls when they reach the fence. I've forgotten why I'm no longer holding his hand and somehow have run past them both. Thavy's shriek pierces the air as she lifts her brother, yanking up a little boy dressed in blue shorts and sandals as if he has taken a routine spill on the playground, as if it were a normal day. I run back to help. I look toward the school buildings, almost expecting to see a shadow, the ghost of that suffering soldier coming after me.

We grab her brother's small hands and run. We methodically clean dirt off Thavy's brother, brushing off his hands and knees to erase evidence that would lead to any suspicious questions from adults. We try to calm him and bribe him with promises of candy, gum, crackers—anything that comes to mind. Anything to get his terrified mind off the school and the decaying corpses, to return him to a normal state of mind as we near our separate homes.

As they leave me at my home, I watch Thavy walk away, an arm snaking around her little brother as she murmurs reassurances. I see their small backs moving up the street. It is a rare parting. The last time I will ever visit my school. Perhaps the last time I will ever see Thavy.

Once home, I try to be as normal as I can, acting like I've just come back from a typical visit at a friend's house. No one suspects my spying, nor the horror that has visited our playgrounds. I keep it to myself and it seems to eat me up, devouring me from the inside out.

The next day the news reaches us—the Khmer Rouge are ordering everyone out of the capital city. The Americans will bomb us, we are told. We have to be three kilometers (about two miles) away from Phnom Penh to avoid the bombing. Since we are not going far from the capital, we are told we shouldn't take too many belongings, just enough to last until we are allowed to return.

Upon hearing of the imminent evacuation, *Pa* asks Uncle Surg and Than to get his mother, *Yiey* Khmeng, and his sisters' families near Olympic Market. His plan is to leave the city together. If we are not allowed to return, we'll head to his birthplace in Year Piar village, the Khmer Rouge's "long-liberated" area where my grandfather, *Kong* Houng, lives. The trip to pick up his mother shouldn't take long, only about ten minutes to reach the families' houses. Maybe an hour or two to pack belongings. But two hours turn into three, daylight turns to cool night, and still we don't see or hear the car or voices of Than or Uncle Surg. Nothing.

Everyone is worried, especially *Pa* and Uncle Surg's wife, Aunt Heak. *Mak* worries about Than, but feels he'll be okay since he's with Uncle Surg. *Pa* decides to go after them. *Mak* insists he wait until morning. *Pa* doesn't say anything to *Mak*, but gets ready, tugging on his shirt and pants. He retrieves his keys and asks me to unlatch the gate. The scooter starts up with a pop and growl, then headlight and taillights wink on and in a few seconds *Pa* disappears up the dark road.

In a short while, he's back. "These Khmer Rouge are difficult to deal with. They pointed rifles at me and made me turn around."

The following morning, April 19, *Pa* walks to a nearby street. After a few hours *Pa* returns to tell us more Khmer Rouge are pouring into Phnom Penh. Their skins are dark from being in the sun, their appearance crude, as if they need a good bath. Their heads are wrapped with scarves like a farmer's turban. Sitting defiantly atop tanks, military jeeps, and trucks, they form a strange victory parade. Renegade floats decorated with ragtag humans. Their uniforms look like black pajamas. Many wear red-and-white-checked scarves wrapped around their necks like mufflers. Their sandals are odd, with soles fashioned of car tires and pieces of inner tube strapping them into place. It fits with their bare-fisted philosophy of combat.

That doesn't really concern my father. What catches his eye is their physical condition, their malnourished bodies. They act tough with guns and rifles strapped onto their shoulders, but their sallow complexions betray their suffering. *Pa* sees not only with his eyes but with his heart. In the evening *Pa* takes a bottle of multivitamins to these malnourished Khmer Rouge. To them, he looks like a Chinese merchant.

A man with good intentions holds a bottle of medicine and a flashlight. He is not fearful of the ones he seeks to help. Aware only that their newly seized turf is being trespassed upon, the soldiers roar and growl like hyenas, puffed up with false bravado to intimidate *Pa*. They stab their rifles at my father as they close in on him.

Pa shines the light on the white vitamin bottle and explains his intention. But an explanation will not suffice. They don't trust him, they accuse him of trying to poison them. One snatches the bottle away. To ease their suspicions, *Pa* pops two red-coated vitamins into his mouth, chewing them like candy. Only then do the Khmer Rouge put their hands out, and *Pa* feels like a child sharing his goodies with bully kids.

Now he has their trust, he asks them if Hou Yuon and Hu Nim,* high-ranking Khmer Rouge members, are already in Phnom Penh. My father knew these men when he was a young boy, long before they became Communists. Perhaps they could pull some strings for

---

* Both were Cambodian Marxists who left Phnom Penh for the *maquis* (underground fighting) in 1967.

him, allow a passage to Olympic Market to retrieve Uncle Surg, Than, his mother, and his sisters' families before we evacuate. But none of these Khmer Rouge men know of them. *Pa* finds out later from other Khmer Rouge coming through the street that Hou Yuon and Hu Nim won't be coming to Phnom Penh. *Pa's* heart sinks.

The next morning brings more hopelessness and we brace for the unknown. The Khmer Rouge come by to remind us to leave. They ask if *Pa* has weapons. He turns over his pistols, requisitioned to him long ago for work. *Pa* gives his word that we'll leave tomorrow, the twenty-first of April, holding out as long as he can in the hope that Uncle Surg and Than will return. For now, we must pack. Everyone has a chore, and we dully follow our duties: prepare meals for the road, hide money and any valuables: watches, jewelry, house title, birth certificates, etc.

Ra hastily assembles cloth belts with compartments where bundles of money will be hidden. Some of us fold clothes and pack them. Others cook rice, cut vegetables, boil a pan full of eggs, which have been incubated by the hens we raised. *Pa* has to kill the hens for us to eat, ten of them.

Tonight is a night of togetherness, the last wisp of freedom. The night presses on. Fatigue creeps up on me. I fall into a deep sleep, drifting off to the sound of chopping.

Day has come. The morning steals upon us with a heavy, overcast pallor. It is as if nature is in mourning. The weather has been dreadful since the Khmer Rouge took over the country. Black clouds have covered the sky above Phnom Penh.

Leaving our home this morning are *Pa*; *Mak*; Chea; Ra; Ry; myself; Avy, seven; Vin, three; Map, one; Aunt Heak, Uncle Surg's wife; Ateek, their two-year-old son; their baby son, who is not yet one; and our dog, Akie. We are one of the last families to leave, setting out on foot. We lock our gate behind us and begin to walk.

I am struck by how slowly we move, held back by the weight of our sorrow. Suddenly *Pa* stops walking the scooter as if tugged back by it. He scurries back to the house without saying a word to anyone. I follow him while everyone else stands on the road, waiting.

Pa unlocks the gate. Dashes to the door, unlocks it. The door swings open.

"Where do we keep chalk?" *Pa* murmurs to himself. "Where is it?"

"*Pa* . . ."

I want to tell him where the chalk is, but he disappears into the house. We've only left it for a few minutes and already it feels abandoned.

Pa reappears wearing wrinkles on his forehead. He leaps onto the deck and begins to scrawl Uncle Surg's name in huge strokes on the wall of the house. Then Than's name is marked in place, followed by a message for them to meet us in Year Piar. In the wall note he tells Uncle Surg not to worry about his wife and two children—that he's caring for them, taking them with us to Year Piar. They'll be fine and he'll see them soon.

"Let's go, *koon*," *Pa* says softly as he steps off the deck.

The exodus resumes. Main streets are closed, patrolled by the Khmer Rouge. Our family walks in a tight cluster, joining a slow trickle of people that becomes a tide. Around me, people move sluggishly, as if slogging through thick mud. Everybody carries something, except the littlest children. *Pa* walks the scooter, its tires squashed under the weight of suitcases and bags strapped to the backseat. Map and Vin stand at the front of the scooter, on the footrail. Chea and Ra walk bicycles with cooking ware and blankets strapped to them. Underneath Chea's, Ra's, and Ry's blouses are three cloth belts containing our money. *Mak* and Ry carry cooked foodstuffs. Aunt Heak carries a handbag of baby clothes on her shoulder, her infant son in one arm, her older son's hand with the other. She frowns as she stares into space, transfixed by the invisible.

Out of the heart of the city, along the roads and streets, everywhere there are Khmer Rouge. They police everyone, tell us where to go. Merging onto a main thoroughfare, my family joins a chaotic mass of humanity. More people than I have ever seen, stuffed onto a paved street never meant to absorb these numbers. We are among a throng of about 2 million Cambodians who are forced from the city in a matter of days. Lines collect at the Sturng Mean Chey Bridge like solid matter jamming the neck of a bottle. From the mouth of the bridge stretches a massive river of humans with their belongings strapped to motorcycles, bikes, pedicabs, cars, carts, anything they've got. It is too crowded to drive. Anything motorized must be pushed. The human river flows on, as far as the eye can see. Around me I see city people, country people, recent refugees. Outsiders who fled here only weeks ago have little. Those who don't have vehicles to transport their belongings carry them, baskets and bundles of possessions tied to both ends of a long stick and balanced on their shoulders. To me the scene seems like a page out of history, though schoolbooks and lessons seem worlds away right now.

Intermingled with the humans are a group of frenzied pigs, dogs, and chickens. I can hear the fear in the incessant squeals of pigs, the protest of chickens carried under arms and tied into baskets. Stationed on shoulders of the street, and on military trucks along the route, are young Khmer Rouge soldiers, mostly men. All dressed in black uniforms with dark blue-checked scarves tied on their heads or wrapped around their necks. Around their waists are loose belts of grenades and bullets. And in their hands and on their shoulders are machine guns. They point them at us, ordering us to move forward, to keep on moving, toward the bridge, not back into the city. There is only out, no in.

Amid this mass of people is a little boy, about three, in gray shorts and a shirt. He cries at the top of his lungs. He is being moved along by the crowd while his little hands are raised in the air, shielding himself from the people passing. As we move forward, I no longer see him. But his cry still pierces the air, and I think of him and his little bare feet.

I notice a sobbing couple fighting against the crowd, trying to wrestle their way back into the city. They look dressed up, as if they've just come from an office. But they're stopped short by Khmer Rouge soldiers on the street. Rifles point toward them like accusing fingers. The couple quickly press the palms of their hands against each other, a gesture of respect and supplication. Pleading for mercy, they implore the soldiers to grant them passage to their home to retrieve their children.

"You can't go, comrades," a Khmer Rouge barks, "It's not allowed. Go!"

Comrade. The word sounds strange to me. I do not understand it. And these young soldiers, younger than the couple they're ordering about, don't use the proper courtesies in addressing elders, don't call them "aunt" or "uncle." The way they speak to the couple suggests they consider themselves their equal. That's not the way we greet our elders, especially in a time of crisis. The lack of respect shocks me. Authority is reversed. Guns now mean more than age and wisdom.

"Athy, Athy!" *Mak* calls out to me. "Keep walking."

My feet move faster, propelled by the tone of *Mak's* voice.

"Walk by your father. Stop looking back, *koon.*"

Mak frowns as she gestures with her head. I notice her stealing a glance at the distraught couple. She walks behind me as if trying to shield me.

Finally we reach the bridge, but still the mass barely moves. My family is mashed against the metal railing of the bridge. I can't see ahead beyond the wall of people, so I look down at the river. It is low, slow-flowing this time of year. Many things float in it, including corpses.

"*Pa*, look." I tug *Pa*'s shirt gently.

"Athy, come here." *Pa* gestures with his head.

We now look ahead, only ahead. As the human river flows out of Phnom Penh, the water carries away the garbage of war. It is as if everything is being washed away.

Then I hear the continuous barking of a dog. It sounds like a cry of frustration, a cry for help. The familiar sound jolts me back to reality.

"*Pa*, where's Akie?" I blurt out. "I don't see him." I bend down, searching for him among the moving feet. Then I see him whimpering, trying to pass through the moving feet. His head tries to forge an opening among them.

"*Pa, Mak*, Akie's behind us!"

"Athy, stop thinking about him. Keep walking," says *Pa* softly. He looks straight ahead. Akie has been a part of our family, and I don't want to lose him again, like during the Viet Cong invasion.

"*Mak*, Akie doesn't walk behind us anymore," I whisper to my mother, eyes teary.

"He's probably lost, *koon!* Stop worrying about him. Keep walking." *Mak* sounds concerned. Her motherly voice soothes me, and I obey.

We make it across the river onto a stretch of paved highway, which is covered with lines of people—thousands and thousands, marching out like a giant flock of birds in forced migration, hurrying to beat the arrival of a storm. Now that we're out of the city, the sky is blue and the sun is shining, and little children cry. Wails of misery and confusion form the background noise to moving feet.

The Khmer Rouge are everywhere. We pass an open field and see them loading people into trucks. On the shoulders of the highway the Khmer Rouge soldiers stand sentry, holding rifles upright. They survey the moving crowd suspiciously, eyes darting among our faces.

In the distance, I can see what seem to be military trucks and people in different uniforms moving in a field off the right side of the highway. When we get close, almost everyone is curious.

"*Pa*, the Khmer Rouge tie Lon Nol's soldiers up," Chea announces.

"*Pa* knows," says *Pa* softly, as if he's afraid someone will hear.

His voice makes my heart hammer. What does this tying-up mean? What will happen to these men? There are about one hundred of Lon Nol's soldiers in green camouflage. They are tied up, hands behind their backs. Walking behind them are lines of more tied-up men, including a few in civilian clothes. But among them are also those with their hands behind their heads, as the black-uniformed Khmer Rouge point rifles at them.

Pa quickly walks the scooter into a thicker mass of moving people, trying to blend in with the crowd. Among them, he's the tallest. He hunches his shoulders and spine, eyes studying the speedometer of the scooter. *Mak* notices this and so does everyone in the family. The worry passes through us all like a sudden chill.

We pass the field, the checkpoint, and I'm relieved. *Pa* is, too. He walks the scooter normally again, his back straight, his eyes looking ahead. Ateek, Aunt Heak's two-year-old son, sobs in misery. *Pa* puts him with Vin and Map on the scooter foot railing, and it's enough. He's quiet.

Ahead of us, people slow down. From a distance, I see Khmer Rouge cadres stop every family. *Pa* stops the scooter. He murmurs something, tells me to stay still, then slips two watches above my wrist under the sleeve of my blouse. *Mak* gazes at him with a sour face. He assures her, "They won't search children."

"Don't say anything," warns *Pa* softly. "Achea, Ara, hide your watches. . . . I'll talk with them."

"Comrade, do you have a watch?" a Khmer Rouge soldier shouts at a man ahead of us. "If you have, give it to me! Have it or not?" The man before us fumbles through his cloth parcel, trying to show the angry soldier he doesn't have any watch. With irritation the Khmer Rouge shoves the man forward, and his family nervously follows behind like dutiful slaves.

Then it's our turn to pass through the checkpoint, which consists of five Khmer Rouge soldiers with machine guns. *Pa* walks ahead, as if he's stepping up to a ticket window for movie passes.

"I have a watch, you can have it," *Pa* exclaims. He stops walking the scooter and secures it nearby. He removes the watch from his wrist and hands it over. *Pa* knows the game. He's cooperating.

"Does comrade have more?" the soldier asks him fiercely as he hands *Pa*'s watch to a younger cadre standing behind him, who looks at my father's watch with interest. His wrists are already decked out with many different watches. He grins shamelessly, like a greedy child who can't have enough.

I stand behind *Pa* and look down, trying to be calm.

Pa politely says, "I have only one watch, no more."

The soldier waves for us to pass through.

Ahead of us, on the shoulder of the highway, are farmers, five of them, standing, holding chunks of pork, still fresh, all bloody. They shout to us to buy their meat, "fresh pork," they bid. *Mak* and *Pa* give an okay to buy some pork. They are relieved, and surprised, to know there's a makeshift market in a time of need—we'll need more food for the days ahead, maybe a week, as we journey to Year Piar village.

At Sturng Krartort Lake, our resting place for the night, we find that hundreds of people have arrived before us. The spires of smoke from campfires rise everywhere. As late arrivals, we have to camp about half a mile away from the lake. After our meal, my parents, Aunt Heak, and some adults who camp near us, sit together talking about the future. Unlike my sisters and brothers, I mingle with these adults. Much is speculation, best guesses. Having some insight into the living conditions in Red China, *Pa* shares it with the group. "In China under Mao Tse-tung, when you want to eat your own chicken, you have to ask permission. Your property is under the government's control. You have to have their permission to do things. Come to think of it, it's better to be an American 'servant' [ally] than to be Chinese—because there's freedom. Russian Communism, I think, is better than the Red Chinese because they use currency."

"How about the tied-up soldiers?" *Mak* interrupts *Pa*. "Those we saw on the road. What will happen to them?"

"I don't know what they'll do to them. But I think the Khmer Rouge won't just take the country. I think a government fights for its nation to liberate its people," *Pa* philosophizes. He wants to believe the Khmer Rouge can be forgiving, that it can become the Cambodian people's government.

After that evening at Sturng Krartort Lake, we journey through many villages and make several stops. Our routine is simple. We walk most of the day and sleep during the night. The sky has become the roof of our home, and the distant stars replace our fluorescent lights. As we crowd together on blankets and plastic ground coverings, the loose tent of mosquito netting around us does little good. Mosquitoes feast on our blood, leave itchy red welts on our hands and legs.

Within a week we approach *Yiey** Narg's house, *Pa*'s aunt, in Srey Va, a small rural village set amid dry, sandy fields on our

---

* Because of her age and the fact that she was *Kong* Houng's sister, it was proper for us to call her "grandmother," even though biologically she was our great-aunt.

way to Year Piar. I'm thirsty and hungry, eagerly expecting good food and comfortable rest on a soft bed like the one I left behind.

But it is just a dream. *Yiey* Narg and her husband are modest farmers who have already lived under the Khmer Rouge for five years. Their wooden house is small and crowded. There are no chairs, only a hard platform and a bamboo counter near it. Instead of lush greenery, the overwhelming color here is drab brown. I stare at a few banana and papaya trees thriving in a dry, sandy backyard. The soil is as worn-out as the expression on *Yiey* Narg's and her husband's faces.

Yiey Narg informs us how restricted her family's freedom has been since the Khmer Rouge arrived. They had touted a promise of equality. And yet, her family can't fish or trade with other people as they used to. They can't travel outside the confines of their own rural neighborhood. As a result, there are deprivations. It seems they have little salt for cooking. And so they've learned to improvise, using ashes from the cooking fire to preserve the fish they've caught.

After we have a simple rural meal, *Pa* wants to head to Year Piar immediately. But *Yiey* Narg insists we all rest overnight at her house. *Pa* is polite but adamant about going to see his father.

"Then your wife and children stay. And Heak and her children. All right, you stay, rest." She makes up her mind for all of us, which is almost always the way it is with Cambodian elders. "Tidsim," *Yiey* Narg continues, "be careful. I've heard rumors. Some families have had to go elsewhere, beyond their home provinces, because the Khmer Rouge are not trustworthy. They'll question you about your past profession. Who knows what they'll do to you. . . . Be careful, don't trust them," she warns *Pa*.

Be careful, don't trust them. The words sound ominous yet abstract—an open-ended warning. But my fear is more realistic now, especially when I hear this admonition from a relative who has lived under the Khmer Rouge for five years.

Pa takes me with him to Year Piar. I'm very tired, but relieved to be leaving. Like *Pa*, who believes in human goodness, I still believe that life could return to what it used to be. Already, as we are about to leave for Year Piar, I look forward to something less grim.

"Athy, *koon*, don't sleep, do you hear?"

Even as I close my eyes, cheek pressed against *Pa*'s warm back, I feel the fog of exhaustion settle over me. But I must leave this place. And I'm happy to be here, clinging to *Pa* like a weary little monkey.

The labored strains of the scooter engine propel the wheels along a dried-mud path while my tired eyes struggle to stay open.

"*Pa*, are we almost there yet?"

"We're almost there, *koon*. Don't sleep now."

"No," I say softly.

I lie. My eyes are barely open. My hands are losing their grip on *Pa*'s waist. Already I'm beginning to doze off. Now and then I feel *Pa*'s hand shaking my back repeatedly. I hear him say, "Don't sleep, *koon*. We're almost there." I open my eyes, then close them once again.

Soon I hear children's voices. Gradually the chorus becomes louder, "Look, those things spin!" The chatter of joyous laughter follows. A wave of young children run toward us as if we were a traveling novelty act.

Pa slows down, then suddenly comes to a stop, causing our bodies to jerk forward. Children swarm around us out of nowhere, hovering the way flies cluster around raw flesh. They chase us, pointing and giggling like fools at the wheels. Some reach out to touch the rubber scooter tires, which hold a strange, hypnotic allure for them.

This herd of half-dressed and naked children, ages two to nine, are unlike anything I have ever seen. The poorest of the poor. Their clothes are ragged, beyond old, the color faded beyond recognition. So many patches have been sewn haphazardly atop each other that their garments are thick and bulky. These are not typical country children but a postrevolutionary product. Dirt is a uniform, and everyone seems to need a bath. The youngest ones approach with noses encrusted with soot and snot.

As filthy and disadvantaged as they seem, their fascination with the tires strikes me as weirdly out of place. It irritates me, at first, to watch them act so silly over something as basic as a scooter tire. I am repulsed, recoiling from these children, some even my own age, as they continue to chase us. It never occurs to me that for many this might be the first time they've ever seen a motorized vehicle.

5

There Are No Good-byes

The New York Times
May 2, 1977
"Refugees Depict Grim Cambodia Beset by Hunger"

BY DAVID A. ANDELMAN

The purges that took hundreds of thousands of lives in the aftermath of the Communist capture of Phnom Penh on April 17, 1975, have apparently ended for the most part, according to the informants. But the new system is said to function largely through fear, with the leadership making itself felt at local levels through what is described as "the organization."

We're met by the familiar smells of the country, and I'm cast back into the past. I breathe deeply, taking in the sweet stench of urine, animal dung, and hay—a powerful formula that reminds me of the times when *Pa* brought me to visit *Kong* (Grandpa) Houng, *Yiey* (Grandma) Khmeng, and *Yiey Tot* (Great-grandmother). I glance down and realize how far I am from Phnom Penh.

Along the path lie flat pools and small hills of verdant, runny dung left by cows, water buffalo, and oxen. I stare at the random drops as *Pa* maneuvers the motorbike around them. It is a crude landscape, where mud and dirt and dung are a fact of life. Houses are built on stilts. Children play not in the dusty road but in the field. Roads are where they go to collect dung for the rice fields.

Pa and I arrive at *Kong* Houng's house before sunset. The hum of the scooter announces our approach. Waiting to greet us is Aunt Cheng, along with other local people I don't recognize. As she carefully makes her way down the steep oaken stairs, Aunt Cheng smiles her familiar, ever-present smile, almost a trademark. Her thick black hair is shorter than the last time I saw her—it's been snipped from waist length to her chin. As in Phnom Penh, she wears a white blouse with a flowered sarong.* She smiles brightly at me, then asks, "Athy, where is everybody, your mother?"

"*Mak*'s at *Yiey* Narg's house. Everybody will come here tomorrow."

I quickly survey my new surroundings. A barn is used as storage for generous mountains of unhusked rice; bundles of hay are stacked near it, and among the fruit trees nearby, a large, branched tamarind tree stretches to the heavens, almost as tall as the barn.

I stand in front of the stairs, looking at a place that was once familiar but now seems strange, for I haven't seen it for five years, half of my life. The house is built on large pilings. Compared with the homes of other country people, my grandfather's house is big; the wooden stairs and a banister skim down the left side. My grandparents are relatively well-to-do people by local standards. They own many cattle and much of the farmland around Year Piar and other villages as well. On earlier visits, I can remember my grandmother explaining how *Kong* Houng would have to go away to collect "rent" from farmland in remote villages. Often the payment came in the form of rice. His success was achieved through hard work, a family tradition. His parents before him had farmed, acquiring property with time and patience.

When the Khmer Rouge came, they ordered him as well as his younger brother, *Kong* Lorng, to give up their property. When they refused, both were tied up and sentenced to be executed. In any society, whether it's capitalist, socialist, or communist, connections do pay off—they were saved by a relative who knew someone who knew Ta Mok, the infamous one-legged man who is one of the Khmer Rouge highest-ranking military officials, overseeing executions.

---

* A long skirt that a woman wears at home; sometimes men would wear them also.

"Athy, Athy."

I look for the eager voice calling my name, only to find a familiar face smiling at me.

"Than!" I croon. I didn't know how much I loved my brother until we were separated.

He looks different than the last time I saw him in Phnom Penh, only two weeks ago. My last image of Than was of him leaving with Uncle Surg to retrieve my aunts, grandmother, and cousins during the chaotic days before evacuation.

I study him. His hair is shorter, and he is darker, the pigment drawn from walking in the sun many days. A peasant color, I think, like that of the local farmers.

Than makes his way downstairs as he holds the railing, watching his step and smiling brightly. I walk toward the stairs, elated to see my old sparring partner, despite the way we used to constantly fight. I've missed him, and the thought surprises me. I realize that I once thought I would never see him again, and my honest acceptance of this shocks me.

If it was permitted within our culture to embrace, I would have thrown my arms around him. But that's only appropriate for someone older who comforts someone younger. Instead, Than tells me to hold on to the stair railing, his own shyness eliciting affection as we both climb into the house. In two large spherical bamboo baskets are different Cambodian desserts wrapped in banana leaves. Also, in colorful steel platters are pieces of dark, sweet glutinous rice with fresh grated coconut and sesame seeds scattered on top. After *Yiey* Narg's modest fare, this is sumptuous. This is Cambodian tradition, greeting guests with a sprawling bounty. With Than around, my appetite seems to kick in. He's good medicine.

"Thy, you can eat as much as you want. They made all of these desserts for our family. They made a lot when I came with *Poo* Surg."

Than's voice energizes me, like sugar on my tongue.

"Let's go see the banana trees. Hurry, pick something, let's go!" he urges me.

Than's separation from us seems to have had no effect on him whatsoever; or maybe he's just happy that it is over. Than persists, "Athy, do you want to see pineapples and bananas?" His eyes are wide. "There are a lot in the orchard. I'll take you there. And there's also a well, and it's deep. You want to go now?"

Before I answer, Than helps me grab some dessert. We hurry to the orchard.

I'm in awe of the lush green pineapples that flourish everywhere in the shade of fruit trees and along the path to the well. Pineapple plants grow bigger than a child, and rising among the long, thorny leaves are the pineapple buds. Some are about the size of a fist, while others grow two or three times that size. Never have I seen such a thing.

I'm still spellbound by the beauty and abundance of the pineapples, but Than is already at the well, like a happy dog wiggling his tail at the prospect of something intriguing. Than calls to me, "Look in there, Athy, you can see your shadow in the water during the daytime."

Surrounding the well are more pineapples, then bananas scattered in rows with long green leaves and buds sprouting out of their trunks. From the barn to the well are tall-branched lamut trees, full with their rough-skinned fruit, that are the color and shape of kiwi. The fruits are still green, but abundant.

"Can we pick lamut?" I ask Than.

"You want some?" Than's eyes glow, his eyebrows raised.

"Yeah!" My eyes widen. On the road, fresh fruit was not to be found, and lamut is one of my favorites.

Than and I hurry back to the house so he can show me where he has kept his private stash, the ones hidden in a rice barrel to ripen.

The next day is a homecoming. *Mak*, Aunt Heak, her two sons, and my sisters and brothers roll into Year Piar in rumbling oxcarts, joining other relatives who have already arrived. Their final arrival seems to mark a family reunion for my grandparents, who look relieved. Now, five of their seven children have returned home with their families. In my own family there are ten of us. The other families consist of my aunts, uncles, and cousins, totaling twenty-nine people, including my grandparents. We now share three large bedrooms. The crowding is not bad, but the lack of electricity bothers me.

Later in the week, more homecoming. Most of *Mak*'s side of the family. *Mak*'s parents as well as her sisters and brothers and their families. Fourteen altogether, too many people for *Kong* Houng to accommodate even in his large home. Sensitive to their situation, *Mak*'s parents and siblings elect to turn the rice storage area into their makeshift home. Everyone learns to cope.

After dinner Chea, Ra, Ry, and I rest in our room, surrounded by our belongings, which lean against the walls like weary travelers. Listening to Chea, Ra, and Ry talk is like a balm. All of a sudden Chea jumps up. She scurries to her school briefcase to look for her watch.

"You guys, it's almost time for the Voice of America." Chea's eyes widen. "Ra, where's the radio?"

Ry and I jump up as Chea and Ra locate the radio near one of the suitcases.

"Athy," Chea exclaims anxiously, "go get *Pa*."

In a minute I have *Pa* with me, along with *Mak*, Than, my aunts and uncles, and Grandma, all crowded into the room and the doorway. Already Chea is fumbling for the Voice of America's frequency. The static crackles loudly.

"Achea, turn it down," *Pa* says, knitting his eyebrows.

The faint, brassy strains of American music come through—the theme song of the Voice of America.

"This is the Voice of America in Khmer," a man's voice announces in English. Then a woman comes on, speaking in Cambodian: "From the city of Washington, I'm . . . Ladies and gentlemen, please listen to the events that have taken place in Cambodia. . . ."

At first I find comfort in her voice, for she connects us to the world, unveiling facts, or what the broadcast claims to have happened. But that sense of comfort is brief. I become nervous when I notice *Pa* frowning. Then everyone else—Chea, Ra, my aunts and uncles—all look anxious, sad. They glance at *Pa* after he sighs. He is a thermometer for our fear.

"Achea, turn the radio off," *Mak* orders. "They'll suspect us."

Chea throws *Mak* a glance, but her hand doesn't obey. *Mak* strides toward the radio and reaches to turn it off.

"Not yet," *Pa* cries, raising his hand to shield *Mak* from the radio.

Then *Kong* Houng's head peeks through the door. He nervously whispers, "There's someone standing below the house listening. He stands right underneath this room," he points, stabbing at the floor, with its wide gaps. "It's a *chhlop*.* You'd better be careful."

Pa turns to his father. *Mak* quickly reaches over and flips the switch off. She disconnects us from the outside world but links us to the mask of horror on her face. By then my father has digested what his father just said.

The next day a Khmer Rouge cadre seizes the radio, his simple black uniform a mark of his authority. He says the radio now belongs to the commune. All I know is fear. At night, following the *chhlop*'s eavesdropping, I'm afraid to speak to my sisters, even to utter words like "hand me the blanket," as if whispering anything at all will cause trouble or bring bad luck.

---

* An informant, usually a full-status Khmer Rouge member, who spied on people and reported on them to *Angka Leu* (the high organization).

At night I lift the mat below me and look through the spaces between the floorboards to see if a *chhlop* is beneath the house, lurking like a demon. Sure enough, I see the shadow of a person standing in a dark corner of the house just below our bedroom. Quickly I drop the mat, recoiling as if I've just scorched my fingers on a hot iron. I snuggle closer to Chea.

Within a few days of our arrival, Year Piar Khmer Rouge leaders, who were formerly my grandparents' employees or tenants, order my father and uncles to work in the name of *Angka Leu*. The office for *Pa* is now replaced by an empty field. A hoe, woven baskets, and a carrying stick replace pens and paper. They order the newly arrived men to dig dirt, to build water canals for no pay, in order to advance their revolution.

After dinner, the evening breeze brings my relatives and me to the solid oak bed—a heavy slab of wood, really—which has been brought outside and down the stairs. With the heat and fieldwork, the men seek relief, yearning for a cool breeze the way some men thirst for a quenching drink of water.

It is here that *Pa* shares his thoughts and feelings about his first day of labor for the Khmer Rouge. "These people are dumb," he mutters, shaking his head. "They use educated people to dig dirt, the kind of work people without education can do."

"In this era," he says, his mouth widening into a smile, "all you need do to pass an exam is know how to dig dirt."

Some of us join in with light laughter.

Mak looks around. "Your father is careless about what he says," she warns. "If they hear what he says, we will be in trouble. Joking without thinking." *Mak* gives *Pa* her patented look of disapproval. Everyone knows what it means.

Mak's words erase our smiles. *Pa* glances around us. "Let's stop talking," he says softly. "Nowadays, walls have ears."

Already the Khmer Rouge, the phantoms of the jungle, seem ubiquitous. They are like flies buzzing around us, everywhere but invisible. They are the breeze that ruffles the banana trees, unseen but powerful.

Angka is now the master of our destiny, it seems. The next morning Khmer Rouge order us to attend a meeting. A meeting for "new people," we are told. As recent arrivals, most of my family must attend except *Mak*, who stays home to look after Vin, Map, and Avy.

We dress as if we were going to visit the Buddhist temple or attend school. I hold my father's hand as we journey to this meeting on foot. *Pa* wears a white short-sleeved shirt with slacks, and I wear my school uniform. After we walk about four miles, we come to a large open field, filled with people dressed in spring clothes—they are not local villagers. There are hundreds of them, and everyone squats or sits on the ground on plastic material or cloth. Together we look like nicely dressed vagabonds, surprised to find we have put on good clothes only to sit in the dirt.

I shake my father's hand. "*Pa*, people sit on the ground."

"*Pa* knows."

We are struck by this churning mass of people sitting on the ground like mushrooms. In the bright pulsing sun we squint, blocking the rays with hands shelved above our eyes, an unintended salute. I gaze at the bulging body of people, sweeping over the scene again and again like a surveillance camera taking snapshots of intruders. In my wildest dreams, I could never have visualized such a meeting, a goofy, dressed-up tribal gathering, a trip back in time.

I glare at *Pa*. Why must we sit on the ground and obey the Khmer Rouge? *We can't just obey them. We don't owe them our respect.* Deep in my heart, there's a fire. I feel that if I sit down, I will forever give in to the Khmer Rouge. In my mind I shout, *You cannot tell me what to think!*

For the first time, I'm defiant, very angry at the Khmer Rouge who are shaping my life as well as my family's. I am no longer sad or afraid. Now I know the taste of anger, for I know I don't want to be in this whirlpool of darkness without reason, yet I get sucked into it.

Behind a mile of people, *Pa* squats, sitting on his heels, and I stand by him. The rest of my family squats near us. *Pa* tells me to sit down. I answer with a single sharp shake of my head.

I don't want to dirty my clothes, I don't want to listen to them, I don't like them. Anger boils in me. Internally, I take it out on my father as I squint defiantly at the makeshift stage, glaring at the Khmer Rouge in their stupid black uniforms and ugly tire sandals. As much as I loathe their backward revolution because it has threatened my safety and security, I dislike their stage even more. A deck covered with gray roofing with two beams in front, each mounted with bell-shaped loudspeakers. It seems a false altar to their power.

Finally the loudspeakers squawk, followed by a man's commanding voice: "Comrades, now we are all equal. There are no longer rich and poor. WE ARE EQUAL. WE ALL WEAR BLACK UNIFORMS."

Black? I look at my clothes, then at *Pa*. He cracks a smile.

"We fought the 'American imperialists' with bare hands, and took victory over them. We're brave. . . . *Chey yo* [Long live] Democratic Kampuchea, *chey yo, chey yo.* . . . *Para chey* [Down with] the 'American imperialists,' *para chey, para chey.*"

Since we are merely the Khmer Rouge's puppets, we are supposed to do the same, shouting "chey yo" with our fists stabbing upward into the air. Then "para chey" with our fists stabbing downward.

Even at nine years of age, I recognize that this meeting is deceptive. How can these Khmer Rouge leaders blindly say things that many of us, even children, already know to be false. *What are their intentions?*

After a few hours of listening to numbing chants under the hot sun, I know only that I feel a defiant seed sprouting deep within me. The entire time, I never sink into the dirt. It is a small act, but an important one.

The next day my asthma returns. As always, *Pa* is my doctor—he's there for me, checking my breathing, listening to my lungs, trying to make things better as my chest rides up and down, struggling for air. At night before going to sleep, *Pa* listens to my labored breathing again, then gives me medicine one more time. As always, *Pa* has a way of putting things right. Good father that he is, he smiles warmly, then says, "*Koon*, when your medicine is gone, let's stop getting sick, okay?"

I look into *Pa's* eyes and know what he means.

Since I've been sick, *Pa* has me sleep outside downstairs, sharing the oak bed sandwiched between him and *Kong* Houng. The next evening as I sleep, I hear *Pa's* voice calling my name, and then his hand gently touches my face.

"Athy, *koon*, do you have difficulty breathing? Sit upright if you do."

I open my eyes and *Pa's* silhouette is beside me. He pats my head, then rests his ear against my wheezing chest, listening to my lungs. Knowing *Pa's* near, I groan a little just to let him know I hear him, then my eyes shut. When I open them again, *Pa* disappears, and I sink back into my restless sleep.

"Please sit down. Yes, please," a voice says.

"Yes, yes," a chorus of three voices exclaim.

My eyes open. And there, opposite me, at the end of the bed, are two men and a woman, whom I have never seen. All are dressed in black uniforms with red-and-white-checked scarves draped around their necks. Greeting them is *Kong* Houng, whose voice I heard earlier. He's sitting near me, illuminated by a dim oil lamp beside him. Feeling delirious and anxious, I get up abruptly. Then I see *Pa* make his way down the stairs.

"*Pa*," I cry out. I feel warm and shaky.

"Stay there, *Pa*'s coming."

After he greets the strangers, *Pa* sits near me, beside *Kong* Houng, facing the strangers, with his legs folded casually on the oak bed. He strokes my hair and tells me to go back to sleep. I obey and close my eyes. But I can no longer sleep. These three people have come to ask *Pa* many questions regarding Uncle Seng's whereabouts and *Pa*'s previous occupation, as well as Uncle Surg's and Uncle Sorn's. I lie facing them, finally understanding what this meeting is about.

Kong Houng has told *Pa* and all my uncles about local people wanting to meet them. Back then, it sounded harmless, a neighborly get-to-know-you meeting. But now it feels sinister. These people are interrogators. Their unwavering, direct gaze burns into *Pa*—an unrelenting eye contact uncommon in Cambodian culture—as *Pa* dutifully explains his own work history and the other uncles' previous jobs.

As soon as *Pa* finishes, the woman quickly attacks, asking *Kong* Houng about Uncle Seng. "Where is your other son, the one who flies an airplane?"

"I don't know why Seng hasn't come home. Most of my children and their children came," *Kong* Houng says gently, appearing genuinely concerned and curious. He turns to *Pa* and says, "Atidsim told me that they got separated on the way here. I don't know what else to tell you."

Pa comes to the rescue. He explains that Uncle Seng was separated from us during the chaotic evacuation from Phnom Penh, lost in the madness of those final days. It is the only lie he utters.

He tells them we waited for Uncle Seng, but that he never showed up. "I figured he can find his way here, so we decided to continue our walk. I don't know why he isn't here yet. We hope he gets to see all the relatives." *Pa* speaks politely and convincingly.

Pa's fabricated story conjures up memories of Uncle Seng leaving our home and *Pa*'s helplessness as he watched him walk away. As I stare at these Khmer Rouge, Uncle Seng's last words replay in my mind: *The Khmer Rouge are my first enemy. I won't stay to see their faces.* This is the delicious power of the mind—they can't stop me from my silent thoughts. They can't interrogate my memories.

Another day, another new thing to learn. Since there are no markets, we constantly have to improvise. It's the frustrating New World Order, the Khmer Rouge way. Ra and Ry are sent to the lake to catch fish for our daily soup. We don't have a proper fishing net, so *Mak* suggests they use mosquito netting. The only fishing they've ever done was for fun back in Takeo, using string and hooks in the water to chase slices of silver fish by my uncle's home. The hardest challenge was touching the earthworm. But what they are now asked to do is to walk through the lake with the open netting, sweeping through the water to trap fish and debris.

Since I'm feeling better, I'm asked to help. I don't want to, but Ra and Ry tell me it's easy. All I have to do is carry a woven basket and follow behind them as they fish. The morning is overcast, a bit chilly. Ra and Ry stand on the bank overlooking the lake, now shrinking in the summer heat, and wonder exactly how they will go about fishing. "Where do we start?" they ask each other. They stare at the water, and I at the tiny green leaves floating on the surface of the lake, then at the tall grasslike plants and dead tree snags poking out like skeletons. Now my task doesn't look easy anymore. I will have to follow my sisters into that water, and I dread stepping on things I can't see, the lurking dangers of thorns.

We start at the lower bank, where there are many tall grassy plants. The water is cool as I tiptoe into it barefoot. It feels strange as the soles of my feet sink into the mud, squeezing between my toes like cool, soft rice dough. I dread going further, but must follow my sisters, who are already far ahead, delicately lifting the netting above the grassy plants. Ra and Ry clumsily try to negotiate timing, deciding when to put the netting down to fish, becoming cross. Like me, they are squeamish but determined. The responsibility of survival rests on everyone.

In time, their voices die down and the only thing I hear is the slurping sound of our feet parting the still water, stirring up sediment from the bottom in a crazy dance. Like the bits of lake bottom, I can almost feel the random collision, the political whirlpool touching us all, occluding the future. Like sediment, I know that life will never fall into the same order again.

Already I'm learning to survive, catching fish as small as anchovies and as large as cucumbers. I cringe at the strange, slimy things that brush against my feet. Inasmuch as I dread walking and carrying the basket, it's exciting to see the captured silver fish flop and shimmy in the netting. Amid all the excitement, something bites my leg. I lift my leg up and on it is a soft dark creature, the size of a string bean, that clings to my shin, bent in a semicircle.

"What's on my leg?" I ask Ry and Ra curiously.

"Ra, leech, le—leech," Ry stammers. She lifts her legs up, one right after another, checking for leeches.

I shriek a long-drawn-out "Ow!" as soon as Ry says the word "leech." The word means nothing to me, but her terrified face and the sight of her dancing in the water, stamping her feet like a scared little child throwing a tantrum, frighten me. I scream, stamping my feet and splashing water, dancing in a mirror image of her hysteria.

"Help me, get it off me!" I run to Ry and Ra.

Ry runs away. "Don't come near me! *Ay, ay,*" she cries.

"Stop moving!" Ra shouts. "Stay still."

I look away, crying, as Ra scrapes off the bloodsucker with the netting.

After all the hysteria, Ra decides that we're done fishing. On our way back to *Kong* Houng's house, I ask my sisters about leeches.

Leeches suck blood—the blood of humans, cows, and buffalo, they tell me. Ry laughs, her face red. Now she's amused as she remembers how silly I looked, stamping in the water, screaming at the top of my lungs. Only now is it funny. I chuckle at the image of Ry running away from me, too. Like schoolgirls, we laugh at our silliness, our new experience, our new way of life.

Now it's a routine. After fishing, I wash up at the well. I've learned not to be scared by it. I lower the bucket, then scoop up as much water as I can carry. Only after fishing and cleaning myself up do I hurry off to breakfast. Usually I have meals with *Mak* and my siblings, cousins, and aunts. *Pa, Kong* Houng, and my uncles eat by themselves, but sometimes the women join them.

It's been two weeks since we entered this strange world and new life. Now *Pa* and my uncles are required to report for "orientation" with *Angka Leu*. They will learn about the new government, they are told, and will be gone for a while—exactly how long no one knows. They must attend and will be picked up in oxcarts. The news is unsettling to everyone, but little is said. By now we've learned to take our worries into our own quiet corners.

The morning for orientation finally arrives, and I've planned to have breakfast with *Pa* before he leaves. Though I never shared my plan, I thought this would be a way to show him how much I will miss him.

After fishing, I go to the kitchen and place the day's meager catch by the clay stoves. I'm disappointed to find *Pa* already eating with my uncles and *Kong* Houng. All I hear is the sound of spoons scraping plates and bowls. Each man studies the spoon as he brings it to his mouth. I can almost feel the weight of their thoughts, even if I can't hear them. Though together, they seem alone, like strangers who have never met. Their stillness sends a strange air through the house, a sadness so heavy that it radiates like thick smoke, choking me. Suddenly I feel lonely, as if something will be taken away from me. I dash down the stairs from the kitchen to the well. I quickly rinse the lake off my legs, then run back to the kitchen. The men are done, the kitchen empty. I want to look for *Pa*, but figure I have time to get a bowl of rice and soup to ease my growling stomach. With the bowl of food in my hand, I run looking for him in the house while shoving a few bites in my mouth. I see only *Mak* and my sisters and aunts.

"*Mak!* Where did *Pa* go?" I ask, feeling scared.

"They brought oxcarts to take your father and uncles." *Mak* speaks softly as she sits on the floor folding clothes.

I storm out, running down the stairs, one hand gripping my rice bowl, the other clutching the railing. I want to catch up with *Pa*, to see him again. I run to the path behind *Kong* Houng's house, but he's nowhere to be found. My uncles are gone, too. No oxcarts. No one there.

My mouth no longer chews the food, but simply releases a sound of immense sadness. I run to the banana grove. I sink down onto the dirt. *Only a moment ago I saw* Pa, *and now he's gone.* I wail, cupping my face, my agony, in my hands.

Looking at the canopy of banana leaves, I beg, "*Pa*, come back. Come back, *Pa*. Come back to your *koon*. . . ."

With each breath, I plead for *Pa* to come back. *No, it's too soon. You left so soon. You didn't wait for me. No, don't leave.*

Never before have I felt so much pain inside my body. My chest, my eyes. My throat. My grief encompasses every cell, touches every limb, every organ. For *Pa* has never left me for more than a day. Never. Now he's gone, and I have the deepest intuition that something is wrong.

Along with sorrow come the companion emotions of frustration and anger. Only nine, I already find myself furious at the Khmer Rouge for taking my father away. I take my burning anger out on the banana tree. I tear at the wilted, papery layers along the trunk, yanking them away and striking the tree with my fist. I rage at the Khmer Rouge. I cry until I'm drained of tears, until my body is limp from exhaustion, in need of the beat-up tree. I lean against it, my head resting on my knees. I feel utterly hollow.

Days have gone by since the Khmer Rouge took *Pa* and my uncles away. I've counted the days until *Pa* is due back, noting them carefully with pen and paper. I draw my own calendar, recording each day without him. A month, *Mak* told me, which was what the Khmer Rouge had told her. During the day I return to the orchard. I cry alone, calling out to *Pa*. Like the earth without the sun, I'm drifting in the dark, thinking of him, wondering where he is, what he's doing. Whether he misses us, misses me.

After the sun surrenders to the night, I'm still thinking of *Pa*. I'm no longer scared of the informant hiding below us. I sit on *Pa*'s scooter, parked under the house where the informant used to eavesdrop on us. Holding on to the black rubber handles, *Pa*'s last handprints, I'm connected to the world as it was when *Pa* was with us. As painful as it is, I journey back in time, revisiting the past as my wet eyes gaze at the tachometer, the red needle aligned at the zero mark.

Zero. Our lives are at zero. Year zero.

I reminisce about better times, when *Pa* took us out to restaurants and to the palace where the royal family lived. I remember nights in Takeo. *Pa* would wake everyone up for pâté sandwiches. He'd carry me from my bed to the dining table. He'd feed me until my mind woke up, then my eyes would open to find a platter of meats, cucumbers, and French bread. My memory speaks until it hurts. Until I break down.

"Athy, why are you crying? Are you okay?" Chea comes to rescue me.

"Chea, I miss *Pa*. I miss *Pa* very much."

"Stop crying, *p'yoon srey*. I miss *Pa*, too."

Chea reaches out and pulls me close to her. In her arms, I cry harder, letting out pain that I've hidden from my family. Chea hugs me tight. Her hand massages my head, a soothing touch that softens my sorrow. It allows me to sleep, lying in the room beside my sisters, hugging *Pa*'s shirt. I hug him in my mind as I inhale his odor from his shirt. I inhale it deeply and hungrily. I love *Pa*—words I've never actually uttered. I miss him; the way I would miss a piece of my own body. I am adrift.

One month has gone by. Still *Pa* hasn't returned. Now the Khmer Rouge order *Mak* to a meeting with the other women whose husbands were taken away. At the meeting the Khmer Rouge ask everyone if they want to go to their husbands and work with them in an "office." All of them say yes. *Who wouldn't want to be with their husbands?* *Mak* wouldn't. She tells the Khmer Rouge that she would rather stay in the village and work for *Angka Leu*. *Mak* would have told them otherwise if it weren't for Som, whose husband had worked for *Kong* Houng before the Khmer Rouge "liberated" Year Piar. Som secretly came to *Mak* the day before the meeting and told her what to say. Even though there was no reason given, *Mak* obeyed, repeating her lines to Khmer Rouge leaders. *Mak*'s intuition to trust Som's words saves my family. In time, those women who volunteered to be with their husbands are taken away.

Walking in the village days later, *Mak* sees a man wearing *Pa*'s shirt—a cream-colored short-sleeved dress shirt with one pocket. In this village of poverty, a simple office shirt stands out. Without fear, she follows the man and demands to know where he got it. Baffled by *Mak*'s abrupt confrontation, he mutters that it has been distributed to him. *Mak* rages at the idea of someone giving away her husband's belongings. Biting back her anger, she turns and heads to Som's hut in search of the truth. *Mak* figures Som will know since her husband is one of the local people who now works for the Khmer Rouge who took *Pa* and my uncles to "orientation."

Som whispers urgently to *Mak*, asking her to tone down her voice. In her hut, lit only by the rays of sun that sneak in, she confides to *Mak*, revealing what happened to *Pa*—a truth that shakes the core of *Mak*'s already wilted soul.

Pa, Uncle Surg, Uncle Sorn, and the other men were not taken to an orientation. They were taken to a remote field outside Year Piar to be executed. Upon their arrival, they were unloaded off the oxcarts and forced to dig their own graves. After they finished, the Khmer Rouge cadres tied them up, then killed each one with a hoe. The bodies tumbled into the very pits they had readied to catch them.

"Your husband fought back while being tied up," Som whispers. "He called them liars and traitors. They killed him right away."

Mak's face gorges with blood, burning with sorrow and anger. The women who wanted to be with their husbands, along with their children and elderly parents, were also executed. Their bodies were buried in the empty field, but their personal belongings were brought back to Year Piar to be distributed among the villagers—*Pa*'s belongings as well as my uncles'. Possessions of the dead passed out as a gruesome prize to the living.

Mak returns, telling us all at once. She is composed, unraveling the bad news carefully. There is no outward grieving, even as a family. Like other emotions, it must be tucked away. She delivers the news in a tone of resignation—relieved that Som has told her. There is no more wondering. And in a dull way, I am not surprised.

But inside, questions bubble up. More confusion than rage. *What has Pa done to be killed this way?* He has never been anything but a caring father, a responsible husband, and a devoted son. Contemplating it all, I'm first baffled by this senseless killing, rather than sad. In this era, the rules are twisted: having education is a crime and honesty doesn't pay. *What will?* I wonder. I answer this question myself. I recall a Cambodian proverb that I heard grown-ups quote among themselves: *Don't give up on the winding road, but don't tread the straight one.*

Mak had treaded the winding road and lied to the Khmer Rouge. Her false act of patriotism prompted by Som's secret warning saved our lives. Despite her fear and her new loyalty to the Khmer Rouge, Som recognized her human obligation, her old loyalty to *Kong* Houng, her former employer, and thus his family, his children and grandchildren.

The Khmer Rouge leaders in the village want to see *Yiey* Khmeng (*Pa's* mother) to interrogate her regarding the whereabouts of Uncle Seng. To prepare her for this, she, *Kong* Houng, *Mak*, and other relatives discuss what *Yiey* Khmeng should tell them. Already we're playing within their rules, hoping we'll survive this life-and-death game. This order to interrogate *Yiey* Khmeng provokes *Kong* Houng: "I already told them about Seng. Atidsim also told them. Now what do they want? These people are impossible."

Yiey Khmeng comes home distressed, agitated and shaking. Slowly she whispers, "They asked a lot of questions. After one of them asked me, the others continued interrogating. They kept asking 'Where is Seng?' One of them addressed me as *Mae*.* He said, '*Mae*, where is your other son and what did he do in the city?' He questioned me sarcastically. 'Tell *Angka Leu* where he is and what he did—that is, if you don't want your son to be in a gas barrel.† Do you want your son to be in a gas barrel, *Mae*?'"

"Why do they speak of such a thing?" she goes on. "These people are cruel. All I told them was that I don't know where Seng is or what he did. All I knew was that I saw him carrying his books to school every day. One of them was furious and said: 'What kind of a mother are you? Don't you know what your son did? Com-

---

* The term for "mother" usually used by rural or uneducated people.
† Refers to a fifty-five-gallon drum.

rade, you lie! Stop asking her more questions. When her son is here, put him in a gas barrel.' And then he stormed out of the hut. These people are coldhearted."

Yiey Khmeng sighs, staring at the floor.

Silence. The Khmer Rouge's dark power renders us speechless, makes us paranoid. We've learned to watch over our shoulders for the *chhlop*. It becomes second nature. Our tightly drawn family community numbers forty-three people, all supported largely by my grandfather's orchard, which is beginning to bear the signs of our dependence. The banana trees are nearly stripped bare; papaya trees and pineapple plants are overused. Still, we find things to eat, to survive.

"Athy, do you want to eat pickled *armmiage*?" *Mak* asks me one day, seemingly in good spirits.

"*Mak*, I like to eat pickled *armmiage* with broiled fish. It's delicious, isn't it, *Mak*?" My mouth waters as I think about it, a green plant resembling watercress.

"Do you want to look for it so *Mak* can pickle it for you? It grows wild along the paths, by people's huts. *Mak* picked some yesterday on the way to work. This is what it looks like. Please go find some more for *Mak*."

I eagerly ask my mother for something to put the *armmiage* in. *Mak* ties knots at both ends of a scarf; draped around my neck, it creates two pouches. She gives me a plant of *armmiage* to take with me in case I don't remember what it looks like. From hut to hut, my eyes take in all the plants and weeds growing on the paths or in the yards. *Mak* is right about a lot of *armmiage* growing wild. It grows everywhere, along the pathways and in front of people's huts. After I pick a patch of it, I look up and see more *armmiage* ahead of me, some growing in clusters, others scattered randomly. Both of the pouches fill quickly, but I am still picking. I know how good it will taste once it is pickled and ready to be eaten.

I am stooping down by the path at the corner of a house when I hear a chorus of women's voices.

"Who else dropped the bombs?" An angry voice demands. "It was him, Aseng, who dropped them. Our families and children were savagely killed because of him. When he comes, we'll torture him and make him feel pain."

Her anger makes me look up. The name the woman spits out sounds familiar. I realize they are talking about my Uncle Seng. The woman who made the first angry remarks was *Yiey* Chea, a woman who I found out later to be related to us—she's actually Uncle Seng's biological aunt. When I saw her before, she seemed nice and friendly to *Mak*. Now I'm startled, scared by the vicious tone of her voice, as well as that of the other women. But the Khmer Rouge have been at work, turning family against family in the name of *Angka Leu*.

"It won't take much to kill him. He'll die just by each of us pee-ing on his head," an older woman quips sarcastically as she steps off the ladderlike stairs of the house.

There are fifteen women in their fifties and sixties dressed in black coming out of the house. It appears they just had a meeting. I'm afraid of *Yiey* Chea, fear she will recognize me and accuse me of spying. With the two filled pouches weighing down my neck, I walk away, trying to appear unobtrusive while contemplating all they've said.

Bombing their relatives? I think to myself. *Uncle Seng didn't bomb them. The B-52s did.* I'm confused by their accusations and sarcasm, but most of all I'm perplexed by their hatred toward him, their utter conviction even when they don't know the truth.

The Khmer Rouge are now focused on turning the people from the city into laborers. At first, most of the adults are forced to build irrigation canals, backbreaking work using only hoes. Everyone must work. My mother and aunts have to gather cow and buffalo dung scattered in the village and transport it to the rice fields. *Mak* has been given a basket to transport the excrement. Separating her head from the animal dung are a layer of the basket and a cushion formed by the scarf folded beneath it. When she walks across *Kong* Houng's orchard, I ask her, "*Mak*, what's in the basket?"

"Only cow dung, *koon*," she says, showing me.

"Yuck! Yuck," I cry, repelled by the dark, drenched excrement. *Mak* smiles, amused. She chuckles, putting the basket back on her head, and resumes her work, which is unlike anything she has ever done in her life. I run over to my seven-year-old sister Avy and tell her about the dung on *Mak*'s head. She wrinkles her nose, and we laugh at the new lesson in our lives.

But more lessons are to follow. There's a meeting for children, and I'm told to go. I dress up in my best navy blue skirt with a nice white blouse. I wear my new leather shoes that *Mak* bought for me just before the Khmer Rouge takeover. I report there alone. To my surprise, children aged about ten to thirteen gather at a barn amid bundles of hay. Among the tumbled straw, the "city children" stand apart from the local children, whose clothes are thickly patched, bulky and ragged, their hair uncombed. I realize my idea of a meeting will never be the same as the Khmer Rouge's.

Three women wearing dark, faded uniforms and old scarves around their heads instruct us to follow them to a rice field, a two-mile trip from the village. While I don't want to go with them, I remember what they did to *Pa*. I'm afraid to protest, and it frustrates me. I continue to follow the group of children, consisting mainly of village children, the Khmer Rouge's faithful slaves. They run barefoot on the elevated pathway between rice paddies as if the rough ground were a cushion under their feet. Unlike them, the city children walk leisurely, as if going to a market.

Like fish drawn to water, the village children dash ahead to the drenched rice paddy recently plowed—a brown flooded field with bunches of soft green rice seedlings. Following the women, the village children troop into the muddy field. This is work they've grown up with, and they know what they're doing as they move quickly to scatter seedling bundles in the paddy. They plant them in rows, in a pattern. Their feet spread apart, legs straddled widely, they stoop down to shove a few seedlings into the mud with one hand while holding the loose seedling bundle in the other. To them, it seems like a pleasant game. To me, the fieldwork looks grim, uninteresting. One of the women yells out at us, the city children, to get into the muddy field. We are hesitant, especially me, when I realize that I will dirty my school clothes. But I have no choice. I hold my breath as I step gently into the field after more commands from these women, leaving my school shoes on the bank behind me.

I'm shocked at the way they speak to me, without the warm, formal endearments that adults typically use, calling young people "niece" or "daughter." I cannot remember women ever yelling rudely at me, ordering me around. In *Sangkum mun* (the previous society), *Mak* or *Pa* would have intervened, confronting and correcting the women. I hold my skirt up and wish the Khmer Rouge never existed, that they were only as harmless as a villain in a movie, gone when the lights come on.

As I wait in the cold, thick water, the mud already making my skin itch, one of the women hands me a bunch of slender stalks. I wad my skirt between my legs, squeezing it safely above the mud. The woman shows me how to plant, dealing out seedlings swiftly and skillfully.

I try to plant like her, but the stalks don't stay put. They float to the surface like bubbles. I only wish I could do the same, feet leaving the mud and floating gently away. I perspire profusely, wipe my forehead with my arm, and swallow the urge to scream. Unlike the rural children, I don't straddle my legs, instead standing with my ankles together—a modest stance when you're wearing a skirt. Other city children do the same. My back and legs are killing me from stooping at a steep angle, as if perpetually caught in a deep, formal bow. One with the city children, I lag behind the village children.

I'm only two feet from the elevated pathway, and they are already halfway across the field. They look coordinated and fast as they shuffle backward. I watch them, observing their work. I try to emulate them, but I still don't get it. Again, I study posture, technique. But I can't figure it out, and this begins to eat away at me, as if I were trying to master a simple game of jump rope. *If they can do this, I can do it, too.* I try to copy them and plant fast, but the stalks float and I almost fall facedown into the muddy water.

"Move this leg this way." I feel a hand grabbing my right leg. One of the women pulls my right leg apart from my left, startling me.

A chorus of giggles erupts from my coworkers. I look up and see the village kids looking amused, as well as the city kids. I laugh with them, feeling less frustrated and angry. I'm relieved that the woman doesn't scold me for being slow. Instead, the women and the village children quietly plant rice seedlings around me and the other city children, closing in on the open areas until we finish. They fix my floating stalks as well as other stray stalks. Since the woman pulled my legs apart, my slender skirt now drags in the muddy water. By now I don't worry too much about my clothes. I figure I can wash the skirt and the spots off my blouse. I've adjusted to what I can't change.

By the time we've planted all the rice paddies, stomping through four fields, I'm exhausted. I'm hungry and sticky from the sun. A small part of me is proud that I've learned how to plant rice, but I hate this way of life. Here, we are moving backward, just as the village children scuttle backward putting down the rows of seedlings. Again, I yearn to go back to school and long for my previous life— even reading about dead kings sounds appealing.

Today Than encounters the most appalling lesson by far. He is among a group of young boys ordered to destroy Buddhist temples and shrines of guardian spirits called *Ronng Neak Ta*, special places typically tucked beneath the giant umbrella of shade cast by huge, majestic old *po* trees (banyan trees), where spirits are thought to dwell. These sacred shrines are made of small wooden boxes in the shape of a house, secured between large branches or in caves created by the massive tree trunks. In each of them is a tin can filled with sand, into which incense sticks are planted during prayers and food offerings. To the sanctuary of *Ronng Neak Ta* women and men would bring food, candles, or incense. Here, they would pour their hearts out to the presiding spirits, imploring them for good health, luck, and happiness.

Than is baffled as he tells *Mak* and our relatives of today's task. With sledgehammers and hoes, they shattered walls and shrines that have stood for years. From village to village they went, the Khmer Rouge urging the boys to shout and grunt as they crumbled walls, like an evil cheering section. Everyone is shocked, at a loss for words. As Than speaks, his expression asks the question, *Is it okay to do that?* It's hard not to remember Tha, who died after the mere slight of peeing on someone's grave. But at eleven, Than has already learned that he has no voice when it comes to the work of the Khmer Rouge. Finally he shrugs, "They made us do it. . . . Kept shouting at us to destroy. . . . Now I'm worried about angry spirits. . . ." He frowns. *If they reject the culture of religion, if they have no fear of the wrath of spirits, why didn't they destroy the temples themselves?*

The Khmer Rouge wish to rule not only our inner spiritual lives but our outward appearance as well. They require girls and women to wear their hair short. The rule is a deliberate slap in the face of our culture, which prizes the traditional beauty of long hair. If we don't cut our hair to our earlobes, they warn, they'll do it for us. Chea, Ra, and Ry decide that they'll have *Mak* cut their hair. My mother takes her scissors and carefully, evenly trims the hair that once fell down their backs to their ears. The hair falls, another measure of loss. I look at Chea, Ra, and Ry with curiosity, as if they were now wearing Khmer Rouge wigs. My own hair barely brushes my shoulders, and I dread the day I must join them. For now, I'm not old enough to worry anyone. The Khmer Rouge's barbers cut hair without thought. A coconut shell is placed over the head. Any hair dangling from below the edge of the shell is snipped away, the shell a crude cutting line. The style was easy to spot—uneven hanks of hair falling randomly, it looked like the handiwork of a five-year-old.

The Khmer Rouge know how to strike deeply. The head is the most sacred part of the body to a Cambodian. To be struck in the head, even to have a younger person or an enemy touch your head, is enormously insulting. And yet our captors seem indifferent to our lives before this moment. There is only the history of the here and now.

Every day the Khmer Rouge set new rules. Now they want to control the words out of our mouths. We have to use the rural terms of address, calling our mothers *Mae*, and our fathers *Pok*. Our other option is to call our parents "comrade," a strange, detached word that, by the sound of it, makes me laugh. *How absurd!* In our culture, we have four or five words to describe the act of eating, to designate an older person, a monk, or a king. Suddenly our very language has changed without our consent. And yet, standing in line for rice rations, I hear the voices of other city children easily slip into the new way of speaking. Still, it amuses me, an ebullience that has to spill out somehow.

"Comrade *Mak*, can I say that?" I curtsy before my mother, causing her to grin. It's so nice to see her familiar smile. This eggs us on. My sisters and I briefly practice our new vocabulary, mocking it in our play. We address each other as "Comrade Athy" or "Comrade Chea" with graceful little courtesies. It is our attempt to cope with what we can't change. However, when no one is listening, we address our family properly. They may take our language from our family in public, but they can't take away the family itself, the bond that binds us. Our private words are our own.

Instead of giving us currency, the Khmer Rouge dole out rations of paddy (unhusked rice). The rations are taken directly from the abundant stores they've seized from *Kong* Houng—hundreds of thousands of kilograms of unhusked rice. They distribute the paddy to us, stingily measured into woven baskets. Older people receive larger rations compared to a nine-year-old kid like me. We have to process our own rice from scratch. Watch and learn. I take the initiative, determined to conform, to survive. I help my mother and sisters crush the unhusked rice. The golden unhusked grains are tossed into a huge cement mortar buried in the ground. Above it hangs a large, heavy vertical pole connected to a horizontal arm. Together we step on the end of the arm, then release it. The pounding pole smashes into the grain like a gigantic pestle, releasing the grain from its husk. Then we winnow it, sifting the unhusked from the husked, and repeat the process. As for meat, we fish when there is spare time, which has become scarce. We harvest vegetables from *Kong*'s rapidly failing orchard and other plants that grow wild like weeds in fields and around people's houses.

Paddy rations are never enough. Most of the time, *Mak* leaves the hut after she helps set up our meal on the wooden deck. When some of us ask for more rice, she sadly puts her spoon down and offers to share her ration. Increasingly, she seems to have errands to run when it's time for dinner. She tells us to eat, and not to wait up for her. We obey, leaving no food. I begin to realize that she never eats. I never think much about it, but wonder why she doesn't seem to be hungry.

Later I find out. All those times, *Mak* has been going around Year Piar asking for meals from the local women she has befriended. To beg means that she has humbled herself before those women. This brutal reality cuts me like a knife. From now on, I know there's no future under the Khmer Rouge.

It is now October, four months after *Pa*'s execution. Rumors have spread. Soon we will be moved to a different place. *Where? Mak* asks around, but no one knows.

The night before we are to leave, *Mak* dreams about *Pa*. He appears without a head. He walks toward her and tries to tell her something with his hands, but she can't understand. As *Mak* asks him questions, he stands there headless, yet he's listening. Then he disappears into the dark night, leaving *Mak* screaming for him to return. This nightmare is a dark omen for all of us.

The next day we gather for our meal of rice and vegetable soup with banana stalk and fish. No one says anything except to make terse requests to pass dishes. I'm scared. I break down, crying. My sisters, too. Through the open hut, where we've been eating our meals, I gaze at the orchard. The empty space where the pineapples once were. The fruit trees, the shady tamarind—my eyes caress them, as if saying good-bye to a refuge where I've found shelter, a place almost outside the revolution.

Even *Kong* Houng and *Yiey* Khmeng must now leave their home, a place he has struggled to protect all these years. For my family, this final act is the beginning of a naked existence. Turning us out of *Kong* Houng's home, built as his bridal gift to *Yiey* Kmeng, represents more than an eviction. It strips us of our last semblance of a normal life, our threads of family community. From here, we are scattered like grains of rice cast in random directions. When we came here, *Pa* was with us. Now he's gone. To abandon the last place I have a physical memory of him hurts me deeply. In Cambodia, we believe the spirits of loved ones look after us. To me, this is where his spirit dwells. It's as if I'm leaving him.

As Chea, Ra, Ry, and I walk outside, waiting for *Mak*, Avy, and our brothers to catch up with us, I sob. I think the words I cannot speak. *The Khmer Rouge will kill us.* I don't want to die, to be killed with a hoe like *Pa*. My tears are contagious, igniting fear and sorrow in Chea. She weeps. The rest join in. Chea puts her arms around me. Together we cry until we can cry no more. The fear remains, but the tears are spent.

Heading down the dusty village road, Chea and Ra carry our belongings the primitive way—suitcases and bags of blankets strapped on either end of carrying sticks. *Mak* balances a bag of clothes on her head, guiding us like a hen herding her chicks. Walking through Year Piar and other villages, I pray to Buddha. *Protect us, protect us.* Then I ask *Pa*'s spirit to watch over us, as I've heard my elders pray to the spirits of their ancestors for protection and luck.

We cross many fields and pass through a succession of small villages until we see a collection of wilted souls waiting by a train track in a barren field. Squatting and standing around are hundreds of people waiting uneasily along the tracks. Suddenly Khmer Rouge cadres dash alongside the freight cars, appearing out of nowhere in their black uniforms with rifles on their shoulders. Some run toward the end of the train. A few open the freight cardoors before us.

"Get in, get in!" they shriek, waving their hands in the air.

We obey. We crowd into the freight cars. We are mostly women. Mothers reach out to find the hands of children, and children reach for mothers. "*Mak, koon,* hurry, wait" are the only words spoken as the steady stream of humans overflows into the freight cars. Then the cries. The Khmer Rouge begin to separate members of families into different cars, as randomly as you would divide livestock. *Angka Leu* is your family now. Mothers implore, children wail. The waves of rifles silence them. Squatting on the wooden floor in the car with

Mak and my brothers and sisters, I'm relieved that I'm already inside, squeezed among strangers.

The door of the freight car slams shut. We move forward, and we move nowhere. I look at the threads of sunlight filtering through cracks in the car's sliding door. The view reveals no details, not even a snippet of landscape. As the day fades, the night crawls in, smothering the dark car with a thick blanket of ink. Around me, tired bodies are crowded haphazardly, with someone's feet planted next to another's sleeping head. Planting filthy feet next to the head of someone else is a sign of disrespect. But no one cares, and that's even more shocking.

Squeezed alongside my siblings, I breathe in the foul smell of sweat, warm bodies, and urine that permeates the entire car. Hours ago, people began peeing behind the water barrel, the only spot affording any privacy. The Khmer Rouge never stopped except to shove in that water barrel. The night comes, and I see only shadows in the shadows. The train slows. My fear escalates.

From a distance, men's voices shout. As they come nearer, I hear "Bread, bread." The door slides open. Two men, one with a flashlight and the other with a bundle of bread, appear in the dark. Warm French bread is passed about. I reach out for a small loaf, the size of a squash, and devour it. The bread settles in my stomach *Why do they give us bread if they intend to kill us? Maybe not yet. Maybe they'll use us first, then kill us.* The bread gives a flicker of hope as the train resumes its course.

Night stretches into day. The revolution of the train wheels on the track sings me to sleep, then I wake to rays of sunlight that flirt through the cracks of the sliding door, telling me that time has passed, even if my own world has stopped, brought to a standstill in this freight car.

The train stops and I'm jerked back to reality. The sliding door is flung open, and we're released, disoriented, wobbling out of our cage. Sunlight bathes us as we trudge behind others across the dry, cracked earth. It is the first time I've been able to stretch my legs in twenty-four hours, and my muscles protest as I struggle like an old woman to master my coordination.

Our lives are like a phrase from a familiar song, *Chivith choun re-ang choun pleang.* "Life sometimes has drought and sometimes has rain."

This is our time of drought.

6

Worse Than Pigs

The New York Times
July 9, 1975
"Cambodia's Crime . . ."

Some twelve weeks after the Communist entry into Phnom
Penh and the forced exodus on foot of millions of urban
Cambodians to distant countrysides, a veil of silence still
cloaks the full horror of what has happened—with the worst
yet to come in predicted deaths from hunger and disease.
The agony and degradation that followed may never be fully
known. Tens of thousands are believed to have fallen by the
wayside, victims of hunger, thirst, exhaustion and disease,
including a spreading cholera epidemic. . . .

*C*an life be worse than it already is? This question becomes a
mental game, a way of throwing down an emotional challenge to
myself: *It can't be any worse. It can't be any worse. This is enough. They can
do no more.*

In my mind, the words become both a dare and a comfort.

Just as we were randomly squeezed into the train cars, now we're
discharged. Hundreds of us march into a desolate field, rushing behind the Khmer Rouge. Carrying our remaining belongings, we
trudge behind them. Children, mothers, and elderly parents hurry
past each other. Little children sob constantly as they're yanked
along, scolded to keep up with the moving crowd. We cross one
barren field into another, propelled by sheer will.

As we enter a green grove of trees and shrubs, they command
some of us to stop. The rest of the group funnel down a path
flanked by bushes and trees. Among these people, I don't see my

grandparents, aunts, or cousins. We've been so hungry and scared that we haven't had time to worry about our extended families. But now we depend so much on our immediate family, and in the faces of my mother, my brothers, and my sisters, I feel a sharpened sense of their value which I've never known before. For the moment we take refuge near clumps of wild vines that snake around shady trees.

A man dressed in black appears. He's tall and slender with dark skin and short hair. He looks smart, different from many of the stocky Khmer Rouge peasants we've seen. Standing before us, he explains that he's a leader of Daakpo village. As soon as he opens his mouth to talk, I'm intrigued by his strange accent. I've never heard anything like it, and it almost makes me giddy.

"*Mak*, how come he talks funny?" I can't help asking as we follow along, carrying our belongings.

Mak smiles and says, "This part of the country, near Battambang province, speaks this way, in *rurdern* [a drawl]."

"It sounds funny," I say chortling, realizing there are actually other Cambodians who speak this oddly, in this drawn-out, singsong way. As grim as our situation is, I find it hard to take him seriously.

"Comrades, this is where you'll stay," the village leader announces, standing under four tall shady trees.

I'm shocked. I was hoping to see shelters, huts or beds where we can rest. But there's nothing except trees, thick woods. It looks like no one has ever lived here before. Green and quiet, it is nature in its naked form. Trees are my walls, the sky my roof.

"Comrades, there's a pond near here. Right over there," the village leader says, pointing. His voice no longer amuses me.

A few days later, bamboo, palm leaves, palm thread made from palm bark, and freshly cut trees are brought to us. Shrubs and trees have to be cleared to accommodate the sudden swelling population, hundreds of us accumulating here and in nearby villages in a matter of days. Local people, farmers, and "old people"—natives of the province who have attained status because of that fact—build the framework of huts, a simple platform on short stilts designed with two rooms separated by palm slats. Each compartment, the size of a small shed, will be occupied by a family. We are assigned to a hut the same size as that of the neighbors beyond our wall, a family of four. On our side, we have nine. *Is this what they mean by equality?*

In a short time, a community of huts springs up amid the forest. Huts appear like mushrooms after a hard rain. Our crude village is a social laboratory, a brutal experiment to test if anyone will survive the Khmer Rouge's utopian theory.

There's a mandatory meeting for the "new people." We assemble in an alley between huts, in the generous shade of a cluster of trees. The village leader orders us to rid ourselves of anything that is of the "American imperialists." "That includes," he commands, "watches, gold necklaces, bracelets, diamond rings." His hand clutches a gray bag in which he'll collect the goods, disposing of these things for us like a monk demanding that we renounce our sins. "These things are impure, which *Angka* dislikes, and comrades cannot possess them. It's okay that comrades have had them before, but now *Angka* doesn't want these corrupt materials around. *Angka* wants comrades to bring these things to me," he emphasizes.

After receiving our instructions, we return to our hut. Safely inside, *Mak* and my sisters talk quietly among themselves, whispering and frowning. They disagree about what to give to the village leader. I take refuge in the shade of a hut near ours. From where I squat, I observe people giving up their possessions to the leader. He nods as if he is royalty. He has power, control over the smallest detail of our lives.

"*Mak!* Only give him my watch. Don't give him everything!" Chea insists, grabbing *Mak*'s arm as my mother is about to take a small bag of fine jewelry to the leader.

Mak shoots her a sour face. She glares at Chea and softly hisses, "You take it to him then."

Chea obeys, relieved to end the heated discussion. She surrenders her watch. Whether she has the watch or not is irrelevant. It's only a matter of time before most of us will die, and it doesn't matter whether we can measure it, counting down the hours on a wristwatch.

In taking our timepieces, the Khmer Rouge are deliberately stealing the last remnants of our connection to the outside world. Increasingly, the atmosphere in our camp is one of unreality—people squeezed into huts next to each other, all steeped in distrust. We're constantly uneasy, wondering who might be listening to us. Traditions are being shattered daily. We are shocked to see that we are separated only by a wall from neighbors who have full-grown sons. In the past, parents and grandparents would have clucked over such an arrangement, worrying about how inappropriate it was. But the Khmer Rouge have no use for formal courtesy.

Still, we see glimmers of what used to be. One day my sister Chea is trying to water the meager assortment of plants we've been growing in the patch behind our hut. Nearby, our neighbor, the oldest son, busies himself tilling soil.

"Look," Chea says, observing with surprise that a squash plant had grown bright white flowers. "Is it supposed to be white?"

He laughs. "Mademoiselle, where do you come from?"

Mademoiselle. A word clue to the hidden privileges of the past. Chea bursts out laughing, delighted to find a hint of education in another person.

"Parlez-vous français?" she inquires.

The discovery creates an instant friendship. Speaking the same language, they share the same culture. Though the Khmer Rouge can control every other aspect of our lives, they cannot scrub out our minds, polish away our intellect like an empty brass pot. In the midst of the daily fear of Khmer Rouge village life, it is a delicious secret. And I'm proud and amused to witness it.

Our lives continue to shrink. Less freedom. Fewer family bonds. Food rations dwindle, just as our living space has been steadily reduced to the small hut, a cage really, where my family now resides. The rice rations are five times less than what we were given back in Year Piar, and they continue to be reduced, stingily measured out in a small tin milk can. In time, the quantity diminishes from a few cups of dry rice to only enough to make a thin liquid gruel, which we supplement with pigweed and salt. The first week of our arrival, we receive a few ounces of pork. Then it too diminishes, just like the coarse salt we initially received, from a few tablespoons to nothing.

Even as food rations are cut, our labor demands remain the same. We work long hours in the woods to ready the fields for planting yams and yucca. Every morning a young Khmer Rouge informant sweeps through the village, bellowing bad news: "Time to get up, time to get up. Go to work!" As we lie in our huts, we hear his shrill voice as he approaches. I squeeze my eyes, wishing to pinch my ears shut, too. But if you don't move, he will sometimes poke his face right into your doorless hut. He's only twelve or thirteen, but he carries the cruel clout of the Khmer Rouge.

Once I hear an older woman—beautiful and elegant before the ravages of poor nutrition and field labor—quietly cursing him behind his back. She goes by the name "Grandma Two Kilo," for the weight of dirt she can carry. And in the early morning, I hear her fierce whispers, "You're the one who will be hit by the bomb. I haven't died [slept] long enough. And here you wake me up. You come again, I'll throw something at your head."

Next door, I hear our older neighbor laughing behind the wall. "Grandma Two Kilo, don't be a blabbermouth," he murmurs. "Be careful. Don't be brave."

Malnutrition takes its toll on everyone. *Mak*'s once-lustrous skin and glistening black hair show the signs of starvation. Her eyes are sunken. Her hair is brittle and wiry, and her skin covers her arms and cheeks like a thin, loose-fitting bedsheet, as if her muscles were being eaten away from within. Her starving body mirrors what the rest of us look like.

Just as the Khmer Rouge suck the life out of us, we drain our pond—a small body of water grown murky with a thick forest of algae and water plants. It is peppered with insects, sediment, and other debris. The water tastes of dirt, but it's all we have—the next pond is miles away. So we drink from it, depleting it quickly, our village acting like a giant elephant trunk drawing even fetid water to quench its thirst. In addition, we must use this pond water for washing, cleaning our pots and pans, our clothes. Those who have no inkling of sanitation discard their dirty, soapy water on the bank of the pond. Some water seeps into the clay soil, the rest dribbles back to the pond.

Soon we have a new neighbor. Death has taken up residence here, moving in like a malevolent, unwelcome visitor. Within months rampant illness begins to touch the newest arrivals. This sickness takes many forms, creeping into our lives quietly, stealthily. Like many adults and children, I squat outside my hut each morning to catch the first sunlight, desperate to warm my body, which is now racked with strange intermittent chills. Rocking back and forth, I'm somehow soothed by the rays of the sun, intangible hands that sway me to sleep in a squatting position. A few hours later, my body moves from being warm to burning hot. I wobble to the hut. Up I climb, my body soaked in my own sweat. Then comes the ache and pain, from my legs to my head. I'm delirious and confused. Finally I'm exhausted and hungry. I gradually regain my senses.

So it goes, this strange routine. No one understands what is wrong. But my condition doesn't seem to improve, my extremes of fever and chill grow worse. I begin thrashing in a delirious stupor. Vaguely, I'm aware of what is happening to me, and yet I listen and observe it as an outsider, unable to control the words as they tumble from my mouth. It is odd to be aware of the fact that I am making no sense. Strangely, I begin crying out, demanding, pleading for a food offering. "A bowl of rice with fried fish with tamarind paste!"

Around me, voices murmur, "These are foods her father would ask for!" My father's spirit has possessed me, they decide. "The ghost is inside her," someone concludes.

As crazed as the situation is, I feel embarrassed. I can hear who is talking, feel the eyes of onlookers—my mother's horrified gaze, a neighbor's well-intentioned suggestion. "Maybe the ghost of your husband is hungry." My mind absorbs this, but my body refuses to respond.

Mak flies out of the hut, desperately searching for someone, anyone, who will trade her for fish and tamarind. She wouldn't dare approach the "old people," only the new arrivals. But no one can help. She returns, offering my father's ghost all that we have—the thin rice gruel. Later *Mak* complains of a fierce stomachache. Everyone concludes that it is her punishment because my father's angry spirit has had to go away hungry.

It is sad, but unavoidable. In Cambodian culture, we try hard to please the spirits of our ancestors. Sickness, bad luck, disappointments—all are often blamed on spirits who have gone away unsatisfied. When I pray to Buddha for protection, I routinely pray to my father's spirit as well. Food offerings are presented as thanks for our good fortune, and as insurance for our continued well-being. My mother is frustrated that she cannot appease the spirit, but there is nothing to be done. Her face bespeaks her anguish, an expression of utter disbelief. "How could one find a fish in this day and time?" she murmurs. Her eyes plead her case. *Here, we have nothing to eat. Why do you ask, spirit?*

Within a half hour, I feel a physical transformation, as if my body has been raised from the floor of the hut and abruptly dropped. I feel control seeping back into my limbs, which now listen to my brain. My skin seems to open, and I sweat profusely. "What happened?" I ask.

Chea explains that my father's ghost possessed me, and I can feel her fear. Her eyes grow large as she recounts it. Then Than speaks up, an expression of relief. "I'm glad I'm not *Pa*'s favorite *koon*," he whispers.

The episode leaves me weak, my fever still an unwavering companion. Even when ill, we don't get anything extra to eat to help nurse us back to health. *Pa*, whose magic I had depended on, has been taken away from me. Food is scarce and so is medicine. The magic is gone. We don't even have clean water to drink. The nearby shrinking pond becomes a scar created by us. It's depleted, polluted, the water evaporating to expose its bottom, a withering carpet of water plants. Unlike the pond, we're more capable, more adaptable in this survival game. We can make another move, seek water elsewhere, even if it's miles away. Even if it isn't clean.

People in the village are now afflicted with severe diarrhea. So rampant is the problem that it defies embarrassment. Signs of sickness are everywhere—staining the fields and stinking in the bushes near the huts. The telltale symptoms are obvious—excrement containing blood and mucus, quickly attracting buzzing flies. Toilet paper consists of any leaf you can grab. The helplessness of sufferers makes them feel ashamed—another form of pain that adds to existing suffering. Sometimes we try to make light of it. Later, when the diarrhea passes, adults mock their discomfort by explaining, "I had a loose bolt."

Others don't seem to rebound from the parasites that plague us. For more than a week, my three-year-old brother Vin has suffered from dysenteric diarrhea. Every day he soils his few pairs of worn pants and the other clothes that *Mak* uses to cover him. On the wooden floor of our hut, his little body lies still, disturbed only by the slow, rhythmic motions of his breathing. He lies sideways, wearing only a shirt. He is naked from the waist down—it's pointless to try to keep clean pants on him, and his tiny bottom is perpetually swamped by flies. We have a new job. Someone must sit near him, fanning the flies away. Thinking back, I remember *Pa* curing one of my cousins of diarrhea. He would have known what to do. Water and salt, to help with the dehydration. But nothing is available to us. Fanning flies away is the only care we can give him. The only thing we know to do to protect him. Helplessness haunts us.

"*Mak* . . . *Mak*, please let me sleep by you. I'm cold," Vin beseeches, his voice small, soft, and sad. "I'm cold, *Mak*. Let me sleep with you for one more night."

"*Koon proh Mak,** *Mak* doesn't want you to make your brothers and sisters sick. Please sleep over there, my son," *Mak* begs.

"*Mak*, let me sleep with you one more night. Only one more night, *Mak*. Tomorrow I'll go to the hospital and then I'll feel better. Please let me, *Mak*, I'm cold," Vin cries out once again.

"*Mak* is sorry, *koon*." Never before has *Mak* been so helpless. So apologetic.

This child whom she brought into the world cannot be satisfied. And this raw fact is slowly killing her.

For the rest of us, it is like listening to the soundtrack of a sad movie that has no end. Lying cuddled beside *Mak*—my brothers and sisters sharing blankets and our warmth when the cool night wind

---

* *Proh* means boy, or man, so *koon proh Mak* is an endearment used by a mother meaning "my son."

blows, wriggling through the cracks into our hut—I weep for Vin. Our sniffles become a melody in the night as each of us suffers with him. He is only three, but the revolution ages us all. Already Vin can articulate his need, his desperate need to survive.

Long into the night, Vin cries as the chilly December wind blows. It beats the leaves of the tall trees behind our hut, creating a chorus of noise akin to Vin's shuddering. Even beneath a blanket, I'm touched by this invisible wind.

When the morning comes, Ry gets Vin ready for a trip to the Khmer Rouge hospital, called Peth Preahneth Preah, a name left over from an earlier time, which means "Hospital of the Sight of God." It is probably three miles from where we live.

Vin's pale, shrinking body lies still as Ry wraps him in *Mak*'s sarong. Sadly he gazes at our mother. Vin's bloodless lips slowly part. "*Mak*, I go to the hospital. Soon I'll feel better, then I'll come back home. I'll come soon, *Mak*."

His words and sad eyes suggest a pensive parting. As small as he is, Vin seems to understand, absolving her, comforting her. His empathy in the midst of his own suffering strikes me to the core. Vin is little, yet so curiously wise. Perhaps it is a wisdom born of a young life that has straddled so much—our life before the revolution, the retreat from Phnom Penh, the life of forced labor. Too much living to cram into too few years. A three-year-old in a boxcar. A three-year-old scavenging for food. He has known so much pain that I can't bear it. I want to drop to the dirt, fall to my knees to beg Buddha to stop his suffering.

I want so much.

"Yes, *koon proh Mak*, go to the hospital and you will get better soon. Then *koon* comes back to *Mak*." *Mak* chokes up, speaking the ragged words she knows will not come true.

"'*Koon* comes back to *Mak*,'" Vin says, repeating *Mak*'s phrase as if it comforts him.

Weeks go by, and Vin is still in the hospital. His condition worsens, Ry reports to us. She is stationed at the hospital taking care of
Vin, a role that would otherwise have fallen to Chea and Ra, who
are older than her. But they are gone, having already been taken off
to a forced youth labor camp. They left a day after an informant
leader, Srouch, came by, ordering them to a meeting. They obeyed
immediately, like soldiers called up for combat. Their responsibility to our family is no longer relevant. Through no fault of her own,
Mak has lost custody of her children—*Angka Leu* has appointed itself sole parent. With their departure, Ry steps in, taking upon herself a motherly role.

Back in Phnom Penh, at age thirteen, she was slim but strong.
Her black silky hair fell below her shoulders, cut evenly. She looked
cute, I thought, in her blue miniskirt with her white and blue blouse.
When she biked to school, her legs pumped her bike pedals like an
athlete's.

Even then Ry was nursing us, taking care of Chea when she came
down with typhoid and a blood condition. Ry was a natural nurse,
staying with Chea so *Mak* could take care of us at home and *Pa*
could work. Though Ra was older, she feared the dead spirits in
hospitals. Unlike Ra, Ry wasn't scared of sickness. Ra was better
off staying at home, helping *Mak* with cleaning, cooking, and grocery shopping.

At fifteen, mature for her age, Ry takes on the caregiving task
again. Just as she used to care for Chea, she now stays days and nights
with Vin. She works in the hospital, a hall that used to be part of a
temple. The floor is dirt, patients lie on slim metal cots. Others are
scattered on blankets or plastic sheeting on the floor. It has the atmosphere of a field hospital, scarcely an aisle to walk through. Vin
is luckier—because of the crowding, he has been moved to an an-
nex, a nearby building with a wooden floor. He is allotted a narrow
space a few scant feet from the nearest patients. Medical scrubs are

replaced by the eternal Khmer Rouge uniform—black shirt and pants, a simple scarf. If these hospital "authorities" have a medical education, it isn't apparent. The only treatment readily dispensed is "rabbit dung," the term adopted for crude "pills" made from bark and honey. Sometimes people request the "rabbit dung" just for the honey alone, something to fill their empty stomachs. It seems that food, simple nutrition, would cure much suffering here.

Like a mother, Ry feeds Vin his meager food ration. Since there is no one else to administer care, she bathes him, dresses him. She gives him comfort and warmth, cuddling close to him at night. But as hard as she works, he is empty. Every day he cries for *Mak*, begging Ry to ask *Mak* to come and see him. Ry passes along the plea, imploring *Mak* until *Mak* cries, "Don't torture, *Mak*, *koon*. I can't walk to the hospital. *Mak* would if *Mak* could."

She speaks the painful truth. *Mak*'s face and entire body have swollen up, inflated by the fluid building up inside her. Her face is an ugly mask of what it once was, as pale as pigskin with puffy jowls. Her eyes squint out from this fleshy landscape, cloudy and dull. No one knows why this is, what is making our limbs so heavy. My mother has a theory. "We don't have salt," she says, shrugging. Before long, she has company. In time, we all get it—the new people. At first it seems like bad fortune, a curse on the most recent arrivals. It takes a while for us to associate this condition with our own starvation. The word is *hamm*, swollen (edematous). I too am swollen. My legs. My arms. My face. Suddenly, a simple task like walking feels like slogging through mud. Like *Mak* and me, Avy and Map also swell up like inflatable dolls, their faces tight and stretched, their legs fat beyond their years. The skin between Avy's toes scares me—so taut and transparent, it looks as if it will surely burst. Still, she is stronger than me, able to walk to retrieve water. I feel helpless, ashamed, weak by comparison. My strong little sister surprises me.

Around us we watch the drama unfold. Sickness touches so many huts. Even the ill-tempered "Grandma Two Kilo" is humbled, her tongue temporarily silenced by the sickness, which robs her of the last delicacy of her fading beauty.

One day Ry returns from the hospital to report that Vin is dying. As soon as she spits out the words, she convulses, doubled over with grief.

"*Mak*, Vin begs for you to see him. He wants to see you one more time."

"*Mak* can't go, *koon*. *Mak* can hardly walk to get water to drink and cook. *Mak* cannot walk that far." Her words are slow, without hope or animation. She is beaten down by her own body.

"But Vin is dying, *Mak*! He asks for you, he misses you. . . ." Ry breaks down.

"*Koon*, did you hear what *Mak* said? *Mak* wants to go see your brother, but *Mak* just can't walk that far." She is too weak to argue. Ry must understand this. And yet the roles are oddly reversed. Ry is like the mother, ordering her child to obey. *Mak* must be there. Doesn't she understand? Her voice rises again, desperate.

"What should I tell him when he asks for you again? What do I do, *Mak*?"

"Tell your baby brother that *Mak* cannot walk that far yet. When *Mak* can walk, *Mak* will see him." Her answer is a long sigh.

"But he's dying . . ." Ry wails.

"*Mak* knows, *koon*. Tell your brother what *Mak* said." Her words are slow and steady. Despite what she feels in her heart, her voice never reflects the hysteria of this moment. She is simply too sick to care. Sitting on the floor, her hands clutching a knee, *Mak* begins shuddering.

"*Mak*." Map reaches out as *Mak* releases her grief. It is as if she has swallowed her tears and her screams, letting only thin threads of it bubble up. Her cries are like jagged glass, and we look on in silence. Suddenly Map wails—his cries breaking her own internal spell of sadness. She looks up as if doused with a pan of cold water. Awakened.

"Don't cry, *koon proh Mak. Mak* stop crying, stop crying." *Mak* comforts Map, holding him in her arms.

Avy's tears rush out to join them, streaming down her pale, puffy cheeks. With the swelling, she looks like a crying statue. The tears are there, but the swelling has masked her expression. Her ragged sobs join the chorus, adding to Map's, *Mak's*, and mine. It is too much for Ry to take. She walks away. Her weeping trails down the alley between the huts until it is a faint echo in the distance. She returns to Vin at the hospital, bringing with her a sad message. I imagine him lying on the floor of the hospital. A three-year-old's heartbroken cries when Ry tells him *Mak* can't come. In my mind, I cry out to Buddha to help Vin: *Preah, please help my baby brother. Please don't let him die—he's only a baby. Please let him live so he can see Mak one more time. Only one more time, Preah. . . .*

I recall Vin's expression of hope and the words he and *Mak* exchanged before Ry took him to the hospital: "*Mak*, I go to the hospital. Soon I'll feel better. I'll come back home. I'll come soon, *Mak*. . . ." "Yes, *koon proh Mak*, go to the hospital and you'll get better soon. Then *koon* comes back to *Mak*." "'*Koon* comes back to *Mak*.'" A hollow game of make-believe. A gentle parting. A promise that cannot be kept.

Vin dies in the hospital from an illness that is curable. But the world is brutal, indifferent. Drawn and dehydrated, his lifeless body lies naked on the wooden hospital floor—a skeleton of a little boy. When Ry wakes next to him, she leans over and shakes him, begging for a weak answer. There is none. Soon after his death, Ry removes his red knit shirt. Even in her grief, she must think about survival, saving the shirt for Map. It is necessary, a desperate act. His last rite. Her final image of him is of a small, still body wrapped in a burlap bag, carried away by two hospital workers. They never speak to her, these custodians of death.

Vin is buried at the edge of a hill called Phnom Preahneth Preah, the Sight of God. It is an impersonal burial in an unmarked grave. None of us are there to mourn. No relatives gather, no monks pray. When Ry brings home this news, no one cries. Not even *Mak*. To weep is to acknowledge what we can't accept. Our minds are already saturated with sorrow. Our silence is our last defense.

Mak is numb. Like the sun surrendering to an eternal eclipse, she simply shuts off. I study my mother now, and it is hard to imagine the happy bride, the rebellious student, the determined mother full of gentle smiles and silent sacrifice. There are no rewards in our life. To be alive and walking every day, to live through another day, is its own reward in this horrible world. Already *Mak* looks old beyond her years. Numbed by suffering, deadened by the death all around us. Too feeble to care.

She can't even walk less than a mile to see to her dying mother, *Yiey* Srem, who has also been brought to our village. As fate would have it, all of *Mak*'s side of the family also end up in Daakpo. But there is little joy in this fact. We hardly see each other. Starvation has given *Yiey* Srem a swollen body much like her daughter's. My grandmother's sagging, wrinkled skin is inflated. Oddly, there is a cruel family resemblance in the edema—we are all becoming a tribe of puffy people, all the "new people" in the village. It is a hideous badge, a way to identify us. We become preoccupied with the lack of food. The memory of it is a living, breathing thing. It infects us. It tires us. It is everything.

Now time becomes hard to measure. We mark its passage in terms of who has died and who is still alive. Time is distilled and recalled by death. *Before Vin died . . . After Pa was executed . . .* This is how we talk. Before *Yiey* Srem's death, I'm able to walk and see her briefly. Such visits are rare, even though our extended family members live close to each other. We have to weigh our desire for such contact against the risk of being punished for exhibiting "family intimacy"—a connection the Khmer Rouge frowns upon. Even while working, we are not permitted to talk with family members. Harder still, we have to sneak visits when we are supposed to be working. And we have to decide whether the energy consumed by walking half a mile should be used instead to find food, for we are all starving.

Angka doesn't care. It no longer gives us anything. No salt, no meat, and no rice. Every day I search for edible leaves, anything to survive. One day I find weeds beneath a tree, duck leaves *Mak* calls them. Only a few months ago, these were weeds that were mixed with rice and fed to pigs. Today, they are a welcome food. "Now we are worse than pigs," *Mak* mutters, boiling the leafy greens.

This is our routine. During the day we clear weeds from fields of yucca and yams, stacking the weeds in piles. Early the next morning, we scatter the debris, tearing through the piles in search of the small black crickets that scurry from beneath their dark hiding place.

"*Koon, koon,* help me catch crickets. I can't run," Grandma Two Kilo begs. "Just two crickets a day, I can survive."

Tadpoles. Crickets. Toads. Centipedes. Mice. Rats and scorpions. We eat anything. As we till the earth, we look upon bugs as buried treasure. Our eyes scan the soil, tucking any edible treat in a waistband, a pocket, tied into a scarf. Later the prize is retrieved, skewered on a stick, and stuffed into the fire. Those who haven't caught anything watch, their begging eyes following each move. We must ignore them, and also ignore what we eat. There is no revulsion. Food is food. Anything, everything tastes good—even the smell of roasting crickets makes stomachs rumble with desire. Yet even the smallest creatures, the rodents, the insects, are becoming scarce. Some days, our meals for the entire day consist of boiled leaves.

Our lives are reduced to a tight circle. Each day revolves around what we can find to eat for the following day. And until it comes, we think about food.

All day. All night.

Hunger owns us.

Chea, seated, with her college
friends, before the Khmer
Rouge takeover.

Pa. Enlargement of the thumbnail-
sized photo placed in a little box
with an ivory Buddha that I took
with me on my way to the New
Camp. This box was all I had to
hold on to for comfort when I was
in the midst of ubiquitous danger.

Ra posed for a picture before her wedding.

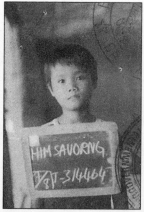

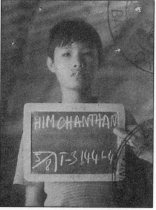

Immigration pictures. (The immigration authorities thought Map was older than Savorng because he was taller, so they switched his name with hers.)

OPPOSITE: The photo taken for Uncle Seng soon after we found out that he's alive in Portland, Oregon. Left to right: Vantha, Ra, Ry, Than, myself, and Map (in front).

Getting ready for my English class at Sakeo II.

BELOW: Photo taken for Uncle Seng at Sakeo II, weeks after Than was beaten by soldiers. Left to right: Map, myself, Than, Ry, and Aunt Eng.

Me at the beach in Mairut.
This was the first time refugees
were allowed to be out of a camp.

BELOW: Immigration photo used as
our family meal ticket, among other
things, in Lompini Camp. Left to
right: Map and Savorng (in front);
Chanrithy, Than, and Ry (back row).
Even while my family was being
transferred to a different camp, we
had yet to be accepted by the United
States. The official stamp on the back
of this picture says: "Under U. S.
Considerations, May 21, 1981."

Myself, as a Cambodian representative, dressed up in Cambodian traditional clothes to welcome tourists from twenty countries who visited PRPC.

Dr. Achilles Tanedo, in a white shirt, with his brother and a friend. He slipped this picture into my hand soon after he said good-bye and wished me good luck. On the back of the picture he wrote: "PRPC—Hospital, 11:30 AM, 11-11-81. You are indeed so nice that the first time I met you I already gave you my sympathy. I really will miss you so much. Please don't forget to write. I wish you the best of everything."

7
Remnants of Ghosts

The Economist
April 16, 1996
"The Real Toll"

A handwritten note is scrawled at the bottom of a document signed by two of Pol Pot's men at Tuol Sleng, the former Phnom Penh school that became the most notorious prison of the Khmer Rouges. It reads, "Also killed 168 children today for a total of 178 enemies exterminated."

The year is 1976. Hunger is constantly on our minds, an inner voice that will not be stilled. Yet the Khmer Rouge lecture us about sacrifice. In a mandatory meeting they tell us that we need to sacrifice for the mobile brigades that are working on the "battlefield." These mobile brigades, they stress, are building *padewat* (the revolution). We, here in the village, are not worth much since we don't work on the battlefield. We've planted rice, yams, and yucca, yet we get to eat little or nothing of the harvest. Most of the food is sent to the brigades. Later, I learn exactly what "battlefield" means— a place where the only fight is to survive the revolution itself.

Mak's swollen body somehow improves, so she can walk short distances now. Like a vulture sensing a corpse nearby, an informant begins circling our hut. He orders *Mak* to a meeting. *Mak* pleads that she's not well yet. But he pounces on her slight improvement. As long as *Mak* can walk, she must go, he demands. *Mak* is angry and murmurs to herself, "When I was sick and hungry and couldn't walk, why didn't it [that creature] stick its head in here? *Ar'khmaoch yor* [The-ghost-take-you-away]!"

Surprisingly, *Mak* comes home in a better mood. The village leader will be sending children to build an irrigation canal near Daakpo where there will be lots of food to eat. Fish, yams, solid rice. *Mak* can't wait to tell me, thinking, perhaps, that her young children will survive after all.

"Athy, *koon*, you should go to the meeting. They'll send you away to work, but it's near here. You'll have more food to eat there. Eat until you are full while there's plenty." It is something to cling to, and she will not let it go. *Mak* sounds dreamy, desperate. "Maybe you can bring *Mak* some food."

"But I'll be away from you, *Mak*. I don't want to go. I'll miss you, I'll cry." Tears burn my eyes as soon as the words leave my mouth.

"Athy! The camp won't be far from here. You'll come to visit me at night after work, you'll have food to eat, *koon*. If you stay in the village with me, we'll all probably die of hunger. Go with those children. Come to see me at night when you miss me, but don't stay here—you'll starve." *Mak* looks into my eyes, willing me to simply listen, her own eyes begging me to understand her intentions.

"I still don't want to go, *Mak*! I don't want to go away from you. I can find leaves and other things to eat. I'll be okay." But it's not okay, I know.

"*Koon*, you have to go. They won't let you stay in the village. If you don't go, they will take you to *Angka Leu*. You don't know what they'll do to you. I don't want them to torture you, *koon*. You go— you'll have food to eat. Go, *koon Mak*, listen to me." Her voice strains, her breath puffs in protest. *Mak* is miserably frustrated. I can only cry.

It is a powerful choice, food or the comfort of *Mak*. In this time of hardship, I can't choose. The lack of food makes me confused, light-headed. There is nothing that I can depend on. In the end, I don't have a choice. I'm ten, and I need my mother. But the mention of food draws me, memories of food I had in Phnom Penh pop to life. With these memories come doubts. Fears. Wisps of questions no one can answer. *What if they lie, like they've done in the past? What if I never see Mak again, like Chea and Ra, who have gone away for months? There are no words, no letters from them. What if Mak starves to death before I return?*

When the evening comes, I go to the meeting. As I get close to the sahakar,* I wipe away my tears, erasing any evidence of weakness. Before the *sahakar* lies a blanket of children, about fifty of them. It's getting dark, and I can hardly make out the faces of the leaders. I take a seat in the back, and a few heads turn to look at me. I'm not alone in my despair. In front of me, children are steeped in their own sadness. We are small, obedient statues. The reek of cow dung and urine rises from the ground. The cool, breezy night is lit by the moon. I gaze at the silhouette of the village leader, and I'm hypnotized by his descriptions of food. He makes life in the brigade sound like going to a restaurant, a daily feast. With words, he casts his spell.

I return home, falling into a deep sleep. A voice drones in the distance, then it gets louder. "*Ko'ma* [Children], go to the *sahakar* . . . go to the *sahakar*."

My eyes crack open and it's still dark. My heart pounds. I crawl closer to *Mak*. The shrill voice keeps coming. I'm afraid they will take me away from *Mak* and never let me come back to her. Lying beside *Mak*, I'm comforted by her warm presence, her soft breathing as she sleeps. *I don't want to go, for now I know I'll really miss her.* I know that I need her more than food.

"*Ko'ma* [Children], go to the *sahakar*. . . ." The voice is two huts away.

Mak is startled and her body jerks. I'm scared, nervous, holding my body still, pretending I'm asleep. *Mak* sits up and shakes my arm. "Athy, get up! Get up, *koon*. It's time to go. Get up!"

* The cooperative wooden building where the meeting is held. It is also where rice is processed and food distributed to people in Daakpo village.

I cry. "*Mak*, I don't want to go away from you. I don't want to go, *Mak*," I plead, looking at the shadow of my mother in the early morning darkness.

"*Koon*, *Mak* explained to you yesterday that you can't stay. *Mak* doesn't have time to explain it again. You have to go, daughter. The *chhlop* is coming."

"Comrade!" the informant shouts, now standing by our hut, "go to the *sahakar*. Hurry, hurry!"

"Athy, here—take a plate and spoon with you, *koon*." *Mak* speaks softly, handing me the package of necessities.

I take the plate and spoon wrapped in a scarf, wishing *Mak* would say more. But *Mak* is silent. I can't see her face or her tears, nor Map's and Avy's, but only their shadows, now taking their places beside *Mak*. Silently, I say good-bye to my shadow family.

One by one, children arrive at the *sahakar*. Each carries a package of plates, spoons, and clothes wrapped at one end of their scarves. Some of the informants go back, working their way from hut to hut to make sure "workable" comrades show up. The Khmer Rouge recruit children as young as eight. This is like harvesting rice that hasn't yet ripened.

Around me stands the new children's brigade—small barefoot bodies wearing little more than rags, our work uniform. All cloth has taken on the same drab tone, from constant use and rinsing in dirty water. Some of the children don't even have a simple scarf, a basic necessity that serves as both a garment and a practical carrying bag. They hold their plates and spoons in their hands, or hug them against their skinny chests. Now and then I steal a glance at them—I wonder if they miss their moms like I miss mine.

"*Ahh*, walk after each other in a line! Comrades, walk in a line," an angry teenage *chhlop* shouts fiercely. "Line up, line up! Straight! No talking. Any comrades caught talking will be taken to reform."

His eyes take in everything, waiting to pounce on the slightest mistake. Like small slaves, we are watched closely by the informants policing the slow-moving human line. I whisper good-bye to *Mak*.

There are no roads, and we make our way through rural land separated by distant green squares, rice fields. I pick my way through odd clumps of stiff grass, a landscape so different from the woods where we live. When we reach an open grassy field, the morning dew that clings to the tough grasses scrubs away the mud, leaving me cold. I wonder why we keep walking farther and farther. *Didn't he say we'll be working near the village? How much longer?* I'm horrified that we've been lured here with lies, but keep in step with the line.

As we march farther away from villages, the trees begin to look smaller. Everywhere there are empty rice paddies, dry and overtaken by grass. Each field is surrounded by elevated paths, small dikes designed to trap water for growing rice. We hike along the elevated paths, then off them again into the empty paddies, stark and barren.

We've walked for hours, and the *chhlops* begin to relax. It is as if they've abandoned us, disappearing far in front of us, assuming that we'll follow. As much as I fear them, I'm more worried about being lost. To lose sight of them is to risk losing one's way, starving to death. Even so, as everyone hurries along behind them, I find myself trudging, lagging behind. My foot, already bruised and tender, meets something sharp. Pain shoots all the way to my skull. I swallow the urge to scream, and drop on the dirt, squatting. Then I see the tree branch, armed with long, tacky thorns, one of which broke into my foot. It's black and deep in my flesh, leaving a point sprouting out of my foot. I pinch it, but it's stuck. I try again, but it's stubborn. I look up and everyone in front of me is gone. Now scared, I cry out, frightened that I'll be stranded here with no food or water.

I try to remember in which direction the *chhlops* were heading, but I don't know the answer. The thorn thrusts deeper into my foot. And my fear of not being able to get to the labor camp intensifies. At this thought, I wail.

"Athy, Athy, why are you crying?" says a soft, small voice.

I turn and see Cheng, a girl my age whom I know from Daakpo village.

"Cheng," I call out, "those people disappeared—we're the only people here. Cheng, I stepped on a thorn and can't get it out." I'm relieved that I'm here with Cheng, one of the "new people," like me.

Cheng brings out a small orange piece of yam root and shares it with me. It is the first food I've seen all day. Softly, she speaks to me. "Athy, stop crying. My legs ache so much, and I'm tired and hungry, too."

"Cheng, can you take the thorn out for me? It hurts when I walk."

She reaches for the package wrapped in her scarf, then unclasps a big safety pin from it. Cheng licks her finger and wipes away the mud from my foot. Gently, she fishes for the buried thorn with the sharp point of the safety pin and carefully plucks at it with her thumb and forefinger.

Cheng seems at ease. "We'll help each other find the way."

"So we'll walk together? Will you wait for me if my foot hurts?"

"You wait for me, too, when I'm tired." Cheng looks up and I nod.

Cheng and I start off again, walking past groves of trees, then into thick, tall, golden grass, taller than either of us. The tightly packed stalks scratch at me. No sooner do we beat back a wall of it than we confront another.

"Cheng, this grass is too tall and we can't see where we are going." Around me, I listen for footsteps, voices, clues that we're on the right path. All we can hear is the constant whisper of parting grass.

Cheng looks tired as her arms—as thin as classroom rulers—push the mighty grass away and her tiny body moves along next to mine. I too am exhausted. Eventually the thick forest of grass ends, and ahead of us are broken lines of children. I'm relieved, almost grateful to be here.

As we trudge closer to a group of trees, we're shocked by what we see. There are hundreds of adults, bent and slaving in a field. Side by side, they dig into the earth, leaving a long excavated ditch flanked by a huge elevated road with sloping sides. Some workers attack with hoes, loosening dirt and scooping it into baskets for those behind them. Others hold their carrying sticks, waiting for the baskets to be filled with dirt. Then there are those who have just dumped the soil at the rising, elongated road, returning for more. The first thought that comes to me is of Chea and Ra.

"Cheng," I say softly, "my older sisters might be here. I want to look for them." My hope floats and hovers above the field.

I scan the busy crowd, but it's hard to see faces. Most are covered by scarves, shielding them from the sun. They either stare down as they work the ground or look away as they carry the baskets. I study each filthy, skinny face, hoping to find Chea and Ra. Motionless, I stand beside Cheng searching, searching for my sisters.

"Athy, Athy!" A weak, hoarse voice calls out. I turn, but find no faces that I recognize.

"Athy!" a scrawny, malnourished person standing among a group of workers shouts, waving eagerly at me.

I move closer, and I'm stunned. It's Aunt Rin, *Mak*'s baby sister. A once-youthful, beautiful woman. Now she hides in the cloak of an old peach scarf and a once-black uniform, now faded a dull gray. Her eyes, framed by long lashes, and her gentle, birdlike grace are my only clues to the person I knew, now a shadow of her former self.

Gingerly and eagerly, she reports, "Athy, your older sisters Chea and Ra also work in this labor camp, but they're over there." She motions away, toward distant tall trees and shelters.

"Athy, who else is coming with you? Only yourself?" Aunt Rin inquires.

"Only me. . . ." I break down as I think about the parting from *Mak*.

"Athy, stop crying. I'll tell your sisters to look for you tonight. Stop crying."

Tears flood Aunt Rin's eyes as she gazes into mine. I feel Cheng's hand touch my arm—she's crying, too. Her ragged sobs and Aunt Rin's make me cry harder.

Suddenly I hurt for *Mak*. She wanted to believe what they promised her. Maybe in her desperate hope she had to believe it. And now this.

"They lied to us, promised that the work camp was close to the village," Cheng sniffs, wiping her tears away with her scarf.

"They told us," I cry, "that there's a lot of food here."

Aunt Rin knows. "They lie, they lied so you'd come. There isn't a lot of food. They give everyone rice rations just like in the village. They work you to death. I'm terribly tired and just want to rest." Her mouth moves slowly, as if there's no energy left in her. A stern woman in a new black uniform approaches Aunt Rin's work group. I alert her. Aunt Rin looks horror-stricken. She wipes away her tears and says, "She's my *mekorg*,* Athy, I have to work. I'll tell Chea and Ra to look for you. . . ."

"Comrade, go back to work NOW! This is not a place for you to talk. Who gave you permission to stop working?"

"I just want to talk to my niece, that's all," Aunt Rin answers submissively.

---

* Brigade leader.

The *mekorg* looks at Cheng and me, then hisses, "Comrades, both of you go to the children's camp, over there! Go there now!" Cheng and I scurry away.

We wander among makeshift tents. They sprout like mushrooms rooted under the shade of trees at the edge of a small mountain, which I think is called Phnom Kambour. So this is a labor camp, the place where mobile brigades are sent. Suddenly, a woman pauses in front of us and points to a large tent as if she knows where we're supposed to go. Cheng and I look at each other, bewildered but relieved. When we get to the tent, it's full, crowded with crying children. Their wails rise in the twilight, calling for their mothers like a sad, chanting prayer.

Chhlops shout at the crying children, ordering everyone to stop. The distraught children only wail harder. Even informants can't stop our cries. Recognizing defeat, they leave us alone with our tears.

Without warning, cooks appear bringing steaming rice and watery soup in round black pots. As soon as we realize they have food, everybody, including Cheng and me, rushes toward the cooks. We swarm around them. My mouth waters, and my stomach roars. Like the other children, I ready my plate for a ration as I stare hungrily into the watery, milky soup and the rice pot. I can almost eat the food with my stare, for the only food I've had all day since leaving Daakpo village was a taste of Cheng's yam, a piece the size of my toe.

After receiving the rice ration, I scurry with Cheng and other children for our soup ration, surrounding the cook, who is stirring a milky broth swirling with flat little fish, with heads and eyes peeking out at us.

The cook drops a plastic bowl on the ground in the middle of the circle, then pours the cloudy broth with a few fish into it. The minute she's done, every spoon collides in the soup bowl. Everyone has the same idea—we all want fish and we all know there are not enough. Whoever is quick gets the fish and whoever is slow cries. We learn to ignore others' sad eyes and eat the fish ravenously.

Surprisingly, the cook gives us another soup ration. Before she finishes pouring it into our bowl, a girl cries out, "Don't take all the fish." Her words freeze me and those who've gotten their share of fish. We don't reach for the bowl until she and two others in our group get their fish. I feel sorry for her, and for us all, that it's come to this, grappling like dogs over a bone. But I'm relieved knowing we've each got a fish. Despite starvation, we haven't completely lost our sense of sharing, a human courtesy the Khmer Rouge have yet to take away.

After our meal, Cheng and I rest, sitting on the ground beneath tall trees since there's no shelter for us. Tonight is the first night in my life I realize that I can lose *Mak* as easily as I've lost *Pa*. Never have I been separated from her, and the distance pains me. Closing my eyes, I can see *Mak* preparing dinner, bending before the flames, coaxing the water to a boil, dropping in leaves. Her words would be a low murmur, gentle instructions to get a bowl for a brother, to wash your face. Ordinary words, but delivered with a kindness that I will never know here.

Once I remember *Mak* daydreaming about food, telling us what she would be grateful to have. She used to say, "Having solid rice and salt is like going to heaven." Tonight I have solid rice and fish soup, even more than her heavenly wish. I've only had one meal, but already I am full of regret, feeling guilty, wishing I could some-how have shared it to ease her starvation. But she's too far away—even my ability to imagine her is fading away.

Out of the darkness, I hear a familiar voice. I look up and see a shadow of a person calling my name. It's Chea! Aunt Rin did tell her that I'm here! And now she has come for me.

I get up, oblivious to everything around me, Cheng and the sob-bing children. She runs and puts her arm around me. I can see little in the dark, only that she seems thinner. We walk away together, almost like in the good old times.

"Athy, when did you get here?" Chea sounds concerned.

"A while ago." I'm comforted by Chea's presence. Her sisterly role.

She wonders why I came to the camp, and worries that I should have stayed with *Mak*. "You shouldn't have left *Mak*. Who's going to look after her? The older children are gone."

I explain to Chea why *Mak* wants me here.

"They lied to you so you would come. They lied to everybody. You should have stayed with *Mak*. You're too small to work here. It's hard work even for older people like me," says Chea, sounding distraught.

Now I'm frightened about what could happen to *Mak*, and I'm scared for myself, whether I'll survive this hard work and live to see *Mak*.

"Chea, I want to go back to *Mak*, I want to go back. How can I go back?" I cry, wanting Chea to help me, but she doesn't answer except to hold me tight.

Chea takes me to her shelter, and I wait there alone while she goes back to finish her assigned task. Everyone must dig a prescribed number of cubic meters of soil each day, no matter how long it takes. I cry until Chea and Ra return to the shelter.

"Athy, I heard my *mekong* say they will send all the children to a camp in Oh Runtabage tomorrow. Did they tell you?" Chea asks softly.

"No," I sniff, gasping for air.

The words Oh Runtabage literally mean a stream struck by lightning. I'm scared all over again. Chea comforts me, saying I'll be closer to *Mak* than if I were to stay at Phnom Kambour with her and Ra. But I can't imagine seeing *Mak*, so the words don't comfort me. Already I miss Chea and Ra, even though Ra has spoken little. She seems exhausted, used up. They are my sisters still, but worn-out versions of the girls I knew. And I'm too caught up in my fears and sadness. I cry until it wears me out; I fall asleep beside Chea, drifting into dreams about seeing *Mak*.

"Athy, Athy, wake up! Wake up, *p'yoon* [younger sibling]."

I open my eyes and it's still dark. The voice is familiar, and for a sleepy moment I think I'm back in Daakpo.

"Wake up, Athy. You have to go," says Chea, her hands lifting my head.

My body aches. Reluctantly I rise and Chea takes me back to where she found me. I don't even have time to say good-bye to Ra.

I hold my tears when I hear a fierce voice ask "Which one of you, comrades, wants to be the brave children of *Angka Leu*? Stand here." I'm shocked, spellbound by the voice of the man and the ghostly shadows of little children standing silently by the fire.

Suddenly I feel a tap on my shoulder. "Athy, *bang* has to go back. May *p'yoon srey* [young sister] encounter only good things as you go to Oh Runtabage. Take care of yourself. *Lea Haey* [Good-bye], *p'yoon*." Chea murmurs her blessing, then her voice is gone. I turn to watch her. She disappears into a grove of trees, and I'm left with heartbroken children.

As we depart from Phnom Kambour, the Khmer Rouge have the "brave children" march on the road under construction, the earthen bridge being built by those we leave behind. The Khmer Rouge launch into a marching chant. Around me, small hands stab the air and obediently repeat the song. Over and over, they call themselves "the brave children of *Angka Leu*." They shout, they sing, they dance.

The journey to Oh Runtabage is tiring and cold. By the time we arrive at Oh Runtabage it's late afternoon. The remote camp is as secluded as Phnom Kambour. Trees create a thick barrier on each side of a stream, casting their tangled shadows over the milky brown water, making it look shallower than it really is. Near the stream, tall yellow grass grows in an open field that stretches far into the distance. There are no huts, only the shelter of trees. I'm hungry and exhausted.

Already there is work. They order us to look for tree branches for the cooks to use as fuel. Some of us have to dig big holes for the cooking pots. Others go to the stream to retrieve the milky brown water for cooking. I help other children to dig cooking holes. I dig until my body trembles. Suddenly I feel dizzy. I pause and take a deep breath.

Softly I say to myself, "I'm feeling sick." A few children glance at me as I sink down to the ground. I close my eyes, resting my head on my knees, hiding behind a row of working children who block the *chhlops'* view of me. Though I fear the informants will see me, I'm too exhausted to care.

Eventually it is time to eat, and I have not been found out. After we eat, the Khmer Rouge direct us to a grove of trees along the stream in which we are to make our shelters. First we have to clear the brush to make a space, then the "walls," nothing more than little branches. Those who have brought extra clothes use them for a sleeping mat while Cheng and I gather leaves for ours. The local children, the "old people," get to choose where they want their shelters to be, and whatever they don't want belongs to us, the "new people." All is done to keep the peasants on the side of the Khmer Rouge.

Being new to this task, Cheng and I agree that we should watch the "old people" build their shelters. We decide to find tree branches near their area, where they're making their makeshift tents. As we study them working, they catch us.

"What are you looking at?" a local girl snarls, speaking in *rurdern*, a distinctive northwestern drawl. In the past, such an accent would have made me laugh. Here, I only risk a giggle under my breath. It is hard not to mock people you don't respect. The trick is not to get caught.

Cheng and I turn away. I murmur to Cheng, and softly drawl what the girl said, "What are you looking at?" Cheng mocks her, too, and we laugh quietly to ourselves. For a moment I feel as if we're back in school, laughing our girlish laughs.

Cheng and I build our tiny shelter away from the other children's, close to the edge of the stream. Like the "old people," we use vines and branches to assemble our roof and walls, so low that we must crawl in and out. But I grin to myself at our small achievement, and I'm glad Cheng is here to help. And I wonder if what I heard back in Phnom Penh is true. Cambodian elders used to say, "At home there's a separate mother, in the forest there's only one mother." In the wild, you have to cling together. Here, Cheng is my family. Hope is our invisible mother, the presence that comforts us.

At night we are like a family, but we can't be while we're working. Every morning at about four o'clock, our brigade leader, along with her "pets," shrill in the air, "Wake up, wake up. Go to work, go to work. . . ." Our leader's voice is annoying, and her face is perpetually angry. She always frowns when ordering us, as if we're not worth looking at. But the feeling is mutual. I don't like her either. She's thin, with short, curly black hair and dark skin. Cambodian elders would say her heart is darker than her skin. She seems to be yelling at us all the time, even after we wake up and march into the field. As our eyes close, open, and close again, her venomous words are all that we hear.

In order to curry favor, our *mekorg* wakes us earlier and earlier.

"Evil woman!" Cheng hisses under her breath. "This creature wakes us up early for work, but it and its evil people go back to sleep. Dogs!" Cheng growls.

"How do you know they go back to sleep?" I ask, astonished.

"I've sneaked out to the cooking area to get fish heads. Then I hide them by our shelter," says Cheng softly. "And I see them sleep. Those dogs!"

Now I know why Cheng always disappears during the lineup time for food rations. I have often noticed how she goes away to eat by herself, or eat with her back to me and other children. *She's brave*, I think, gazing at her toiling in the morning's shadows.

The next day as she waits in front of me for her rice ration, I assume Cheng has fish heads in her scarf. I want to ask her for some fish heads, but I'm scared of the *chhlops* standing by the cooks. I glance at her, then at the *chhlops*, anxiety making my hunger gnaw deeper. I'm nervous, but bold. I walk over to Cheng and whisper.

"Can I have some fish heads?"

"Athy, stop talking to me. The *chhlops* will see us," Cheng hisses softly.

Now I draw a *chhlop*'s attention. He turns, surveying the food line, and I quickly look away, pretending I haven't said a word. As the line moves a step forward, I take a step, acting like everyone else. When we get our food, I sit down to eat by the other children, not beside Cheng. But as soon as that *chhlop* goes off, I move next to her.

I whisper, "Cheng!"

I wait. There's no answer, then, finally, "Here!" Cheng's hand slides out, touching me. I grab the fistful of fish heads, no bigger than a thumb. The little fish heads taste good, ashy but substantial, and I want more.

The next day during the rice ration, again I don't see Cheng in the lineup. I look around and see only one *chhlop* helping the cooks with the rations. I sneak out to the stream, looking for a place where the cooks might dispose of their garbage—including anything left from fish cleaning, guts, fins, heads. There, I hope to find Cheng, but I'm nervous about being spotted by my *mekorg* or her "pets." I discover Cheng and two other girls scavenging through the garbage by a clump of trees. They tear through the cold, slimy garbage even faster when they realize that I'm coming toward them. Clawing at the bits of flesh, we're like four vultures circling ravenously over a corpse. When Cheng's hands are full, she turns away from the garbage and us, then stuffs her fish heads in her scarf. I grab two heads with the guts still attached to them.

"You took my fish heads! Give them back!" a girl insists, grabbing at me.

I ignore her demands. Instead, my eyes search as rapidly as my hands, scanning for even the smallest scrap of dead prey. Soon the girl stops demanding. By now she has learned that the fish heads are not hers. She turns her attention to the garbage. I wish I could just give them to her, but I'm starving, too. We're worse than beggars.

Before returning to the lineup for the rice ration, we look for a fire in which to cook our fish heads. Among a few cooking holes near the stream, there are slumbering embers covered by flakes of ashes. Into the hot holes we throw our fish heads, and go back to the lineup.

The next day Cheng and I sneak out early, perhaps two hours before lunch ration. Upon our arrival near the cooking area, we spot a few female cooks preparing our meal. One cook is alone, away from the others. We approach her, slowly like a turtle, testing to see if our intrusion is permitted. She looks over her shoulder at us, and speaks to us with motherly concern. A peasant, her voice lacks the typical sting of the Khmer Rouge leaders.

"Why aren't you at work? You'll get in trouble when they catch you."

Her gentle tone invites me in. For the first time, I have the urge to tell a Khmer Rouge about my hunger.

"I'm so hungry. I want fish heads. Aunt, don't throw them away," I plead, addressing her as "aunt" instead of "comrade." I trust her, feeling at ease as she reports to us what the food ration for today will be. Lunch will be rice and fish soup. But for dinner there will also be a vegetable, green mustard-like leaves.

"They woke us up to work very early this morning," says Cheng softly as the cook scoops the cleaned fish into a basket. "Every day I'm very tired. Hungry."

Suddenly the cook scrapes fish heads and guts toward us with the knife. Without repulsion, we grab the heads, trailing slimy guts from the tree stump. Then, making a makeshift pouch with our shirttails, we stuff them inside. To my great surprise, the cook hands us each two fish, which she has beheaded.

"Here. Go before they catch you. Before they punish us. Go now." She motions her head nervously at Cheng and me, shooing us off.

As we're leaving, more "vultures" emerge. A group of kids scurry from the trees toward the cook, sending her to her feet. She hurries over toward the other cooks, calling someone's name in her jittery voice: "Nak! Nak! More . . . more children are coming for fish. I . . . I'm scared," she stammers, pointing to the starving children scavenging at the fish area.

"Comrades, go back to work or I'll report you to your *mekorg*," Nak warns, striding toward the children.

The children disperse quickly into the trees, and so do Cheng and I. After this incident, I stop sneaking out for fish heads. It's too little food for me to risk my life.

In the evening after dinner, Cheng and I wait until the food ration is over. Before the cooks take those big black pots to the stream to wash, we dash over to them and ask if we can have the burned rice crust. Sometimes they peel off the sheets of crust and hand us each one, or they allow us to help ourselves. It is bitter, but it's food. Later, everyone discovers this idea, and again there are more children than there is rice crust to go around.

We constantly try to find more food. One day as I am drinking water from the stream, I see schools of small fish parade in the shallows at its edge. On hot days they hover close, bunched amid the cool shade of overhanging branches. I'm eager to catch them, wishing for a fishing net so that I might simply scoop them up.

That night I tell Cheng of my exciting discovery. The next day we slip away to my secret spot, struggling to push our way through intertwined trees that cast a continuous deep shade into the stream. We grin at each other when the brave fish swim slowly in our direction.

For the first time, I'm happy—just to be here, to enjoy the proximity to nature and Cheng's friendship. I feel like a kid again—a rare privilege. Here, no one yells at us, ordering us around.

Later, Cheng and I have a plan to catch the fish. During lunch we confide in Larg, one of the other "new people." Early on, she drew our sympathy, and we befriend her. After work, the three of us would bathe in the stream far away from the shelters, where no one can easily see us. There, we would talk about missing our mothers and about our problems. Together we've shared rice crust when one of us gets more than the other. The three of us plot to fish with our scarves tied together as a fishing net.

On the way to the stream one evening after work, we walk like thieves, looking over our shoulder to see if we're being watched or followed. The spot where I've seen fish is too small to fit all three of us. Instead, we hike farther until we come to a quiet spot with an open space.

We tie our scarves together with thin vines, then Cheng and I fish while Larg tries to scare the fish in the direction of our scooped net. We walk slowly in the cool, shallow water as Larg herds them toward us. We try again and again, but we don't catch any fish. The final time we try, Larg stumbles, then falls facedown, splashing water toward Cheng and me. For a moment I panic, paralyzed, as I watch Larg's body slowly sink into the shallow stream. Cheng and I run to help her.

"I felt light-headed," says Larg softly, "then my legs just sank."

Still recovering from shock, Cheng and I watch Larg shiver after we help her out of the stream. We return to the camp as empty-handed as we came.

I keep trying to figure out how to catch the fish. After bathing in the stream in my worn-out clothing, I notice that a metal snap from my cotton shirt is loose. I break it off the shirt and study the shine. Without a needle or thread, there is no way to sew it back on. But I notice the tiny wire snaking inside the back of the snap. Suddenly an idea takes shape. I hurry back to the shelter, looking for a safety pin on my shirt. Like a goldsmith, I carefully pull out the hidden wire, now a precious resource. I straighten the button wire. Sharpen one end with a stone. Then I bend it to form a fish hook. A tiny, tiny fish hook—probably an inch long, but made of a stout little wire. It is a glorious invention. Tomorrow, I'll head to my secret spot, but tonight I need to hold my excitement, hoping my plan will work. I don't breathe a word of it to anyone, not even to Cheng.

As soon as the *mekorg* goes on patrol after lunch, I slip away with a hoe, carrying it on my shoulder. If I get caught, I'll announce I'm going to *bot chhurng thom*, "fold big leg," a polite way of saying "pooping."

Alone at the fishing spot, I take out the fish hook and a length of polyester thread—my fishing line salvaged from an old rice bag—and a small ball of rice I've saved from my lunch ration. Now I need a fishing pole. I break a tree branch and pick off the leaves. My fingers mash the rice to make a bait. I gently sink the fishing line into the water so as not to disturb the fish. A few fish make sudden moves. Their tails wiggle faster, propelling them forward. In my mind, I speak to them, coax them: *Come on, eat the bait, eat the bait.* I recite my chant over and over while trying to hold the fishing pole still.

One fish approaches, studying the bait. Suddenly its jaws open and the bait vanishes, and I pull. Into the air flies a silver fish the size of a tablespoon, jerked free from the hook but landing on the bank. I run over to it and cover the fish with both of my hands. Then I pinch its head until it stops moving. For a moment my fingers are frozen in victory.

Holding the fish beneath my hands, I know the life has seeped out of it. But it takes courage to move them, for I fear that it will somehow leap from my grasp and tumble back down the sandy bank out of my reach. To be safe, I move it, setting it back several feet, and return to the water. I gently lower the hook again and promptly catch two more fish the same way. Again, I sink the rice bait, and as soon as the next fish gulps the bait, I pull. My eyes follow the fishing pole in the air, then to the ground, but I don't see the fish. I look into the water. There goes the fish and the polyester thread, the bait and the hook. *Ah, the fish must have been hungrier than I am,* I decide. Still, I have my catch. I roll up the three fish into the elastic waistband of my pants to hide them.

Cheng's eyes open wide when I show her the fish. Her eyebrows rise when I tell her how I caught them. And her hand reaches out to see the hook. I tell her about losing the hook and the string, and promise that I'll show her and Larg how to make fish hooks. The three of us sneak into the underbrush to make more hooks. Now our shirts are held together with bits of vine or safety pins. We fish whenever one of us can sneak away. Any catch is shared among us, sneaked into the embers to be cooked a little. For a while our extra catch helps. Later, everyone is closely watched and we don't dare try to leave our work. Still, we have each other.

Months have passed. We operate on a cycle of endless longing. A yearning for the lunch ration pulls us through the morning. The desire for a dinner ration tugs us through the remainder of the day. It's a circle of hunger. It obliterates everything—the heat, the exhaustion, the loneliness. Every day we slave for the Khmer Rouge in a vast barren field, digging irrigation ditches, hauling dirt in woven baskets. But we're also slaves to our own hunger.

Hungry and exhausted as I am, I can hardly lift my feet up as I carry two baskets full of dirt balanced on either end of a carrying stick that rests across my shoulder. When I turn around, Cheng is right behind me, tipping her baskets, dumping the dirt out. She whispers to me.

"Athy, do you want to eat sweet grass? When I went to pee, I sucked on this long grass and there is juice in it. It tastes like sugarcane."

Cheng gestures with a quick motion of her head.

My mouth waters at the thought of sugarcane. These words seem old, far distant. It's been more than a year now since the evacuation from Phnom Penh. Suddenly the word "sugarcane" triggers images of good times. Eagerly, my mind slips away to Takeo.

Here is *Mak*, emerging through the gate, baskets full of groceries, bending against their weight. Avy, Than, and I race over to her. Each of us is eager to find out if *Mak* has bought our desserts. Eagerly, we call out "*Mak, Mak*," squealing like baby birds in need of worms.

Than digs into the baskets. Already he finds bags of sweet puddings. He hands me one. I hum in contented pleasure as I untie the bag. *Mak* places the baskets on the cement floor, then strides to the stairs, looking up with a smile at Avy, whose shrill voice adds to the din. She reaches out her little arms to *Mak*, eager to be picked up. Memories past. Now they are like good movies, a distant, comfortable place to which I escape. A moment's fantasy simply triggered by a familiar word, "sugarcane."

"Athy?" asks Cheng, snapping me back to the heat and our reality. I'm going to ask our *mekorg* if I can go pee. You ask her after I leave. . . . I'll wait for you." Cheng looks cautious, then disappears into the crowd of children in search of the *mekorg*.

Cheng meets up with me in a distant grassy field, away from the labor site. Each of us carries a hoe, our eating ware, which we'll be using to cut the sweet grass. We hike to bushes of tall cream-colored grass, which look nothing like sugarcane. Cheng picks a clump and I pick the next one. Without hesitation, we raise our hoes in the air, cutting down the grass. I pick up a crisp stalk, the size of my index finger, and suck the sweet juice out of it. Cheng and I say nothing, temporarily lost in the frenzy of our hunger—we continue to drink the juice, grazing at one clump after another.

Suddenly the heads of the *mekorg* and a *chhlop* emerge among the swaying stalks of grass. I freeze. My jaws are stuck as the fierce, angry stares weigh down upon me. I want to alert Cheng, but I can't spit out a word.

"Comrades, what are you doing here? You're supposed to be working!" the *mekorg* roars, her giant steps approaching.

Cheng turns. Her body jolts. Her hands drop the hoe.

"Take these comrades to reform!" The *mekorg* yanks my arm. She shoves me, sending me sprawling onto the ground. I struggle up, and stumble forward as fast as I can. Cheng glances at me in terror and I at her, through my tears. We knew the risk. But the fear, pain, and exhaustion are too strong to hold inside, spilling out in harsh sobs. I know we should have gone back to work sooner. *It's too late*, I think regretfully. They must have watched us closely, and we were too hungry to notice. Now we're at their mercy. They shove at our backs as they march us to the shelters.

"Tie both of them up and don't give them food! Have other comrades watch them so they won't follow their bad example," the *mekong* orders the *chhlop*, pointing to a stump near the entrance to the girls' shelters.

Against the rough bark of the stump, my ankles, arms, and hands are bound tightly behind my back. Then my chest. Never before have I felt so utterly defenseless, so humiliated. The *chhlop* snakes the rugged rope, half the size of my wrist, around me over and over again. There is no struggle left in me. As soon as the *chhlop* leaves, having finished binding Cheng against the opposite side of the stump, my grief tumbles out.

"Athy, don't cry too hard," Cheng sobs. "Stop crying. . . ."

"Cheng . . . I . . . I miss . . . my mom. . . ." I gasp for air.

"I miss my mom, too. . . ." Cheng weeps.

The sun sets. My legs go limp. The rope bites into me. I feel delirious, drowsy. Suddenly I hear a voice approaching. Slowly, I turn my head to see the *mekong*, *chhlops*, and an army of children marching back from the work site. Like obedient soldiers, they walk single file, passing us. Each head turns briefly, throwing a glance at us. We are their lesson.

"This is what will happen to you if you don't follow *Angka Leu*." The dark, ugly *mekong* jabs at Cheng and me with a stick. "Observe, comrades. . . ."

The night is here. The food ration is served. The children are asleep. But we stand through the night, without being given food or water.

The night turns to morning. The children pass us, escorted by the *mekong* to the work site. With shallow breaths, my ribs fight against the ropes around my chest. My body slumps against the stump. *I'm on the verge of death*, I think, and the very words terrify me. I breathe slowly. Every breath I take is for the deadened weight in my arms, wrists, and legs—they're hungry for air.

It's so quiet. Cheng is already dead. She must be. She has made no sound since the children passed by on their way to the fields. I call out her name. Every part of my body braces for an answer. Finally a faint groan. I'm relieved, but my body feels strange, numb. It can no longer hold itself up, and I fear that the lack of circulation in my limbs will kill me.

When night comes, the same *chhlop* releases us. He warns us of tougher punishment if we repeat our offense. After he leaves, a shadow appears. It's Larg. She brings us rice rations, placing them by the stump. Slowly my legs and arms awaken, burning, as blood and oxygen find their way back. Cheng and I go to our shelter. In the dark, we devour our food. I thought I would never again know the taste of rice. Or salt.

We are now watched closely. Working conditions get worse. Every day we are awakened long before sunrise and return only after the sun surrenders its light. Their goals, our leaders stress in mandatory meetings, are for us to beat the "set date." To exceed the quota. To compete with other brigades digging irrigation ditches that will join ours. I measure our progress in inches. The few feet of the elevated roadway and the depth of the canal in which I work every day. Almost around the clock, dirt is my landscape.

The long days of forced labor have taken its toll on us. Many children grow ill. Some come down with malaria. Others with fever or diarrhea. At night I hear the sounds of pain, of sickness. Near the shelters are signs of diarrhea covered with flies. Soon I too have diarrhea, then it gets worse. I have what Vin had, amoebic dysentery. Every day I lie in the empty shelter, which is built close to the open field near the work site. I'm drained, weak from days of losing fluid. I constantly soil my pants. Two pairs, that's all I've got. Every night I think of *Mak*, Map, and Avy. I close my eyes and imagine lying in the hut beside *Mak*. The longing is a physical ache, competing with the pain in my own belly. I try to console myself, *I'm lucky to have Cheng*. She takes care of me.

At mealtimes I wait for Cheng to bring me my ration. At our shelter, she kneels down, reaching out to help me up. Pointing at a plastic cup, she reminds me that she's also brought water, cloudy like a light milk-chocolate drink. In a short time, a *chhlop*'s voice roars, ordering children to return to work. Cheng obeys, but I know she will be back—the one thing I've come to count on. In the evening she washes my soiled pants, then covers me with her only scarf. She leaves her own head bare, working in the hot sun. Never once has Cheng complained. Her silent sacrifice fills me with a deeper gratitude than I have ever known.

The follow night Cheng wakes me. Her footsteps storm out of the shelter. In a few minutes she returns with stomach cramps. She curls up behind me, groaning. Her body feels unusually warm, a sign of illness. I'm scared for Cheng, scared for both of us. How will we survive if both of us are sick? *Who will get us rations?* Certainly not the *mekorg*, even though she's in charge of us. She is indifferent, only interested in us when we have strength. If you are weak, you are useless. I know we can't rely on Larg. Since our punishment, we've seen less and less of her.

The next morning, as always, the *mekorg* wakes everyone. She peeks into our shelter and orders Cheng to work, not me, since she knows I've been sick. Cheng tells her that she has diarrhea. But she says Cheng has to work.

Cheng obeys. Quietly, she gets up, then disappears among the shelters. At lunch, her face drawn and pale, she appears with my ration. At night she has to get up several times with diarrhea, the next symptom of amoebic dysentery. The next afternoon Cheng brings my ration and explains to me what she has been plotting since last night.

"Athy, we've got to escape from this place," she begins softly. "You're very sick, and I'm getting sick like you. If we stay here, we'll die. We need rest and medicine."

Cheng speaks like an adult, the kind of strong, comforting tone I would hear *Pa* or *Mak* use when I came down with a fever or an asthma attack. "If you don't escape with me, you'll never see your mom again." Cheng looks into my eyes. She knows. And so do I.

The Khmer Rouge have never given me medicine. Now they simply glance at me—I'm not worth their breath. But as harsh as their indifference is, it's better than being beaten to death, I reason, recalling their warnings about what happens to those who attempt to run away. As much as I want to see *Mak*, I fear this more. But the odds are grim. I face the chance of dying here in camp of an illness I can't control, or risk the punishment of death if I'm caught escaping. Back and forth I work the choices in my mind, but nothing becomes clear. How odd to be wrestling with the question of how I might die.

"I must escape. If I stay here, I'll die. I might not die if I escape," Cheng states. "I'll help you tomorrow if you want to go with me, but, Athy, I won't stay here." She looks sad but determined.

"But I don't have the energy to walk. I can't walk fast enough, Cheng. And so they will see us. They'll see us walking across the open field. There aren't enough trees to block us." I imagine us running away. My mind is willing to go with her, but I don't know if I can trust my legs to carry me, to keep up.

"I'll help you walk. I'll come and get you, and we'll escape tomorrow while they're eating lunch. I have to go back to work." Cheng hurries out, returning to work as the shrill voice of a *chhlop* rings out in the distance.

Our day to escape comes. I get ready for Cheng, readying both my mind and my body. Sitting in the shelter, I rehearse our escape in my mind, visualizing Cheng and me running, or rather walking, for I can't run. The cool morning turns into another warm day. Without watches, we must observe the sky. When the sun is bright above the shelter, Cheng comes looking anxious. She frowns, squinting from the harsh sunlight.

"Athy, are you ready? They are lining up for food. We must go now."

"Ready," I quickly answer. Inside I'm scared, trembling. I want to tell Cheng, but something holds my words back. *I must not tell her now, not now.*

Cheng whispers, asking me for my plate. Together with her own, she slips my plate under her jacket, securing a drawstring at the bottom. I watch her with wonder. *Why take plates when we must run? Shouldn't we travel light?* But Cheng has thought this through. We carry out her plan. Silently, Cheng motions her head, signaling to me to crawl out of the shelter. She holds my right hand and we walk slowly, cautious as we pass other children's shelters. Cheng slips an arm around my shoulders, helping to steady me as I struggle to walk on my weakened legs. On her own shoulder Cheng carries a hoe, making it appear as if she is helping me to go defecate in the open field. In the distance, about a mile away, is a row of trees—our first goal. We hope to make it at least that far, a natural screen to cloak our escape. At any moment I expect to feel a hand on my shoulder, or hear the shuffle of another pair of feet behind us in the grassy field. We try not to look behind, only ahead. With every step, the trees seem further away. I imagine the *chhlops* or our *mekorg* chasing after us, almost expect it. This time, I think, I'll never survive any kind of physical punishment, being as ill as I am. The more I think about it, the more fear moves me—a rush of energy surges through my body, propelling me forward with a force I didn't know I had.

Now we are too far from the shelters for anyone to believe that we're going to defecate. If the *chhlops* see us now, surely they'll know. I walk even faster. Cheng grips my hand tighter. We walk, then we run—an awkward, hobbled hopping, but in my mind I want to move the trees closer to us. As soon as we reach them, Cheng drops the hoe to the ground and commands: "Athy, walk faster. We must walk faster." She begins to run, pulling me forward.

Cheng drags me, and I let her. I drift behind her like an anchor as the pull of her hand tows my frail body. Through the fear, I somehow feel free. I no longer think only about the *chhlops* or the *mekorg* coming after us. Nor the dry grass that licks our ankles or my own weak muscles. I think about what I'm running toward, not what I'm leaving behind. I think of *Mak*. And the thought pulses through my veins like a newfound power. With each step, something loosens in my soul.

I am free.

Even though we've passed the trees, our first obstacle, the horizon seems so far. Not a sound passes between Cheng and me, only soft, labored breathing. She pulls, I follow. We keep on walking fast, using the clump of trees we've passed as a visual block.

We've covered quite a distance already—a few miles, I think. Over the sound of our shuffling footsteps, we hear voices approaching. We pause, crouch down, looking at each other, horrified. Spontaneously, we both sprawl flat on the ground, like soldiers listening to enemy voices.

Cheng grabs my hand. We run, stoop, hunker down. By the time we reach the bushes, we have to stifle our gasping breaths. The voices are men's, coming closer. Already I know the terrible torment that will befall us. As they near, I'm surprised to hear them talking about fishing, not about us. I feel reassured enough to peek: one man carries a fishing net on his shoulder, and the other an old bucket. Cheng and I look at each other, relieved.

Without a map, we let the landscape guide us, looking for clumps of trees, letting memory lead the way. As Cheng and I figure how to get to Daakpo village in the twilight, my emotions run high, mixed with fear, nervousness, and excitement. We pass two villages. Then the path begins to look familiar. Fearing informants, we keep to back pathways, zigzagging, trying to stay invisible. Somehow, in the darkness, Cheng and I find our way back to

Daakpo village. But the discovery brings uncertainty. What if we don't find our mothers? Before we go our separate ways, Cheng makes one last request: "In case they catch me, if you see my mother, tell her that I escaped with you." Cheng's shadow turns once again, as if to study me, then begins to fade. I run through layers of darkness to find her, to make the same request: "Tell my mother, too, if I don't see her."

Alone, I'm again on guard. I'm nervous, but I'm also eager to see *Mak*. I swallow the urge to run back into my mother's arms. Instead, I walk to the hut, cautious. Like an adult, I've learned to anticipate obstacles, to avoid drawing attention to myself. When I see the tall trees near our hut, my personal landmark, I'm exhilarated. The cooking fire in the corner casts a dim glow around the entrance. At last, I see her. *Mak* sits beside the fire—so typical, so ordinary, as if I never left. Her gaze transfixed, she is studying the contents of her cooking pot like a fortune-teller, as if something will be revealed in the tangle of leaves that swim within it. For a moment I'm frozen, stilled by my own joy. Then, the impossible. I walk up to her, reaching out to embrace her.

"*Mak*, I'm back!" Just to speak those words fills me with pride and jubilation, a swell of feeling I haven't known since they took me away. To be so near her. To smell her familiar scent. In an instant, I realize the depth of my love for her. I know exactly how much I need my mother. How much my family means to me. To my survival.

Mak turns, startled. She jumps to her feet and her voice explodes with delight, "*Koon*, they let you come back! You're finished. . . ." *Mak* gropes for words.

"*Mak!*" I whisper. "Don't speak so loudly." I glance around the hut, and so does she. At that moment I notice Map and Avy gazing at *Mak* and me nervously. I lean closer to *Mak* and whisper into her ear, "I escaped from the labor camp."

Mak pulls away, horror-stricken. Her expression scares me. Freezes me. I look at Avy and Map. Their silence triggers more fear in me. Hunger has wrung out their spirits. My heart races as I realize the repercussions of my escape. Now I fear what my homecoming could mean to my family. At the Phnom Kambour labor camp, Chea had warned me that I should have stayed with *Mak*, Avy, and Map and looked after them. At the time her words made me feel guilty and fearful, like a bad omen. Now that I'm here, I hope to stay, to make right what should never have happened. After a dinner of boiled leaves and salt with *Mak*, Avy, and Map, I lie down beside *Mak*'s warm back, just as I envisioned. Silently, I pray to Buddha and *Pa*'s spirit that the *chhlops* or the *mekorg* will never come take me back to Oh Runtabage.

To avoid my being spotted by the *chhlops*, *Mak* warns me not to leave the hut while she's at work with Avy and Map. I'm to stay in the hut at all times. She leaves me boiled leaves so I don't have to go outside to cook. Even so, the *chhlops* can check the hut whenever they want to. Knowing this, I brace myself when I hear footsteps, flattening myself against the palm-thatch wall, afraid even to breathe for fear that my slightest movement will rustle the dry palm leaves. Only when the footsteps subside do I relax, lying down again, cherishing every moment of my rest time. In the evening, as the sun drags into twilight, I look forward to *Mak*'s return.

In my self-imposed isolation, news travels slowly. Though I don't dare ask around—I'm too caught up in my need to stay hidden— I assume that Cheng must surely be finding the rest and comforts that I am. But I am wrong. Within weeks I learn through her younger sister that Cheng has died from edema. *How? The strong girl who pulled me through grass and woods, who helped me escape? How could she go so fast? Was it the amoebic dysentery that had so scared her back in the camp?* My heart cries out to her as grief rises in me. Pictures of how she took care of me return in my mind, of the days when I was groaning and delirious with fever and Cheng had lain beside me, patting my arm. She saved me from the death camp.

There is no modern medicine, but *Mak* tries to cure me with folk remedies. She boils guava bark to extract a bitter juice for me to drink, to help stop the diarrhea. I am the good patient, diligently drinking the concentrated fluid, so strong that my brain seizes up. Gradually, *Mak* nurses me back to health. Soon a *chhlop* discovers me. His young, splotchy face peeks into our hut, spotting me. Mysteriously, I'm neither tortured nor sent back to Oh Runtabage. Instead, they send me to work in a rice field close to the village. Perhaps the Khmer Rouge's disregard for the individual works in my favor—they have simply forgotten who I am and where I'm supposed to be.

8

When the Owl Cries

I'm more than willing to plant rice. When the *chhlop* leader, Srouch, orders me to work with *Mak* and other women from Daakpo, I'm deeply relieved. Every morning I rise early with *Mak* to report to the rice field while Avy stays home with Map. I've learned to accept what cannot be changed. Living on scanty rice rations in the village—less than at the labor camp—is still better than the alternative. I trade food and cruelty for some sense of family.

With *Mak*, I head to the dark, flooded rice fields each morning. There are no rest days, no holidays, no breaks, unless we are forced to attend a required meeting. I comply, even when my body is weak. Thoughts of food push me, and I pin my hopes on the promise of shade and a scanty lunch of leaves and rice. In the fields, I go hunting. Tiny field crabs, a slender snake, a crawling snail—any living tidbit can make me scramble after it.

Like the older women, I step into the muddy field, heading for the tender green rice seedlings, spears poking out of the water like young grass. By now I know the routine, unlike my first time planting rice in Year Piar. I help with work that doesn't need to be explained—scattering rice seedlings, transplanting them alongside *Mak* and the rest of the women until we're finished. Then the next field, drenched with black, muddy water mixed with cow dung. I walk along the elevated pathway between rice paddies. My mind is elsewhere, dreaming about food, but my feet carry me to the next field. One foot sinks into the soft mud and onto a sharp point. Pain slices across the top of my left foot.

I know I'm in trouble—a cut in contaminated field water and no medicine. In a second I want to undo my last steps, to remove the injury that is already spilling warm blood over my foot. Reaching down into the mud, I fumble to find what hurt me, a tree branch hidden in the mud. I want to take it to dry land so no one else will step on it. I struggle to crawl out of the rice field. I wipe the gray-black mud off my injured foot, a steady red river breaking loose. With an open, bleeding gash, I'm afraid to go back into the paddy. I know this will invite infection. But as an escapee, I have no choice. To stay invisible, I must transplant the rice. Everyone is working. I can't risk another punishment. I don't want to be taken away from *Mak* again. And I can't let *Mak* see my foot. I know she'll worry. I swallow my thoughts and wade back in.

Infection develops quickly. It gets worse every day, from the long walk through the woods to the field and back to the hut. Sand, soil, mud. From standing in the manure-soaked rice field, transplanting rice seedlings all day. The infection ignites like a flame. At night I can't sleep. It becomes itchy and painful. So painful that I scream out at night. Over and over, I call out to *Pa*. To ease this pain. To stop my tears. To be my doctor. Or just to be here with me. In my mind, he is so close, almost within my grasp. I yearn for his strength.

Soon the pain becomes unbearable, erasing everything else. I cry out, begging, "*Mak*, help me, please help me." Her shadow comes to me. Softly, she scratches around the wound. Her gentle touch soothes me to sleep, but the pain wakes me again, as if a large fierce bird is tearing at my foot, pinched tight in its claws. My throat hurts, raw from my own cries. I bang on the wall made of bamboo and palm. For one week, I cry every night. I'm used up, and *Mak*'s getting ill from lack of sleep and fatigue. I can't help it. I keep calling for her, begging her to rub around my wound; she helps me many times, but when she is exhausted, she goes back to sleep, leaving me to scream alone.

The sharp stabs throb from the inside out, pulsing up my leg to my waist and head. *Mak* can't sleep. She asks me to sleep away from her, Avy, and Map. All alone like Vin before he died, I'm banished to a small alcove. I realize now how helpless he must have felt. With no medicine, I know that I too will die. My wound is caked with pus. At night I study my foot, scratch around it, try to massage it, and cry. I beg for *Mak* again and again. But she doesn't come.

In the morning the fog of pain lifts long enough to allow me to make a decision. If I am to live, I must find *slark khnarng*, sour leaves, an ivylike vine that grows wild in the woods. It's a valuable leaf, typically used for cooking. But I have my own ideas. When boiled, sour leaves produce a sharp acidic juice that used to sting my fingers when I had an open scratch. It reminds me of the rubbing alcohol that *Pa* used to clean out my scraped knees. Maybe the juice of the sour leaves could work a little of *Pa*'s magic as a disinfectant. At the same time, I can't rely on *Mak*, can't expect her to find sour leaves. The leaves grow in the woods, not in the rice fields. She barely has the strength to work for the Khmer Rouge and keep up with her trips in search of edible leaves to supplement our scanty rice rations. She's doing all she can to keep our hearts beating.

I cannot walk—since my left foot can't take any pressure—so while others work in the field, I crawl on my hands and knees away from the village, past a grove of mango trees to a hill where the dead are buried. I follow a tight path carved to fit oxcarts. Past guava and bamboo trees I crawl, searching for sour leaves, the leaf of life.

Finally I see some. Big green leaves sprawling on the ground, climbing up over other shrubs on the other side of a thorny fence. I try to reach them but can't. Tree branches armed with sharp thorns shield the sour vines. I crawl around the bank until I see a small hole in the fence, through which I wiggle into the field.

In joy, I grab the thick stem, stripping away all the leaves into my hand. Hands flying, I grab the other sour vines, pulling leaves, shoving them into the pouch in my scarf. I am lost in the movements. I fall into a rhythm, for a moment forgetting even about the pain in my foot.

"Comrade, what are you doing? Are you stealing?" a fierce voice demands.

I turn. Before me stands a tall, skinny man, dressed in black, carrying a long curved knife on his shoulder.

"No, I'm not. I'm not stealing. I'm only picking *slark khnarng*," I say timidly, frightened by his accusing words, his sudden appearance.

He grabs me by the arm and drags me around the yucca field like a bag of rice. My arm feels as if it could be yanked off. I beg him repeatedly, "Please don't hurt me," but he says nothing. Reaching a tree, he drops his long knife to the ground and pulls my arms behind me. Snaking a rough rope around my skinny arms, he binds them tightly from wrist to elbow. Ignoring my pleas, he yanks my scarf from my neck and throws it on the ground. He pushes me down on my knees and binds me to the tree, the posture of a criminal soon to be executed. He must see the sour leaves, now all over the ground.

With cool indifference, he announces my sentence. "I will kill you at sunset," he says, delivering his verdict from behind a tree.

I beseech him, my voice rising. "Please don't kill me. I wasn't stealing. I was just picking *slark khnarng* for a swollen foot. I'm telling you the truth! Please spare my life!"

"Don't lie, comrade," he shouts. "I don't believe you. I will kill you. Say no more!"

I sob, "If you don't believe me, just look at my infected wound. I don't lie. I need *slark khnarng*. My foot hurts at night. Please spare my life. Don't kill me. . . ."

I wish I could bow down to him, sink into the dirt before his feet, begging his forgiveness. But it's too late. My words don't reach him.

His voice trails off, shouting in near-triumph, crowing like a bully who has had his way, "I'll cut off your head at sunset so people coming from work can see you—they won't follow your bad example." His footsteps crunch on dry leaves.

I look at the sour leaves scattered on the ground. I keep thinking how it's the small things that get me into trouble. Sucking sweet grass with Cheng. And now this. How can I be accused of stealing when there's nothing in my scarf—only sour leaves. I stare at the hole in the fence where I sneaked through only moments ago. Now I wish that whoever made it had left more thorns in it. I wouldn't have gotten in. As time passes, I cry hard and loud, tears of fear and frustration. In time, my sobbing becomes softer. My destiny awaits.

The sun is now behind the tree, its rays filtering through branches in a shifting dance. Suddenly I'm awakened by birdsong. *Maybe they cry for me.* I listen to them and I remember an old Cambodian warning: "When the owl cries, it will take someone's life," the spirit winging away with the bird. Now I hear birds cry. Later, perhaps the owl will hoot, announcing the fact that I will be beheaded.

As the sun begins to set, I speak to my heart, to Buddha, to *Pa's* spirit, silently begging for a second chance at life. *I'm not ready to die.*

My prayers are broken by my fear of the man in black. I imagine him returning, raising that long curved knife in the air. I can feel my own body cringing, feel the hiss of air as it swings toward my neck. Fear chills me. I shut my eyes and lower my head, looking for the courage to face the blade.

Suddenly footsteps echo on the dry leaves. I drop my last tears, my eyes dry with fear. The air is warm, but I'm shaking with cold. I look down at the ground and shut my eyes. I tighten my body, bracing for pain. I don't know whether I should scream or bite my lip. When he comes closer, I get ready to die.

All of a sudden, I feel a tug on the rope that snakes about my arms. I cringe. I squint my eyes tighter. Soon my arms swing free, released from the trunk of the tree, and I slump to the ground. I open my eyes and turn.

The man in black speaks sternly. "Comrade, now I set you free. Don't do that again." He says no more.

He loosens the rough rope from my numb wrists. I grab my scarf and put it around my neck, leaving the spilled sour leaves on the ground. I struggle to get up and walk but can't; in the unimaginable excitement of being freed, I have forgotten that I cannot walk. I crawl back as fast as I can through the hole in the fence without turning back.

Around me, birds sing in the woods. Every sense is sharpened, and I'm amazed at my own energy. I struggle down to the ox path and slowly crawl up the other side. I pull myself up, grabbing vines along the bank. I'm numb with my good luck, can't believe that I have been released. It seems like a strange, powerful dream. The voice of the man still echoes in my head.

As I crawl past the grove of trees, dragging my swollen left foot along through the dirt and dung, I'm elated to see our tattered community of huts. Never before have I seen the beauty in them. I'm anxious to tell *Mak* about my brush with death, my release. I'm giddy with the joy of survival. As I approach our hut, my eyes run hungrily over every detail. I can't stop looking. A short time ago, I faced a certain death. Now I'm home. "My hut," I call softly, crying, as if the palm walls were human, a close friend whom I've missed.

From the ground, I look up to see the pale, thinning shape of my mother's face, old at thirty-five, peeking out at me from the hut. In the twilight shadows, her face is a dream.

"Oh, *Mak*," I cry in joy and disbelief, "I thought I wouldn't see you again."

My words spill out, a tumbled, babbling story about leaves and a man in black cutting my head off. In that moment I feel I must never let her out of my sight. My heart clings to her, my eyes can't let her go.

Mak strokes my hair. "You're lucky. I'm so glad that you weren't killed." Tears stream down her cheeks. She reaches out to hold me, tightly embraces me. I feel *Mak*'s love. Her fear of losing me. Suddenly she stops crying. She wipes her tears. Then mine. Sitting near *Mak*, I'm lost in indescribable happiness. I'm oblivious to Avy or Map. I don't feel the throbbing in my foot, the pain in my puffy leg. Only an unreal sense of gratitude.

Mak says, "Stop crying, *Mak* cooks leaves for you. Stop crying, *koon.* . . ."

The next day *Mak*, Avy, and Map come home with *slark khnarng* packed in the pouch of her scarf, wrapped around her neck. I'm grateful. Eagerly, I greet them. Their presence is medicine to me.

My foot gradually gets better from the daily cleaning with the *slark khnarng*. Guided by vague memories of my father, I prescribe for myself the care I think my foot needs to heal. Twice a day I disinfect it with the stinging acidic juice. With my thumb and forefinger, I gently scrape and pinch away the crusted yellow pus that has formed overnight, releasing a fresh stream of blood. *Mak* is like the head doctor, checking my foot almost every night.

I'm relieved, almost grateful, not to be forced to work. I sleep soundly, trying to make up for the restless nights caused by my throbbing foot. One morning I'm pulled from slumber by a fierce voice. The next thing I see is the ugly *chhlop* looking down at me.

His voice strikes like a fist. "Comrade, why don't you go to work? Go to work, or I'll take you to reform! You must go to work."

I don't know what to say to him—I'm ambushed before I have a chance to think. Tears come before words, but I abstain from crying.

Finally I spit out the words, "I can't walk. My foot is painful, it's swollen. I will work when my foot gets better." Submissively, I show him my foot. Red blood spurts out the side of the yellowish curve of my wound. The bleeding is probably the result of getting up so quickly. The blotchy face glances briefly at my foot, recoiling from it. Then he is gone. I know he'll keep an eye on me.

In time, my foot improves. In the cool evening I stand in front of the hut. For the first time, I feel as if I need to inhale more air. Suddenly I sense a weight upon me. The ugly *chhlop* is out hunting again. I hop up into the hut, frightened. "*Mak*, it's him again!" I flatten myself against the front wall of the hut, hoping he won't see me.

In a cold, detached voice, he barks at *Mak*, his elder. "Comrade, where is your daughter? Your daughter has to work."

"She's still sick. Her foot has not healed yet," says *Mak* meekly.

"But she can walk some," he snaps.

I listen to them, my body shaking. He sticks his face inside our hut.

"Comrade! Get out of there and come with me," he orders.

I obey. I burst into tears as I move away from the wall. I plead to *Mak*, "*Mak*, help me. Help me!" He grabs my arm and yanks me out of the hut as I grab *Mak*'s hand.

He threatens, "If you don't go, I will take you to *Angka*." He speaks the words we fear. The mysterious *Angka*. I don't know where he wants to take me—another distant labor camp, nearby fields? All I can do is cry.

"Go, *koon*, so they won't harm you." *Mak* lets go of my hand.

I limp beside this awful boy who thrives on his small measure of power.

"Don't hurt my daughter," *Mak* begs, appearing behind me. Her sunken face bespeaks pain, added to my own.

The next morning I'm herded with a pack of malnourished kids by a group of *chhlops*. After an hour's walk I limp onto a rough, barren field. Another labor camp. I sob silently, wishing *Mak* could stop them from taking me away. I wish *Pa* were still alive to make my foot better. I'm the slowest kid, lagging behind a scattered crowd of children. As if the hard labor weren't enough, pain is again my working companion. It's only morning, but the sun is fierce. I'm fighting the pain. The sun. This time there's no Cheng to help. I don't know how I'll survive another labor camp.

The new labor camp, near Phnom Srais, isn't far from Daakpo, perhaps five miles. We must stay here, they command, but there isn't any shelter. Before we have a chance to rest, they order us to work. They throw hoes, baskets, and carrying sticks at us. Even the youngest know better than to disobey or talk back.

As in Oh Runtabage labor camp, a *mekorg* breaks the children into groups of four or five. I'm assigned to a group of five, one of whom is elected to be the group leader. She oversees everyone's work and reports to the *mekorg*. At least she's one of the "new people." The *mekorg* hands me a hoe since I can't walk well. I break up the hard dirt and scoop it into everyone's baskets. I repeat the task over and over, and the vibration from the hoe as it strikes the earth sends an echo of pain that crawls up through my foot, to my leg, and all the way to my waist. Dust swirls and settles, threatening more infection. The intense heat is suffocating. Everyone moves slowly, a weary production line, an army of ants that could be crushed under the heel of *Angka*.

I have a fever. I announce to no one in particular, "I'm very sick and my foot is painful. I want to stop a little." I squat down, allowing myself the brief luxury of leaning my shoulder against the hoe. The group leader takes over my task. She begins to break up the dirt. She looks at me urgently.

"Comrade, why aren't you working?" A loud, forceful voice erupts behind my back.

"That comrade said she's very sick," answers the group leader, pointing at me as I struggle to get up.

"Now, you dig the dirt," she says, pointing at the group leader. "You"—she points to me—"carry the dirt. No more resting."

I carry the baskets filled with dirt, struggling feebly up the bank with the weight. The scene is a familiar flashback: *Mekorgs* and *chhlops* stand among us, watchful. I wonder if I'll ever be free of their constant scrutiny.

The hot, scorching day changes abruptly. By late afternoon the sky turns cloudy. More clouds move in and it gets very dark. Thunder roars. Lightning strikes, flashing bright jagged lines, lighting up the dark sky. Everyone stirs, anxious and agitated. We look for anyone with the authority to dismiss us, but two *mekorgs* order us to continue working until, they say, *Angka Leu* tells us to stop.

Thunder echoes again. The rain falls in dense plops, beating down on me. Then it falls in heavy sheets, stinging our arms. We run in a frenzy. The *mekorgs* and *chhlops* vanish. Everyone, all at once, runs. Knowing I can't run, I plead for help, "Please wait for me. Wait for me!" I'm scared for my life. Everyone scrambles. The lightning strikes brutally across the sky, revealing chaotic crowds of frightened children moving through the drenched, muddy field. Some cling to one another. Others trudge by themselves, scattered bodies in the field. The only way we can see where we're going is by the flashes of lightning. I lag behind.

Another lightning bolt lights the sky. I see a group of four children holding on to each other, with dark clothes covering their heads, walking beside me. I grab a girl's soaking scarf, draped over her head. Then I switch, grabbing her arm instead, making sure I won't be lost in this tempest. She turns. Glances at me, startled.

Now the sky is totally dark. The intermittent flashes of lightning stop. The sky roars, thundering. The angry rain still falls, beating, slapping my body. Everyone shudders. My jaws chatter. I'm cold, yet I feel warm with fever. We stumble into a ditch, slamming into baskets and hard pieces of wood. Screams erupt in unison: "*Mak*, help me. *Mak*. . . ." My words mingle with the other pleas. In the chaos of mud and baskets and the collision of bodies, I struggle to stand. I reach out in the dark, looking for the kids I've been with. I feel a hand, grab it, and say, "Please wait for me."

The sharp, pinching pain in my foot is immense, but the fear of getting lost, swallowed up in the cold darkness, cannot be measured. I cry the pain away. My own suffering is lost in this madness. Somehow we rise and move on. We must move on.

As suddenly as it started, the rain is over. The darkness lingers, daytime tumbling into night. Some children's cries pierce the night, other children whimper. I release my long-held fears, calling out to *Mak* in my mind. A man's voice from a distance rises over the children's cries. It sends a wave of hope. The group I'm with steps up the pace, shifting our bodies in the direction of the man's voice. We cling together, a chain of human links. As we get closer, we can make out the man's words of warning.

"Don't cross the water! Stand there! I'll help you one by one," the man's voice commands, loudly but with compassion.

"Ow, help me!" a voice bursts out, choking. "I fell in the water. Help me, Athy. Help me. . . ."

Who is calling out my name? I rack my mind, trying to think. Suddenly it clicks—the voice is Ary's, a girl I know from Daakpo. I saw her earlier, when we were working.

"Ary! Ary! Where are you?" I yell at the top of my voice. I want to pull her out of the gushing water, but I can't see anything in the darkness. I can hardly move. My body is as stiff and cold as a corpse. I feel my way with my hands, threading through other children, reaching forward in the dark, trying to get to her.

I shriek, "Where are you, Ary? Where are you?"

"I'm in the water. . . . Help me, Athy," she cries, choking and coughing.

"Ary, wait, I'm coming." My feet slowly sink in the slick, muddy soil. The cold water gives me chills. I stoop, my hands working as eyes. Suddenly the man's voice shouts, breaking my own fear of getting swept away like Ary. "Don't get into the water," he commands. "I'll get her. Stay there!"

I stop, relieved and grateful. Everyone else, it seems, has abandoned us. He somehow manages to get Ary out of the water.

The man guides us with a flashlight. We squeeze together, shivering. As we walk through the field, I suddenly feel concrete beneath my feet—a distant memory of a more civilized world. I know we're now in a village, but I can't see anything before me except the curtain of darkness. A woman's voice guides us up a wooden stairway to a darkened building. I'm exhausted, yet with every step I take I encounter a rug of children, sprawling and packed closely together.

I resign myself to the darkness and sink down amid some mysterious metal objects, hugging them like a soft pillow.

In the morning I awake, horrified. The sunlight filters through a small, dirty window exposing thick cobwebs intertwined along the ceiling, the walls, and the old bicycle parts that litter the floor where we have slumbered. Around me, children are squeezed close together, like small lumps of human dough. Like me, other children have had to sleep sitting up, leaning against bicycle parts.

I need to get up to pee. My legs are numb and weak. I gingerly stretch them out, then limp over the sleeping children and down the stairs. Outside the shop, tree branches, coconut leaves, and other debris are scattered in disarray, still wet from the rain. *This is a real village, a place where people actually used to live. Real houses, real shops, not makeshift huts. Now empty.*

I limp back up the stairs and go back to sleep.

"Wake up. Wake up, comrades. It's time to go to work. WAKE UP!" a female voice yells from the bottom of the stairs.

I want to obey, but I can't. My wound is throbbing and my body feverish. I steal glances at three children on the floor by the corner of the wall. By the sounds of their groaning, I know they're very sick, and I'm relieved that I'm not alone.

After most of the children have left, the brigade leader demands, "Comrades, why aren't all of you going to work?"

"I'm sick. My foot swells and I can't walk," I say.

"I have a fever," another girl reports humbly, her voice soft and small.

The other two sick children roll over to face her and report their illnesses.

"That's enough. That's enough! All of you stay in here and don't go anywhere. Later, a comrade will take you to *peth* [clinic]. Nobody leaves this place," she emphasizes.

We go back to sleep. Later in the day, I'm awakened by a soft, gentle voice.

"*Ey*, wake up. Wake up. I'm taking you to *peth* to give you medicine. Wake up!" A woman mildly shakes a girl's shoulder.

I sit up, gazing at her. Dressed in a black uniform, she has short black hair that hangs no lower than her earlobes. She's gentle. A lady, a doctor, disguised in the Khmer Rouge uniform. Her hand touches the girl's neck as if checking her body temperature.

"Are all of you sick?" she asks gently, looking at us.

We answer by saying yes or nodding our heads.

"Come with me and you'll stay in *peth* until you get better," she replies.

"I can't walk that well. My foot is hurting me. It swells up," I announce. I show her my foot, and she is aghast at the sight of the raw wound. She is the first comrade who has ever reacted to the sight of my foot with compassion.

She carries me to a small hut nearby. Her warm arms embrace me against her chest, holding me as if I were her little sister. She looks young, perhaps in her late twenties. Her complexion is light, as if she has never been exposed to hard labor, to the sun.

She squats next to me and touches my shoulder while I lie on a shelflike bed made of old slabs of bamboo. She asks, "*P'yoon srey* [Young sister], how long have you had this wound?"

I'm touched by the tender way she addresses me. It's a term I have never heard from a Khmer Rouge. For the first time, I wonder if some Khmer Rouge are actually nice, quietly hiding among the ranks of the cruel.

"I've had it for a while. It almost healed before I came to work in Phnom Srais because I cleaned it every day with the juice from *slark khnarng*. My father used to put penicillin powder on my knees when my wounds got really bad. Does *bang* [elder sibling] have penicillin?"

It is an outrageous request, considering how far we are from civilization. She gazes at me briefly with a trace of a smile, amused, perhaps, that I even know the word.

"I'll go and look. I'll be back," she promises.

She disappears into a cubicle at the other side of the hut. She returns quickly, holding something in her hand.

"I have penicillin. I'll put it on your wound for you." She shows me the vial.

I can't believe my eyes. It looks just like what *Pa* kept in his medicine drawer—a vial with a rubber cork and a shiny metal band wrapped tightly around the top. The last time I saw modern medicine used was before my father's execution, during Lon Nol's time. It seems like another world.

She opens the vial and holds it above my left foot. She warns, "It will sting." Again, I'm surprised by her knowledge of medicine. But I welcome the pain of healing. "Don't cry, *p'yoon srey.*" She cringes, wrinkling her forehead as if to brace herself for me. She taps gently at the mouth of the vial, then again, but the powder is stuck. She taps harder, and an avalanche of white powder crashes into my hollow wound.

"Oh, all the medicine is in your wound! Wait, I'll scoop some out for you." She rushes away.

In seconds I scream in pain. I scratch crazily around the wound. "Oh, *bang*, it hurts," I call out. "*Mak*, help me, *Mak*, it hurts so much!" My palms slap at the bamboo slats and I bite my lips to control the sharp, pinching pain, which I can barely stand. I blink back tears as I study the wound. She scrambles back, trying to calm me down.

"Don't cry, don't cry," she stammers softly. She rubs around the wound. When I grow quiet, she gently tilts my foot to let some of the powder fall into the palm of her hand. About a third of the medicine falls into her hand. Carefully, she guides the leftover medicine back into the vial—surely as precious as gold.

For days I apply penicillin to my wound. About two weeks later, it looks better. The tissue starts to grow, slowly filling in what was once hollow. I'm in awe of the power of the body to heal, given the simple ingredients of rest and medicine. Most of the bloody pus disappears, and I can walk and get my own food ration.

The kind doctor has offered to apply penicillin powder to my wound, to care for it herself, but I politely decline. The offer of nursing care is sweet, thoughtful—a gesture of personal kindness I haven't seen among the Khmer Rouge. And yet, she has already helped me more than I could have dreamed possible—the clinic, the medicine, bringing me a ration of rice gruel when I couldn't walk. She checks on me every day. Her kindness begins to reshape my view of the Khmer Rouge. Not everyone has a heart of stone, only living to serve *Angka*. Not all thrive on the power and cruelty. Some retain a seed of human goodness.

When my foot is nearly healed, a brigade leader orders me to return to work near Phnom Srais. The doctor comforts me. She says I'll be okay as long as I clean my wound after working and apply penicillin to it at night. She acts as a surrogate mother, as good a friend as any child could ever ask for.

We toil under the unwavering gaze of *chhlops* and brigade leaders, dressed in black uniforms standing on the bank. Yet I see them through different eyes. Is their cruelty a mask, hiding humanity deep within? The world is no longer as black as their uniforms, as white as rice. At least I have shelter and better food rations, solid rice rather than the rice gruel. I only wish I could share this rice with *Mak*, Avy, and Map.

Each day is the same. They wake us early in the morning. During the working hours, they watch us. A stretch of children laboring in the fierce sun like a mass construction line clawing the earth, leaving a long, wide ditch that lengthens slowly each day.

Later, Communist leaders announce that a mobile brigade is coming from Phnom Kambour to help us. The arrival of this brigade means I might see Chea, Ra, and Aunt Rin, if they have survived.

My wish comes true. As soon as the brigade leaders shout that it's time for lunch, we peel away from the ditch, scattering into the open field, heading to the cooking area located a mile away. Suddenly the wave of children in front of me starts to run. In the distance, I see a mass of people in gray, discolored uniforms swarming around the cooking area. Some stand in lines while others are sitting or squatting on the ground.

"We should hurry before they give all the food to the mobile brigade," says a girl, running past me, followed by others.

"Athy, Athy! Wait for me." I turn. I stop when I realize it's Ary. She waves tiredly at me, her face dark yet white.

Out of breath, she reports, "Athy, I'm tired. I can't run anymore. Let's walk instead."

I tell Ary to walk faster, worried that the food will be gone, distributed to the troop of the mobile brigade. I can hear her lungs labor, her mouth gulping air. We both hobble on, stiff-legged. Our stomachs growl.

Hundreds of children and young adults cluster around the cooking area, which is open, without a shelter to shield it from the rain or sun. The natural landmark is a dead tree, leafless with only the brittle skeleton of tree branches sticking out. People hover close by, sitting and squatting on the dirt, shoving rice into their mouths. Ary and I wait in a children's line, our eyes stealing glances at the rice and thin fish soup people are already devouring. Suddenly a faint eager voice calls out my name, "Athy!" again and again.

I turn, looking for the voice. I see Chea emerging from the waiting lines and people sitting on the ground. It's hard to believe this is my sister. The image makes my heart ache—she's thin, her face darkened and worn by the sun. Her clothes are very old, grayish-black pants and a rag of a shirt with an old faded scarf around her neck.

"Chea, Chea," I croon. I'm giddy with jubilation and frozen with shock at the deterioration of my sister's beauty. I've heard that many in the brigades have died from exhaustion and illness. Yet she's running to me, her eyes glowing. She would have opened her arms wide to embrace me if space permitted it. I don't care about being in line, I don't care about eating. Chea is food for my soul.

"Athy, where are you staying?" Chea inquires urgently. Her face closes in on mine, but she recoils, horror-stricken.

"Your eyes have white lines of tissue in them." She gently lifts my eyelids with her fingers, then spits out her blunt conclusion. "Your eyes look bad. You could go blind, Athy."

Her words scare me, and I blink hard—my eyes suddenly feeling heavier than they felt before. Chea has to leave right away, but she promises me that she'll look for me. I find my way back to the food line. I know I've had problems with my eyes. When I wake, my lashes are glued together. And it's been hard to see, my eyes squint painfully under the sun. I'm frightened about the possibility of going blind.

The following day Chea sneaks over to see me briefly during mealtimes. One evening, during the ration, Chea seems anxious. She waves, signaling me to come to her. "Athy, do you want to go with Ra and me to see *Mak*? We're going to see her and bring her rice."

The thought overwhelms me. "I'm scared, Chea. I want to go, too, but I'm scared. I'm afraid they'll catch us on the way."

"It's okay. We're going at night, and we'll walk in the woods and not through villages. My coworker knows a way. Don't worry. I'll come to get you at your shelter when it gets dark. I have to go now," she says, touching my shoulder, a gesture of reassurance that comforts me.

Night sets in. Chea, Ra, two other women, and I stoop and crawl past shelters, out of the labor camp. The only thing I hear is my own breathing and theirs, soft whispers of air. The sound of our footsteps is muffled by sandy earth. The trees along the oxcart path cloak us, but they also darken our way. My eyes, which strain in bright sunshine, are of little use at night, but we don't run into anything. Chea's coworker must know her way around these villages. I wonder if she's one of the "old people." I can't tell. In the dark, I see only shadows, the dim silhouettes of Chea and Ra. I recognize Chea only by her voice. There, I put my trust.

We leave the oxcart path, turning onto a different path flanked by trees, bushes, shrubs. It looks familiar: This is the oxcart path that snakes through many villages, leading us close to Daakpo village. Though we are still in the woods, there is more light. Our fears lessen as we get a glimpse of the familiar community of huts, all in shadow.

The two coworkers go their separate ways to their families. My sisters and I head to our mother, cautiously weaving past the sleeping huts. We walk quietly into the hut, trying not to scare *Mak*, Avy, or Map, who are already asleep.

"*Mak*. . . ." Chea sticks her head into the doorless hut, whispering.

"*Mak!*" Ra echoes in an enthusiastic whisper. I join in, climbing into the hut for our secret homecoming.

Scooting close to *Mak* in the dark hut, it's hard to believe that I'm actually back with her, Chea, Ra, Avy, and Map. *Mak* awakes, confused to find us all in the hut.

"*Mak*, we've brought you rice," I whisper, producing a pouch of rice the size of a small melon from my scarf. She puts her arms around me. Chea and Ra sit by her side, their eyes gazing at *Mak*'s silhouette, loving her in the Cambodian way. In our voices, *Mak* can feel our longing to be near her as clearly as any physical embrace. Our escape, the effort to bring food, speaks louder than any warm words we might offer.

"Achea [Chea], did you all sneak out? Aren't you scared the *chhlops* will catch you?" *Mak* softly inquires, her voice concerned.

Chea answers, "There are other people who sneak out to see their families, not just us." Her voice is at ease, reassuring.

Tenderly, *Mak* warns us, "Always be careful. Look after *p'yoon*, Athy, too. She's small." If they torture us, she says, it will kill her. Again, she warns us to be careful.

Chea reassures *Mak* about how careful we are. *Mak* turns to the rice. She asks Ra to wake Avy and Map up to eat, too. The moon wanes, its luminescence fading near the entrance to our hut. *Mak*, Avy, and Map eat quickly. Into their mouths the rice flies.

"*Preah*, the rice is delicious, sweet," *Mak* softly exclaims, her voice grateful. "I haven't had solid rice for so long. Having rice is like going to heaven."

After eating, *Mak* updates us on their life in Daakpo. All they have to eat are leaves from the woods or the fleshy tubers from water plants nine-year-old Avy picks in a nearby lake. Sometimes they're lucky—*Mak* or Avy catches a few crickets or toads. *Mak* speaks of their hunger easily, as if it were a natural condition.

It's very late, perhaps after midnight. I can tell time only by how silent Daakpo is. Quickly I fall asleep. Before long I hear Chea's voice. "Athy, it's time to go. We have to go back. Those two people are here. Get up, Athy."

Chea helps me off the platform of the hut and into the woods, safely back to the labor camp through the inky early morning darkness.

Here in the labor camps, Chea is our mother. She, Ra, and I continue to sneak a scant ration of rice back to *Mak*, saved from our rations. Every week I look forward to this escape, to spending as much time as we can with *Mak*, Avy, and Map. Since *Angka* orchestrates our lives, we don't know how long our good fortune will last. But for the moment we allow ourselves a small sliver of pride.

Just the hope of seeing *Mak* creates a horizon for me in a world with no horizons. Even during our short visits, she cares for me, comforts me. For my infected eyes, she tells me to use my pee, caught in a leaf folded into a cone. She instructs me on how to do it, holding the point above my infected eyes, releasing the stinging yellow liquid in slow, steady drips. She says a woman's milk will also help—I've heard that before, too, but where do I find a woman with milk? There are so few babies.

The only time I see adults show any interest in each other is among the Khmer Rouge *mekorgs*, the children's brigade leaders, who flirt with each other. Workers would watch and nod. "They have the flesh," they explain. "Without flesh and blood, there is no desire."

There is only work. The irrigation canal is near completion, to be finished by an adult brigade. I'm surprised that children are being allowed to return to their respective villages. My eyes have healed from the infection, "cured" with my own pee. In addition to the infection, I've suffered from an ailment called "blind chicken," which caused my eyes to stop working at night. During mandatory meetings Ary had to hold my hand, guiding me there and back to my shelter. As the infection subsides, so does the night blindness.

With my sight restored, my eyes again open. There is more to see.

9

Now I Know the Answer

$\mathcal{U}$nder the Khmer Rouge, reunions are precious but brief, appearing like a sudden summer shower that opens the sweet plumeria, and ending just as quickly. After Phnom Srais, children are sent back to villages to work with the adults, mostly mothers now, to clear woods and to weed fields for planting yams. The work site is within walking distance, perhaps two to three miles. But at least we are together again. We fall back into comfortable chores, gathering leaves to cook with rice and salt, going on forays for firewood or water. Back in Phnom Penh, we did household chores without thinking, and the conversation was casual—Chea talking about a history test or plans with her friends. Now we perform our daily tasks mostly in silence, lost in our private thoughts and afraid to look too far into the future. At night I lie on the floor of our hut and try to absorb the feeling of those I love held tight under one roof. The soft sounds of night breathing, a concerto of crickets, cicadas, and small frogs. I lock these things into my mind for safekeeping.

In weeks, Chea and Ra are gone, sent to another labor camp. The day the Khmer Rouge line them up I see them off, my feet dragging. I've learned to hate these good-byes, for with them comes the fear that I'll never see them again. As they walk to join the end of the line, I'm shocked to see Aunt Rin also standing in line. My pretty aunt, her eyes flooded with tears, her body thin and pale. I say nothing but her name. She turns away, coping with her grief, her feelings so raw that she can't face separation again. I let her be, praying for her to summon the strength and courage to fight and stay alive.

In a matter of minutes—too soon—the line begins moving. Before they leave, I want to say good-bye to Aunt Rin. I want to run and hug Chea and Ra, or even just hold their hand one last time, or call their name, but my tongue freezes. Only my eyes work. I search for Aunt Rin, watching her until I can see no more than her feet moving, fading between people before and behind her. Chea and Ra drift away, too.

Our family ebbs and flows like the tide. With one wave, Chea and Ra are gone, but Than returns from a labor camp, a relief to *Mak*. Again, Ry finds a refuge at the hospital Peth Preahneth Preah by pretending to be sick. It is a tricky gamble. By staying behind, she escapes possible death from exhaustion and labor, but she must be clever to avoid amoebic dysentery, grown rampant among patients at the hospital. The rest of the family—*Mak*, Avy, Map, and I—have to survive our own way, working in the woods since we're not in the age group needed at the labor camp. Than does whatever the informants and village leader tell him, plowing the rice field or working in the woods with the quickly shrinking pool of men, mainly fathers.

These days, we clear small plants, weeding out grass in open fields surrounded by trees, one of which is wild, a mango tree. During lunch break under a generous shade of trees—while the Khmer Rouge leaders sit among themselves away from us—*Mak* and the other women reminisce about old times. Following their meals of rice gruel with edible leaves and salt, they talk about their favorite foods. It sounds like cruel torture to talk of things we cannot have, but there is a comfort in these conversations.

Rice ration is at its lowest point again. Edema is also widespread. Avy's body is swollen, her eyes nearly shut. Sprouting between her eyelids are her long eyelashes, her hair wiry. Her skin is wan, inflated with fluid that seems ready to burst through her thin skin. The rest of us have edema, but not as bad. This is the randomness of starvation. She has been spared the rigors of labor camp, but still her body is protesting, giving up.

To supplement our small ration, Than sneaks out to fish. Only thirteen, two years older than I am, Than seems to have taken on the role of a grown man, head of the household. Late at night, he walks a long way to a lake where he has planted a fishing net, staked out in the shallows and hidden away where no one can see or steal it. One night he brings home a dozen fish, each the size of a tablespoon.

Mak asks Ry—who usually comes back from the hospital to see us at night—to clean the fish. I pour water for Than as he washes mud off his skinny legs. *Mak* gathers the firewood to cook the fish. We have not had fish or any real meat for weeks, aside from occasional toads, crickets, tadpoles, or tiny lizards in the woods.

The fish is ready, brown, shriveled, a small spread on a plate before Than. Than hands *Mak* a few fish; Map two, Avy one, Ry one, and me also one. He keeps four for himself. I savor the fish, biting a little at a time as if I'm licking cold ice cream. Than also eats it slowly, his mouth busy telling about his trip to the lake.

Mak watches Than, proud of him. Avy has already finished her fish, her hand reaching, her swollen eyes imploring. She interrupts, "Than, can I have a little fish?"

Than's distracted but goes on with his adventure. I notice Avy's patience, her ability to stifle her hunger. I can't remember the last time our family really sat down together and just listened to one of us.

"Than, can I have a little fish?" Avy persists, her hand weakly reaching forward.

Than breaks off half of a fish and murmurs, "She eats everything, ants, anything, that's why her face is like that," Than says, irritated. "I tell her not to, but she's stubborn. She doesn't listen." He looks at *Mak* as if wanting her to agree with him.

Mak tenderly suggests, "Don't be mad at *p'yoon*. She's hungry, *koon*."

Than glares at Avy, then spits out, "Stubborn!" He throws half of the fish at her. It falls through the crack in the floor. Avy scrambles. She hops off the hut, her head moving, her eyes searching hungrily. I can't fathom what Than has just done, the cruelty. We are all shocked. Yet Than is somehow enraged, his body almost trembling, seemingly for no other reason than the mild disrespect of his young, starving sister. His face churns with emotions even as we watch.

"Why did you do that, *koon*?" *Mak* finally says.

Avy cries, sobbing desperately. Ry and I help her find the fish beneath our hut. Gently, we lift small tree branches, one by one, from the pile of firewood where the fish fell. When we find it, she desperately blows away the dirt that has coated it. She eats it, and she cries, trembling, as if losing and finding this scrap of fish would make the difference between life and death. As soon as she finishes her fish, her body relaxes. Her disfigured legs, now blown up to absurd proportions, slowly carry her into the hut. She says little, accepting her condition and treatment.

Than is quiet, but we can feel remorse in his silence. Tonight has brought us brief joy, then grief. Agony at the realization that the Khmer Rouge have shaped us, made our tempers brittle and our hunger sharp. Led us to the point where we could be as cruel to one another as they are to us.

The rice distribution comes to a complete stop. Starvation revisits us. Avy's edema gets worse, the fluid seeping out from pink cracks between her toes. She walks slowly, like a turtle, her body stiffened with the fluid that continues to build behind her thin, bloodless skin. One day *Mak* and I return home from the woods and she's gone, disappeared to Peth Preahneth Preah with Ry. There, she gets a food ration, not much, but better than nothing. *She'll die there*, I fear. I don't know of anyone who has ever returned. To our knowledge, there's no proper medicine, yet we send her there, to this crude excuse for a hospital—filthy and unsanitized, humming with flies that congregate on patient's eyes, the sick squeezed onto the floor between rusty twin beds. However, Ry's there to take care of her.

Time passes. It's been a month since Avy left for Peth Preahneth Preah. At home, we fight our own battles. *Mak*, Map, and I are also afflicted with edema. Than has again been sent somewhere to work, but my thoughts don't stray to be with him. Starvation has blurred my mind too much to care for anyone. Each day I barely have the energy to keep my heart beating.

Ry returns to Daakpo, her eyes empty, her stomach protruding with sickness. With the weariness of an old woman, fifteen-year-old Ry sinks to the floor of our hut. Her eyes are dry, her face guilty and sad as she reports to us Avy's death. Softly, she explains: "Last night I noticed the change in Avy's body. Her jaws locked, her body stiffened. I wondered about it, but I didn't understand why she was that way. This morning I got up and looked at her, she's changed. Stiff, very thin. Her edema's gone. When I looked at her feet, I saw ants around the webs of her toes. The fluid oozed out of her burst skin, through her feet. I gazed at her bony face and I wanted to cry, but I couldn't. I don't understand. I couldn't even cry when the hospital workers took her to be buried. Maybe I've seen too many deaths."

Mak doesn't cry, her eyes fall upon Ry. Map looks on, too young to speak and too little to understand death. Listening to Ry's description of Avy's death, I fear the fluid building even now within me, within *Mak*—our arms, faces, and hands grow taut. I can feel panic rise in my throat. Avy's death cements my determination to live. In my mind, I tell myself that I must search for edible leaves, toads, mice, crickets, whatever I need to stay alive.

Avy's death lingers in Ry's mind. Her inability to mourn continues to haunt her. In desperation, she turns to Buddhism, an institution long since destroyed and disdained by the Khmer Rouge. In spite of that, she finds a way to make things right for herself. She remembers reincarnation, the idea that after death we are reborn. She reconciles her internal conflicts this way, as our parents and elders did before the Khmer Rouge's takeover. She talks to Avy's spirit.

"If *bang* lives to get married, may *p'yoon*'s spirit conceive in *bang*'s womb. *Bang* wants another chance to take care of you." Ry finally sobs, her heart beseeching, her soul comforted. Her mind is at peace, she tells me.

I find myself thinking about Buddhism, too. I think of those who've died and hope they will be reincarnated to make up for this life, returning when freedom and peace have been installed in Cambodia. Like Ry, thinking this way, I'm more at ease, comforted that I'll see my family again.

Mak and I become very ill. In addition to edema, malaria has returned. The day is warm, but *Mak* and I shiver with cold that seems to seep from inside our bodies. I lie behind her watching her back tremble as my own body shivers. Three-year-old Map sits by us baffled, as if he wants to help us but doesn't know how. Now and then, I fall asleep.

"*Mak* and Thy are sick." My mind picks up Map's soft, small voice.

I vaguely feel the vibration of feet climbing into the hut. It seems like a dream.

"*Mak*, I'm back. . . . Athy, Athy, wake up," a voice commands, stern but anxious. I feel a hand shake my shoulder. *It's Ra*, my mind acknowledges, feeling delirious.

Ra lifts me and *Mak*, assuring us she'll "coin" our backs, a traditional remedy in which a coin is rubbed repeatedly along both sides of the spine and other areas to promote healing. Then she performs another procedure, a remedy Cambodians call *choup*. Placing a small ember of burning wood into a vial, Ra presses it horizontally against my forehead, above my eyebrows. Being so sick, I can't feel the hot vial. But my forehead is burned badly, leaving a permanent scar.

Energy gradually comes back to me. Looking at Ra tending to *Mak*, I'm grateful. Deep down I think that *Mak* and I would have died, but Ra has come, pulling us back from the hands of death.

Ra tells us grim stories of Phnom Korg Va, a disease-stricken place where many laborers have died from exhaustion, inadequate rest, and lack of medicine. The work camp had become a mountain of death. Among those who have perished is Aunt Rin. I'm sorry to hear this news, yet in an odd way I'm not really sad. Death is a constant, and we've become numb to the shock of it. People die here and there, all around us, falling like flies that have been sprayed with poison.

I brace for more bad news, news about Chea, but Ra quickly assures us that she is still alive, but being forced to work hard. She is closely watched by her brigade leader, the same woman who has viewed Chea as an enemy since the day Chea defended the quiet chatter of Ra and Ry at the work site in Daakpo.

A premonition prompted Ra's return. Her conscience kept telling her something bad was happening to *Mak*. She knew she needed to leave. For days she stayed at a clinic, asking for malaria medicine, with our family in mind. *Modern medicine? Does it still exist?* I'm surprised that the Khmer Rouge endorse its use when they loathe everything modern. Ra talks like a storyteller, with great animation in her eyes and gestures, almost like a small child sharing an exciting story. *Mak* asks how she was able to leave Phnom Korg Va and why Chea couldn't come with her.

Ra smiles, a warm smile, her eyes bright. She reports, "I forged a letter saying my *mekorg* allows me to return to the village because you're very ill. I signed her name." Ra smiles again. "I ran from Phnom Korg Va at early dusk and showed the letter at every checkpoint. They let me through, no questions asked. I hitchhiked, riding on oxcarts from village to village, until I got close to here." Ra takes a deep breath, her face relieved, her eyes gazing into *Mak*'s.

Finally Ra shows *Mak* the white medicine tablets. Small, round. *Mak* takes a few, swallowing them greedily. She tilts her head as if trying to help them down. I watch her, my heart constricting as I observe her bloodless, swollen face, her wiry hair. Slowly, her hand reaches toward Ra.

"Give *Mak* more, maybe it will make *Mak* better soon."

Ra holds her scarf out to *Mak*. "*Mak*, that's too many," Ra cries, alarmed.

Ra cringes as she watches *Mak* toss the tablets in her mouth. I don't see how many pills *Mak* is holding in her cupped hand, but later in the night, I can only imagine how many she must have taken. *Mak* grows very ill, her body writhing, agitated, gagging. The sound of her dry retching makes me sick to my own stomach. I'm relieved to have taken only two tablets for my own malaria. Silently, I say a prayer. I pray to *Preah* that she'll survive the overdose of this medicine. In the morning I'm relieved to see her looking better.

A month later, Chea returns. Miraculously, she brings food: uncooked rice and dry salted fish. She also has a container with cooked rice and cooked dry fish, a luxury long past. I didn't recognize Chea at first. She looks so different, her complexion healthier, her face crimson with robust color. Her hair is thick, now touching her shoulders. She has gained weight, looking more like she did before the Khmer Rouge's takeover.

With her, Chea brings us more grim stories. Weeks ago, while clearing the dense woods in Phnom Korg Va for a cotton plantation, a tree branch cut her foot, resulting in a small wound that quickly became infected. She couldn't walk and therefore couldn't work. Chea knew her days were numbered—her brigade leader now had a chance to incriminate her, scold her for not "fulfilling her duty to *Angka.*" With this in mind, Chea devised a way to save herself.

Alone in her shelter, she composed a fight song for her brigade leader. A song about nature, green vegetation, and fruit, on which she had been laboring all these months. It's a song of hard work at Phnom Korg Va.

"One evening I went to see my *mekorg,*" Chea recalls. "I asked her how she was doing. She was surprised. Then I flattered her, complimenting her on how attractive she was. I told her that if it were during *sangkum mun* [the previous society], men would be crazy about her. They would whistle at her, flirt with her. Do you know what? She relaxed." Chea smiles, her eyes bright, satisfied. "Then I sang her the song. She liked it!"

My eyes widen, a mirror image of Chea's animated face. "She's pleased that I wrote it, especially for her. After that she never gives me a hard time. She treats me nicer, giving me food to eat. She let me come back to the village when she saw my foot. It doesn't matter which era, *p'yoon srey,*" she says, looking at me, "people want others to compliment them. And many like bribery."

But now, in 1977, more changes are taking place. *Angka Leu* sends us a clear signal, letting us know that we will have no privacy at all. We're told in a meeting that there will be no rice, salt, and vegetable distributions as before. Everything will be sent to the commune kitchen. Foods such as vegetables and chickens, which any of us might raise, belong to the commune.

With the new rule, we move to a new hut half a mile away from the old one. It is similar to our first hut, built from bamboo poles and palm leaves. It's even a little bigger, about eleven by thirteen feet. It is situated among a scattering of other huts, all of which seem to have more space in front and back—open land on which we can cultivate vegetables, the fruit of my family's labor which I want no Khmer Rouge commune to have. I brace myself for the day they come to harvest it.

I have almost recovered from malaria and so has *Mak*, but she grows steadily worse in a different way. In our new hut she's with us, eating our dinner of rice with yam leaves and salt, but she stares into the distance, her eyes fixed on something invisible. I know *Mak* is mourning. It was May 1975 when *Pa* was executed. It's been nearly two years since his death, and she has never spoken of him until now—spring 1977. Reminiscing, she talks about *Pa*, saddened for him. She wonders out loud how painful his death was, talking to herself more than to us. Since Avy's death, she has changed. She has become disheartened, complaining of headaches, dizziness, and fatigue. Being sick for nearly a month, she feels useless, and simply eats and sleeps. It's all she can do. Her face spells out her frustration.

One morning I wake up to *Mak*'s voice. "I'm going to weed, do some physical work," she murmurs to herself. "I don't want to be cooped up in the hut."

Mak hops off the hut. Chea and Ra have gone to work, only Map remains on the hut platform. With a knife in her hand, a tool she uses for everything, *Mak* tills the dry soil in front of the hut, weeding, pulling the grass. Maybe being outside in the sun will help her, but I'm fearful of her being exposed to the watchful eyes of informants.

"Comrade, why aren't you at work?" a voice snarls. My heart quickens as my mind recognizes this familiar demand. "Everybody works and you're staying home! Do you want me to take you to reform?"

"I've been sick, and I'm swollen all over." *Mak*'s voice rises, softly, protesting. "I'm hungry. I just want to weed a little, perhaps my children can raise vegetables. It's hard just sitting in the hut," *Mak* pleads. "I can't work like others when I'm still sick."

The informant snaps, "Go to *peth* if you're sick! Don't stay home."

"Two of my children died there. No one could help them. If I go, who will take care of my children? I've a baby son who needs me. I'd like to stay home and take care of my children. Would *Angka Leu* please understand and let me take care of myself at home? If I go, I'll die there like my children."

Mak's imploring words don't reach him. He gives her an ultimatum. "If you don't go to *peth*, I'll have people take you there. If you can't work, you stay in *peth*!"

In the evening when Chea, Ra, and Ry return, *Mak* announces the bad news.

"They want me to go to *peth* and die. They won't let me stay home. All of you take care of your *p'yoon proh* [young brother]. He's little and doesn't understand. Don't get mad at him. Take care of each other. I don't know when I'll come back. I don't want to go, but the *chhlop* threatened me. I don't want him to harm us. . . . Life is so hard. . . . I've asked *Preah* to let me live for one more year. . . ."

Mak's voice subsides. Inside the hut, silence. For a moment we're all lost in despair, our own words suffocated by her acceptance. Quietly, we've feared the day when *Mak* would die, but none of us has spoken of it. Chea finally breaks the silence. "*Mak*, don't worry about us. You take care of yourself and we will take care of each other."

"I've asked *Preah* to let me live one more year." A wish so modest, so small, so unselfish. Only a year, so short. I wish that she hadn't told us this prediction of her fate. I don't want to know, am not ready. Her wish reminds me of *Pa*'s years ago.

Back then, our world was already in chaos—the invasion of the Viet Cong,* our Takeo house decimated, our dog Aka Hom killed, Tha dead, then Bosaba. *Pa* was afflicted with appendicitis, worsened by the lack of medical care in a time of war. His simple, desperate wish, he told us, was, "to live until forty-two so *Pa* can see you grow up." He got his wish. At forty-two, he was executed by the Khmer Rouge. Now I fear *Mak*'s wish will come true. That *Preah* will grant it. One year, and no more.

The day *Mak* goes to Peth Preahneth Preah, my mind is crowded with thoughts and fears. As I work in the woods, my hands slowly clearing away plants and grass, my mind is absorbed only with *Mak*. The family separation is now reversed. Instead of my brothers, sisters, and I being separated from her, she's the one who's taken from us. I dread going back to the hut, picturing Map waiting in the hut by himself.

Without *Mak*, Chea becomes his surrogate mother. At night he cuddles next to her, his arms thrown wide embracing her or hers embracing him. In these moments I see a child's desperate need for comfort, and a sister who dispenses all the love that she has. Since our mother's departure, we've drawn close to each other, hearts and minds bound by an invisible thread. When we come together from work, we read one another's eyes, as if checking to see if the other misses *Mak* or is sad about her. We serve our evening meal of rice and weeds on plates like small adults, passing food to the others, polite, respectful. We keep our thoughts to ourselves, swallowing words. To speak of our fears only reinforces them, opening up a dark path of possibilities.

---

* The United States as well as the South Vietnamese invaded Cambodia in their attempt to stop the Viet Cong, but they instead drove the Viet Cong deeper into Cambodia.

In the hospital, patients must struggle to find the self-reliance to survive. Those who succeed learn the tricks. Their competitors in the game of survival are mice and rats, the hospital's residents who remain hidden during daylight. They range in size, as little as a toe and as large as a papaya. At night the games begin. From somewhere beneath the hospital, they emerge, the sound of their soft moving feet magnified in the silent night. They crawl, then pause. *Mak*, like many starving patients, mirrors their behavior—pause, be still. With a cloth draped over her head and body, a few grains of rice scattered beneath as bait, she waits, her hungry hands prepare to pounce. The rats smell the bait. Hunger draws them to their death as *Mak*'s hands grab them. Quickly she kills them, snapping their necks until they're motionless. It is a strange cycle—the rodents come to gnaw on the weak and dead, the dying wait to trap those who would feed upon them. They will be her next day's meal only if other patients sharing the crowded floor space don't steal them.

Ry tells me about *Mak*, her tricks to survive in the hospital. But I already know. This is what I've been doing in our own hut— covering myself at night with a blanket and baiting a small tin can with a few grains of unhusked rice, waiting for mice. Lately I've traded my sleep for food, dozing lightly until I felt movement or heard their feet on the can. Sometimes I get two or more, even four on one occasion. In the morning I skin them, taking the guts out and tying their small bodies to a stick. Each mouse is a small, savory bite, and I try to eat the bones and all. In the evening, at the commune, I roast them on the fire. There, some boys steal envious glances, whispering among themselves. They wonder how I catch mice at this time of year.

At first there are many. Then my supply becomes scarce. I no longer have them to supplement my ration like *Mak* at Peth Preahneth Preah. A few weeks after arriving there, her edema worsens. Her stomach grows larger, swelling like that of a pregnant woman. Ry describes it to me, her eyes reddened.

Another week passes. Ry comes back with more news. A hospital worker has suggested that she take *Mak* to a hospital in a village called Choup. Unlike Peth Preahneth Preah, it has modern medicine, the worker promises Ry. We've never heard of it. Even though it's painful to imagine our mother being at an unknown place, the prospect of *Mak* being treated with modern medicine eases that pain. It gives Ry hope, and she wants to persuade us. She waits for family consent.

The day before *Mak* leaves for Choup, Ry takes Map with her to Peth Preahneth Preah. Map spends the night there with Ry and *Mak*. The next day they say their good-byes, Ry recalls, her words painting the scene:

Beneath the shade of a tree, hidden from the hot afternoon sun, *Mak* squats on the dusty earth in front of the hospital, waiting to be taken to Choup. *Mak* bids Ry good-bye, her mouth slowly articulating advice, her arms embracing Map.

"*Koon*, *Mak* doesn't know when *Mak* will see all of you again. Take care of each other. If Map does something wrong, please let him finish eating before you discipline him. He's little, doesn't understand—pity him. . . ." *Mak*'s eyes are red, burned by gathering tears.

When her last word leaves her mouth, her head turns, eyes on Map. Her tears spill over. Map's arms break free from her embrace, wrapping around her neck. Finally a high, ringing cry tumbles out of his mouth. Their good-byes are brief. A horse cart approaches. *Mak*'s head turns, her arms releasing Map. His cry rises to a wail, his legs wrapping around her leg. Ry pulls him away from *Mak*, then two black-uniformed strangers from the cart take *Mak* away.

Map screams, "*Mak*, don't go!"

Ry freezes, hypnotized by *Mak*'s frail body as she's helped into the cart like an old woman. She watches the cart pull away as she anchors Map, preventing him from running after it. His free hand grabs and flails toward the cart, fingers stretching for it as it grows smaller until it is a distant speck.

At three, Map is left alone in the hut each day to fend for himself. He sits motionless in the center of the doorless entrance like a tiny statue in a shrine. When Chea, Ra, or I get back from working in the woods, Map checks our scarves, his hands shuffling through the weeds we've picked, searching for things to eat—a yam or yucca root. When we tell him there's nothing to eat, he doesn't cry. His eyes resume the distant stare, a small, detached statue once again.

At about lunchtime, Map carries his spoon and sets out on foot. He has learned how to find Peth Preahneth Preah. There, he goes to Ry. She shares with him her meager ration of rice gruel, but it is still better than what we've been getting in Daakpo.

Sometimes he returns with a stomach full of food. Sometimes Ry sends him away with food for the evening. It is a risky act of compassion. Because she is a patient, she worries that the Khmer Rouge will catch her sharing her ration with her brother. The penalty, she fears, could be her return to a forced labor camp. "Feverish rabbit"—it's the term the Khmer Rouge use for workers who pretend to be sicker than they are. Fatigue and starvation don't matter. Ry hasn't been well, her stomach is puffy with edema. She worries that giving away part of her ration will send the wrong signal and mean punishment for both of them. Despite her fears, she continues to feed Map whenever it's safe.

At the hut, the vegetables we planted are now thriving, pushing up shoots of green around the hut. In front of the hut stand rows of tall corn; their cream-colored tassels are blooming, silk hair spilling out and weighing down their stalks. On the right side of the hut and in the back are chili plants. Alongside them are a few small rows of pepper and *mvorng* mint. In the front near the corn rise a few mounded rows of yams. Thick vines from pumpkin plants spread out like wild ivy, blossoms opening to brilliant gold, leaves green and prickly. Though *Angka* says these vegetables are for the commune, everyone harvests from their own garden.

I wake up to the opal haze of summer morning. Chea tells me to stay home today. She asks me to show Map how to get to the hut belonging to *Yiey* Om, *Pa*'s favorite aunt, who is *Kong* Houng's younger sister. Somehow her family has ended up in a village called Poi-kdurg, located near Daakpo.

When Map and I arrive at her house, she and her daughters, whom I call *kao* (aunt), are working at what seems to be weaving, passing crosswise threads under and over lengthwise ones, which are already secured to the wooden frame. I've seen this before, long ago when *Pa* took me to her house. I was about three years old.

Yiey Om greets us with a long gaze, her eyes peering above half-glasses, studying what stands before her.

"*Chao* (Grandchildren/child) you come to visit *yiey*?" she asks, her voice rising with concern.

"*Yiey*, Chea asked me to bring Map here," I finally say, hesitant to say more for fear I'll insult her. "Wants Map to trade chili and mint with you for something to eat." I repeat almost exactly what Chea told me to say. I feel as if we're not related as the word "trade" passes my lips.

"Well, what do you have in there, *chao*?" *Yiey* Om reaches out to my scarf filled with a small harvest of our chili and *mvorng* mint.

She looks into the pouch of the scarf and raves about the red chili and mint, effusive praise so like what I used to hear in her voice when my father would bring her a gift of soap or detergent. It is a forgotten echo of a grandma's excitement. Bending over a steamy pot of water bubbling over the fire, she picks up a flat woven basket, then scoops up tiny enclosed sacs afloat in the liquid.

"Go ahead and eat, *chao*." She motions to me and Map.

I pick out a warm sac the size of a peanut. Its texture is coarse like a soaked cloth. I hold it with my forefingers. I finally speak out, "*Yiey*, what is this? How do you eat it?"

"Like this, *chao*. . . ." She pauses from her weaving, her fingers tearing the sac open.

She hands me what's inside, a shriveled, cream-colored worm the size of a bean. I shiver, my body recoiling at the sight of the pale, motionless worm. She chuckles. Her daughters join in. It's a silkworm, she says, and people eat them.

I place it in my mouth. I cringe, chew quickly, then swallow the creamy tofu-textured insect. It tastes good. But the idea of eating the silkworm is repellent.

Map likes it; his small fingers peel the cocoons like peanuts, his mouth munching it like a soft candy.

Yiey Om's family is more privileged than most "new people" in Daakpo or any of the nearby villages. Instead of staying in a makeshift hut like many "new people," her family stays in a large wooden house built on stilts. It seems the Khmer Rouge accept them more than most of us. They have skills the Khmer Rouge want. *Weaving.* It's the basis of what the Khmer Rouge value, the old ways of life which *Yiey* Om's family mastered long ago. None of them seems to suffer from edema.

Yiey Om lets us eat as many worms as we want, then she wraps a handful for Map in a banana leaf to take home.

This summer yields a crop. The corn cobs grow larger, their plump kernels, light yellow, packed like snug rows of teeth. It's the first time we have raised many vegetables, yet *Mak* is not around to enjoy them.

"Athy, take some corn to *Mak*. Take Map with you." Chea commands, her voice decisive, her words tumbling out as if she has been waiting to say this for a long time. "Don't go to work. Take corn to *Mak* and take Map with you to see her. She hasn't seen him for a while."

The thought of seeing *Mak* is comforting, but I'm frightened. I remind Chea of the *chhlop*, of the village leader, of possible punishment. She turns to me, her expression wise. This happens whenever she wants to teach or share something with me.

"If taking food to one's mother is a crime, I'll be responsible for it. I'll talk with the village leader. You are only taking food to our mother, not to an enemy of *Angka*."

I put my trust in her. When she tells Map about the trip, his eyes glow. He follows me around as I pick eight ears of corn—four for *Mak* and two each for Map and me. In the pot I boil the corn. Map helps add the firewood from tiny tree branches to the cooking hole while I make tamarind paste, grinding the sour green tamarind fruit and coarse salt.

By the time we leave, it's midmorning. I tuck the corn cobs in the pouch of my old scarf, still warm, pressing against a small package of tamarind paste. We walk quickly, my eyes on guard, frequently looking over my shoulder. My hand holds Map's. We have long since passed Daakpo, entering a stretch of gritty road without any huts nearby. My fear of getting caught eases, but my body and Map's grow weaker, slower, from the strong sun.

The hot road burns our feet. I carry Map until I'm too exhausted. Drawn by his cries, an old woman stops us to give us cool water. I'm struck by her kindness, which helps give me the courage to continue our journey. We reach an old, worn-down barn, surrounded by greenery, where a family has planted vegetables in front and in back of their hut. In front of the barn, there are rows of corn, pumpkin, and yucca root plants. But something is wrong. There is a reeking odor, like the stench from a field scattered with feces from cases of dysentery and diarrhea.

"Thy, *na Mak* [where is *Mak*]?" Map inquires, his voice quivering with apprehension.

As we approach the doorless barn, the pungent smell intensifies. The sound of groaning greets us. Walking ahead of Map, I hold his hand as we enter the barn. In the muted light, we're met by the sight of pale, swollen people, perhaps thirty of them, lying on bare, rusty metal beds lining the wall. Patients are crammed into the aisle between two rows of beds, perhaps twelve of them, separated from each other only by a few feet. They lie on the dirty earthen floor, some on plastic sheeting, others on filthy clothes. Under the beds near them are flies swarming over runny feces pooled on the floor. The flies settle on eyes, on wounds, around nostrils, on the sides of mouths, gorging on human filth, on the dying.

I peer from one bed to the next looking for our mother, but I can't find her. I pull Map's hand, guiding him down the aisle. He is rigid with shock; it is like pulling a bag of rice. Slowly I study each patient. Even though it horrifies me to be here, my eyes take it all in—snapshots of the sickness and the filth and the crowding—yet I can't find my own mother.

"Thy, *na Mak?*" Map begins to cry. "*Na Mak?*" Again and again he repeats it, his voice on the verge of hysteria.

Finally I answer, "I don't know."

A little girl scurries toward us. She says, "*Bang,* she's your mom." She points. For a few seconds my eyes fix on her face.

Who is she? How does she know my mother? And me?

"She's over there," the girl says, pointing again, her urgent voice snapping me to reality.

I follow her finger, and I see a frail woman sitting on a bare rusty bed. Her forehead rests on her knee, her face is pale and her swollen eyelids closed. *That's not Mak!* I turn to the girl, searching for reassurance. She looks at me, then at the swollen woman. I study the frail, ailing woman again, then recognize the clothes she wears.

"Thy, *Mak?*" Map pulls me, but I'm trapped by what I see, a nightmare.

"Yes, *Mak yurg* [our mother]," I softly answer, then my hand opens, freeing Map's fingers from my grip. My eyes fall on her floral blouse with its once-brilliant pink hibiscus and green leaves. Now old, the flowers have faded to a flat, muddy gray-brown.

Mak slowly raises her head from her knee, her ears tracking our voices.

"*Koon srey Mak, koon srey Mak. Koon proh meas mdaay* [My beloved son]. My little son. Come to me, little son. I miss you so very much."

"*Mak.*" Map reaches out to our mother, both of his hands holding her arm, his eyes gazing at her face.

Mak embraces him, her swollen arm slipping as if it is too heavy.

"*Mak*, I'm Thy," I say, staring at her bulging eyelids. I'm afraid she can't see me. It is like studying a contorted version of my mother's face—the stretched, pale face of an obese person, indentations where her temples are, her hair sticking up like tough wire. Her movements are slow and heavy, like those of a very old woman. Instead of asking her questions, I look at her. My jaws are locked, I struggle for words to fit what I see. For I know I am looking at death. I have to say something to her to give her hope, even if it can never be fulfilled. At least she can cherish it for the moment.

"I wanted to bring Map to see you, *Mak.*" The words slide out of my mouth. I want to comfort her, to make her feel better. I settle on words that seem so ordinary in this strange place. "I've brought you corn on the cob, and I also made you tamarind paste. *Mak*, you'd like to have tamarind paste with rice—that's why I've made you some."

"*Koon, Mak* can't eat tamarind paste. I have dysentery," she softly whispers. "You and your brother eat it. *Mak* will have corn, just give *Mak* corn."

My hands untie the knot on my scarf, my heart aching. I wish I knew magic. For a moment I am a small child, back on our sofa watching movies about Cambodian magic, wanting to go to the Himalayas to find some of my own. But the only thing I see here are tears, building up behind my eyes.

"*Mak*, here is corn for you."

"Only corn, *koon Mak*." Her voice is sweet and longing.

"*Athy, koon*, this corn is not cooked. It'll make *Mak* have more diarrhea," *Mak* says, her tone frustrated. Slowly, she hands it back to me.

Heat from my body emanates up toward my face. I am hurt, frustrated, mad at myself that the corn is not cooked. I look at the bite she's taken from that corn and check the rest—they're uncooked. I'm so mad at myself. *How stupid!* I cry. *Why do I have to make Mak suffer more, why didn't I check them better?* I thought I had.

As *Mak* requests, I go to the back of the barn looking for embers to cook the corn, passing by groaning patients, the casualties of *padewat* (the revolution). In one dug-out cooking hole, I find a few small, fading embers. I gather tiny sticks of firewood nearby, piling them up gently. Kneeling on the ground, I blow at the pile, coaxing streams of smoke. I add larger firewood, then bury the corn in the ash, below the burning fire.

When I return with the roasted corn, Map is sitting beside *Mak* on the bed. While he eats rice with the tamarind paste, she strokes his hair, her eyes closed. For the first time, I see Map's face shine. His body relaxes. He looks at ease, sitting with *Mak*—even here, on a rusty, dirty bed.

I clean up the stench below *Mak*'s bed, covering it with ashes from the fire pit while listening to her conversation with Map. It seems as if we're home; her voice sounds gentle, motherly, and caring. Despite her own suffering, her words march along calm and normal. If she shares my fears, she doesn't show it. "*Mak* misses *koon proh*

Mak," she says, her hand patting Map's back. "Do they give you enough rice to eat, *koon proh Mak?*"

"*Otphong* [No], I'm hungry every day," says Map, his eyes gazing briefly at *Mak*.

Mak is silent, her mind working.

I come to her rescue. "They never give us enough, but Map picks chili and mint to trade with *Yiey* Om for food. He's smart, *Mak*. He knows how to find *Yiey* Om's house after I showed him just once." I see a glimmer of *Mak*'s smile, just a hint of it. Her face remains as swollen and as still as a statue's. Her eyelids hang closed much of the time. She reminds me now of a blind woman, of *Yiey Tot*, my great-grandmother.

"Do they give you modern medicine, *Mak?*" I ask, happy to see even a glimpse of her smile.

Suddenly *Mak* weeps. "*Koon Mak*," she sniffs, "they haven't given *Mak* water for four days, and I can't walk. *Koon*, life here has been difficult without anyone taking care of me, not even my own children." *Mak* sobs.

Gazing up at her, tears well in Map's eyes. "Many times I wished that one of you were here, just to get me water. That's all I've wished, *koon srey Mak*. . . ."

Mak's tears squeeze out from between her swollen eyelids, streaming down her cheeks; her mouth stops chewing the corn. Map's hands cling to her arm, his head leaning against it, his face reddening.

My eyes are blurred by my tears, but my mind clearly remembers how beautiful *Mak* once was. I remember her all dressed up one day, wearing a slim, shiny black silk skirt with embroidered flowers at the bottom. Her ivory-colored sleeveless blouse rested lightly against her smooth, youthful honey-colored skin and her soft chin-length dark hair. Even at age four, I was taken by my mother's beauty. But now I hurt as I gaze at her, my tongue tied, my heart aching. In her swollen face I can see her destiny. Already I feel my-self bracing for the day when she'll be gone.

When she dies, how much will I cry? I've asked this question before and I ask it again. Now the answer seems close. The only thing I know for sure is this—there will be agony.

Time is against us. Though we haven't been here long, it seems what we've shared with each other is mostly pain. Now Map and I have to go.

Mak makes a request: "Athy, *koon*, when you go back, ask the co-operative leader to let you come here to take care of *Mak*, get *Mak* water. At night you can sleep outside on the bench." *Mak* slowly motions her head. "Please don't forget, *koon srey mdaay*. Ask Chea to help you talk to the leader. Don't forget, *koon*. . . ."

By now I've learned. I've seen it so many times. To the dying, you make promises that cannot be kept.

"*Cha* [Yes], *Mak*, I won't forget. When I go back, I'll tell Chea to help me talk to the cooperative leader. I'll come back soon." My mouth forms the words to assure her, then I repeat them again.

"*Mak*, we're going." I don't want to say good-bye; my throat tight-ens.

"Hurry and come see *Mak* again, Athy. You too, *koon proh Mak*."

Map says his good-byes, his head turning, eyes wet. *Mak* doesn't say "good-bye"—all she says, again and again, is "Come back soon . . . don't forget." I assure her we will, tears falling freely.

The orange sun shines behind us, edging above the horizon. The trip to Daakpo is short, the dirt road now cool beneath our feet. My mind thinks of nothing but *Mak*.

As *Mak* has requested, I ask Chea to help me. Together we go to see the cooperative leader. In the open communal shelter, I stand beside Chea as she explains *Mak*'s situation and her request to the leader. He looks away, listening, then says, "Comrade's sister can go if comrade's mother will recuperate from her illness. But if comrade's mother dies, comrade's sister will be punished."

We walk away. Chea's face burns with anger.

"What should I do, Chea?" My mind summons up images of *Mak*.

Chea wraps her arm around my shoulders, a warm comfort. *Who will get Mak water? How sad will she be, waiting for me and Map to return?*

"What about *Mak*, Chea?" I can't escape *Mak*'s words. Her pleas echo in my head.

"When they give us more food," says Chea, her voice soft and calm, "*bang* will go to *Mak*. *Bang* will tell her that you didn't forget."

Through the nights I lie awake, staring into the sheet of darkness thinking about *Mak*. Her words are clear, still ringing in my ears. The picture of her sitting on the bed is vivid. Her fading flowered blouse, a map, a clue, that marked her as my mother. I gaze at her in my mind, as if looking into a magic mirror. *She's all we've got, yet we can't take care of her.*

For several nights her words and pleading continue to echo in my head as if she's calling to me from afar. But soon starvation and forced labor wring out my energy, blur my mind—I think less and less of *Mak*. Instead, I think about the scant watery soup ration I get from the communal kitchen, and my own survival.

Angka has ordered the communal kitchen to make noodles with fish soup—a rare luxury we only get when *Angka* wants us to attend its meetings. For many of us, the meeting simply means a resting day. We don't have to work, just sit, listening to whatever *Angka* wants to preach at us. Production. Revolution. Threats. My eyes watch them obediently, but my mind mocks them. I recall the saying I used to hear *Mak* say: *Doch chak tirk leu kbaaltea.* "Like pouring water on a duck's head." They are wasting their breath.

Within the thatch-roofed shelter, both children and adults sit anxiously waiting at four long wooden benches. The noodles are already cooked, and the warm smell of the fish soup with ground lemongrass, *kchiey* root, and turmeric powder flows through the shelter. To smell these spices is to sniff heaven. Perhaps it's nine o'-clock. I have to guess, since none of us own a watch. Suddenly I can hear bodies stirring as we catch a glimpse of the cooks coming toward us, women lugging baskets of noodles and pots of fish soup. They ration the thin white noodles, handing us three draped clumps. I save some of mine, shoving some aside on my plate for Chea to take to *Mak*. By the time I get back to the hut, Chea and Map have already gone to see *Mak*, Ra and Ry tell me.

I want to go to see *Mak*, too. I want to explain to her myself why I couldn't come to take care of her, but only Chea and Map can go, given rare permission. The rest of us must attend the meeting.

The meeting takes place on a patch of open ground surrounded by tall shade trees. Among the clusters of people, I see a "new person," a man in his late fifties, squatting on the ground beside the Khmer Rouge. His face, eyes, and complexion suggest he is of Chinese descent. He wears an old faded shirt and pants, muddy brown like our clothes. He looks relaxed, as if he's somehow connected with these Khmer Rouge leaders. The Khmer Rouge point to him as a model worker. He speaks to us shyly. His candor coaxes smiles from us. This is the first time since the Khmer Rouge's takeover that I hear and see people around me laughing and at ease. But the smiling faces fade as soon as the Khmer Rouge leaders get up to speak, lecturing us about rice production, the people in the "battlefield," and *Angka*'s goals.

The meeting ends. The leaders quickly dismiss us, but we can't go home yet. We must go to more meetings, one for children and the other for adults.

Suddenly I hear a soft voice behind me. *"Bang! Bang!"* I turn. From the deepest shadows beneath the shade trees, the silhouette of a little girl scurries toward me. I pause, lines creasing my forehead—I'm sure she's calling me because there's no one else around except trees.

The girl looks up at me. "They—they threw your mom in a well . . . a well of the deads," she struggles to catch her breath, panting the news. "Your mom was still alive. . . . She groaned when they took her away."

My heart thunders, rising against my chest. I think I hear what she has said, but nothing registers. It is as if something has lodged between my ears and my brain. I stare back. "What did you say about my mom? What happened to my mom?"

"The Khmer Rouge threw your mom in a well . . . and she was alive," sputters the girl, her sharp eyes looking into mine.

Her words sink in. *No!* The core of my soul screams out from a deep hidden place. My legs carry me away before my brain can command them. Across a dusty path, toward a distant woods, I run as fast as I can, the fingers of anguish squeezing my soul, pumping out pain.

"*Mak*, oh, *Mak*." I drop on the ground, landing by a bush underneath the shade of trees. "I'm sorry, *Mak*. Sorry I couldn't help you. . . ."

Alone in the woods, I call out to my mother, my mind summoning up the last images of her sitting on the bed talking to Map, to me, begging, reminding me to remember to return to her. In frustration, my fist strikes against the ground as *Mak*'s words replay in my mind, stabbing inside my chest with each syllable. My head hurts, swollen with sadness. My heart aches. "Oh, *Mak*, you've left me. . . . *Koon somtoh* [I'm sorry]. . . ."

The pain of losing *Mak* comes fiercely, without respite. It lingers inside me, lodged like a root. *How much will I cry when Mak dies?*

Now I know the answer.

10

The Spirit of Survival

The sun penetrates through the cracks of my shack. Alone, I curl up, covered by a scarf; my eyes fix upon the fine particles of dust that drift through the morning light. Most of the day, I lie here, staring into the dark until I tire. The next day the sun rises, and my eyes return to the twirling dust, again awaiting the blanket of night. I think, but I'm not sure what I'm thinking. I don't remember how I arrived here—a labor camp, I don't even know its name. I vaguely remember what happened to *Mak*, but the wound of her death is fresh.

Nights and days pass. I wonder what happened to my siblings. Who brought me here? I am weak, yet I don't feel like eating. Outside the shack I hear voices. The words, the commands never reach me. A woman in black sticks her head inside the shack. She softly says, "Comrade, go to work." I glance at her, then away.

A voice within me speaks up: *Something is wrong. You must eat.* Finally it awakens me, and I obey.

When the sun is blindingly bright, I rise. Out of the shack I walk with my spoon and plate in my hand. I wobble, trying not to fall.

I'm drawn toward a grove of trees. There lies a crowd of children; some line up for food, others squat on the ground eating. I trudge to stand in the food line, my flattened stomach slowly rising and falling.

"Comrade, which brigade are you in?" a food-ladling woman inquires, her forehead creased with curiosity.

"I'm sick," I reply softly, taking my place in front of her. The woman scoops a bowlful of rice onto my plate, then drops a pinch of coarse salt beside it. I feel her stare, her eyes questioning. But I walk on, one hand holding the rice.

"Never seen her before," says the woman.

"That comrade has been sick, huddling in her hut all the time," a voice replies.

"I gave her the same as the workers!" The woman complains.

The food begins to change me. With each bite, some life seeps back. My brain clears. The idea of my own survival had almost been erased from my mind. But I'm still too hollow to work for the Khmer Rouge.

While everyone labors in the hot field digging irrigation ditches, I sit in my shack, a squatty thatch shelter. Beneath my legs I can feel the itch of loose dry grass scattered about. I stare through the doorless entrance. My mind is pulled outward. I want to talk to *Preah*:

Preah, why is the day bright, yet seem so dark to me? My life has no meaning, I hear myself say. *Why am I so empty, so sick inside? Was this how Mak felt? Did this cause her to get bad so quickly?*

As I ask these questions, my mind readily summons the image of *Mak* in the Choup hospital, offering no resistance. *Did Mak sacrifice too much for us? Did she miss Pa, Avy, and Vin? Preah, stop letting people die, put an end to this suffering.*

For the first time in the twelve years of my life, I don't pray to Buddha requesting him to stop the suffering. I demand his action.

I want to have a say in my suffering, my family's, and others'. *How much more do I have to endure?*

Do you care?

I question his mercy, his divinity, like I used to argue with my own father. Even now, I can remember one summer back in Phnom Penh when I asked him if I could go to a private school.

Pa didn't say yes or no. He simply said I was young (eight) and didn't need to go to a private school. Smiling, *Pa* explained, "If all my children want to go to private schools, with book costs, school costs, *Pa* will be dead [broke]."

I couldn't accept it. I told *Pa* that if Chea could go to a private English school and buy expensive hardbound books, why couldn't I too go to summer school?

"I want to improve my math. Why can't I do that, *Pa*?" I said, standing before my parents while *Pa* was having breakfast.

Pa was quiet, his mouth chewing. *Mak* gazed at him. Still, he was silent. I needed to leave for the first day of class, my hands already holding my notebook and pencil. All he had to do was pay.

Silence.

I burst out crying, "*Koon* wants to go to school and *Pa* doesn't want to pay. I'm not important." I sobbed, my nose burning.

Pa was surprised. Never before had he known any child my age who wanted to study this badly.

"Stop crying," *Pa* said, grinning. "*Pa* will pay. Little, yet ambitious."

Mak beamed. I smiled through tears, then hurried to class.

This was my earthly father. He understood when I reasoned with him. A Buddhist nun once told *Mak* that I was *koon Preah* (God's child). If I am, then *Preah* should understand my suffering. Stop my suffering.

I shut my eyes. My heart aches.

On the dusty ground by the entrance to my shack, I look at the distant red sky. The sun is setting. Strangely, no one has made me work. Perhaps everyone is repelled by the way I act, the way I look, and how lost I am in my own mind. For a long time I used to worry, but I don't now. I'm not even scared of my brigade leader—don't even know what she looks like. Maybe she's the one who often sticks her head into my shack, calling me "comrade." She can call me, but I'm hiding in my mind. Sometimes I think of *Mak* briefly, in no more than small bits and pieces. Then a door in my mind slams shut. Again, I'm as quiet as the night.

As the sun retreats, I'm drawn back into the corner of the shack. Suddenly a shadow crawls in, too, and my heart jumps.

"Athy!" a woman's voice whispers. "I've brought you rice crust."

"Ra?" My voice cracks louder than I intended.

Ra hisses at me. Hastily, she tells me she'll come back tomorrow, then she disappears—here, then gone. In the dark I hold the rice crust, still paralyzed by Ra's sudden appearance. *How did she know where to find me?*

My stomach growls and my mouth waters as I inhale the brown-burned smell of the rice crust. Piece by piece, I eat it, savoring the chewy coffeelike flavor. With each bite, hope. I look forward to tomorrow—something I haven't felt in a long time.

The day is overcast, still early. Children's and mobile brigades have gone to work. Ra comes as promised. Scurrying into my shack, she issues stern instructions, "Hurry, go to Zone 3." She grabs my hand and guides me, or rather pulls me, out of the shack. I let her tug at me, every part of my body tensing, increasing speed.

"Hurry, walk faster," Ra commands, her voice anxious.

I trail behind her, watch her legs shuffle along. I want to stride as fast as she does, but my step covers one third the distance of hers. The bottom of her faded black pants slaps at her legs. Her old cotton shirt with the sleeves rolled up reveals a light golden flash of her youthful hands and arms. Their smooth beauty shocks me, delights me. Her arms swing fast, back and forth as if she is rowing herself forward. Hard labor hasn't robbed her of her fine "city" features. Even in the tattered remnants of a faded uniform, Ra looks healthy, somehow vibrant. She's more energetic than I. She's like a rabbit and I'm like a turtle. I can't keep up.

"Ra, why are we going to Zone 3?"

"To ask for food. Walk faster!" she barks. *"Dar muy, muy* [Walk slowly], the *chhlops* might see us now! Make big steps, hurry!"

Ra looks down at her own legs, as if showing me how to walk faster. I try, stretching my legs stiffly forward. I can't make long strides. Ra steals glances behind us, worried. She commands me to walk faster again, her voice sharp with irritation.

"But I'm smaller than you, Ra, and I'm weak!" I'm angry at her. With Chea, it would have been different. My mind orders me to hurry. I give Ra everything, but she doesn't seem to notice, moving ahead of me.

The sun is now shining. Beads of sweat stream from my scalp. Lagging behind Ra, I run, I walk. Tears well up and burn. I feel as if we are being watched by invisible eyes. Soon, I imagine, a forceful voice will command us to stop. The thought of it drives my legs. Suddenly a long, open depression emerges just ahead. The landscape changes. I hold my breath. Ra slows down, and I pant. A green bridge is on the far left.

A river! I marvel. A great liquid ribbon with shimmering ripples. Alone in our discovery, it is as if the river is ours. I feel free, standing on the riverbank. Tall shaded trees and shrubs are on the other side of the river. All green. They thrive far better there than on the side we're standing on—which is barren, only dry grass and rocky ground. Peaking in the distance between clusters of tall tree branches are palm and coconut leaves. This vegetation looks pretty, yet there's a sense of danger lurking in the comfort of this natural beauty.

"Athy, why are you standing there? Climb down. *Yeeh* [Gee], look at you standing there looking," Ra says, her voice raw with disbelief.

Her scolding tugs me back to reality. For a moment I forget why we're here. A shower of small rocks and dirt tumble down the steep bank as I climb down behind Ra. My hands hold the earth, my feet hesitate, I'm afraid of falling.

"Ra, there's a bridge over there," I say, motioning my face toward it. "Why don't we cross it?" I tense my body.

"Are you crazy? *Chhlops!*" She glares.

"Wait for me, Ra. I'm scared!" I sit still, my hand reaching out to her.

She climbs back up and steadies my hand as I crawl down. I wish I'd never come, trapped in this journey in search of food.

Be brave, I urge myself. If we go back, I reason, we might get punished and starved by the Khmer Rouge at our zone. If we move forward, we must face the river. And possibly be captured by *chhlops*. But maybe we'll be lucky and find food. In a heartbeat, I resolve to go with Ra.

Staring at the flat green water, I'm scared again. "How are we going to cross the river? I can't swim." I study the cool, moving current. I know the answer but don't want to hear it.

Ra plods into the water, her feet making a sloshing sound. I stand watching her, my feet rooted to the solid ground. *I can't swim*, I remind myself.

"Athy, come on. It's not deep. See?" her head nods at the water that laps just above her knees. She gives an encouraging look, waiting for me. But I can't seem to think beyond the image of being swept away, knowing how weak I am.

Ra returns, and I make a suggestion. "Go ahead and ask for food, and I'll be waiting for you here. I'll be okay."

If I stay by the river, she warns me, I'll be spotted by *chhlops* from Zone 3. I will be fine, she says. She doesn't know how to swim either.

I squat down, drawing my knees under me in a tight ball, so Ra can't pull me into the water.

"You won't fall!" Ra scolds. "I'll cross beside you and you can hold my hand."

I shake my head. My fear mounts as Ra urges me forward, her hand waving, her feet planted on rocks exposed in the shallow water. Finally she points to a long stick on the bank. I won't fall, she assures me, since I'll be using the stick to help me cross and she'll be holding my hand. With the security of having something to hang on to with both hands, I agree to try.

The water is cool. When it reaches my chest, the coldness of it makes me inhale, taking deep breaths. It's okay, Ra assures me. I glance at her and she's not scared. In time, it is as if the water washes my fears downstream. I feel my feet slipping on rocks, my body floating. But the water has only reached my shoulders, and we've already crossed the center of the river. The slapping sound of our wet pants is magnified in the midst of the tranquillity of the river and woods. My eyes follow the riverbank, this time a wall of soil and rock thatched with vines and shrubs.

Ra climbs the bank, clutching at vegetation like a ladder, and I follow her. I cling to the wild ivy and the sturdy buried rocks anchored in the earth. The only things I hear are the birds chirping and the dancing leaves.

"Athy, hurry," Ra hisses.

As we push through thick underbrush, we emerge near a large wooden building. It resembles a warehouse surrounded by tall shaded trees. The wooden walls seems new, the color of freshly painted brick. This is where Ra says we are to meet a man she and her coworkers call *Pok* (father), someone who has given them food before.

Already I imagine food: rice, marinated broiled fish, and soup with fresh vegetables and fish. Ra whispers to me to wait while she goes into the warehouse looking for *Pok*. My mind summons up more images of food: beef curry noodles, banana-tapioca pudding, juicy, sweet pineapples, and my favorite pâté sandwiches on crisp French bread. My appetite grows and so does my impatience.

I lean against the wall and pray that Ra and I will return safely to our zone. My stomach grows tighter, more nervous. I can't escape the anxiety growing inside. With or without food, I ask *Preah* to bring Ra back to me.

"Athy, Athy," a whisper interrupts the prayer.

Ra waves for me to come. She wraps her arm around me as we enter the warehouse, its concrete floor covered with piles of bricks and decorative concrete blocks stacked neatly along the walls. I study this warehouse, making a mental note of how tidy and clean this place is. How strange to find a building full of bricks planted in the middle of nowhere.

"Pretty soon *Pok* will come. He went to get us food," Ra says softly.

I hear her, but I pay little attention. I'm fascinated by this place. How different it is than the forced labor camp. It is modern, like places back in Phnom Penh or Takeo.

Though I haven't met him, I envy *Pok*. I wonder how he fits in with the ideology the Khmer Rouge have long preached to us. *There are no rich and poor. There will be equality. As comrades, we are all one.* Looking back, I remember how doubtful I was when I first heard them speak in Year Piar. And now this warehouse reinforces my doubts: *There's no equality. There will never be,* I think darkly.

"Athy, *Pok*'s coming," Ra alerts me.

She introduces me to him. "*Pok*, this is my young sister."

"*Chumriep sur, Pok*," I say, pressing the palms of my hands to-gether, raising them to the tip of my chin. A courtesy the Khmer Rouge can't take away from me. I didn't consider his approval, whether this is appropriate or whether he's one of the Khmer Rouge and despises this formal culture.

Instead of greeting me with words, he looks at me, then at Ra. Back in *sangkum mun* [the previous society], he would have returned my *chumriep sur*. But since both of his hands are holding a pan and plates, I can understand. I'm more than content with his kindness, his willingness to bring us food.

"Ara, you must be careful when you bring your sister here, and when you take her back. There are a lot of *chhlops*," *Pok* warns as he sets the foodstuffs on the concrete floor. "If they catch you, they'll torture you. Be careful."

His words reveal much. His tone is gentle, like a father address-ing a child. And by not calling Ra "comrade," I know he is not a Khmer Rouge. I study him—tall, strongly built, with dark olive skin. His black hair, neatly combed, is mixed with scattered gray strands. I would guess he's in his early fifties. His physical features suggest he has never suffered any hardship or lack of food. He seems educated, privileged, even though he wears the Khmer Rouge uni-form: new black pants and a long-sleeved shirt with a cotton scarf wrapped around his neck. I watch him in wonder. *Who is this man?*

Pok invites us to sit down. We hunker down, squatting on the concrete floor. Suddenly a slender young man, perhaps eighteen, with dark eyebrows and thick black hair approaches us. I look up, peering at what he's holding in his hand.

Pok explains, "Sun works with me. He brings more food for you."

Before us Sun sets down a large soup bowl filled with chunks of golden pumpkin, its withered blossoms and green shoots. Near it lies the crisp, reddish-brown smoked fish, nestled back to belly as they were when they were smoked. Then there's a saucer with about three tablespoons of fish sauce the deep color of tea. Its smell is strong. *Good.* I savor the aroma and my mind reels.

I have not tasted fish sauce since we were driven out of Year Piar—more than two years ago now. At first I didn't recognize it until my nose prompted me, detecting the pungent smell. Then my memory arouses me, my eyes widen, fixing on the food.

Pok picks up a plate from a stack. He lifts the lid of a small blackened metal pot, revealing white steamed rice. The sweet aroma reaches my nose, the familiar scent of a new crop of jasmine rice. My stomach growls, my mouth waters. My eyes follow *Pok*'s hand as he dishes up the rice with a spoon onto the plate. My mind, my whole body, yearns to snatch that plate from him.

"Can you eat this much?" asks *Pok*, his eyes looking into mine.

"Yes!" I answer, my head nodding as the word tumbles out of my mouth. I'm relieved to finally have the plate.

The rice piled on my plate is as high as rising dough. I want to gorge on it, shoving it in my mouth, but I have to wait for *Pok*, who is dishing up another plate of rice for Ra. I'm anxious, studying the movement of his hand from the pot to Ra's plate. It takes every bit of self-control to not fidget and scream out "Hurry, hurry."

Finally *Pok* hands Ra her plate, and she reaches for it with both hands, a polite gesture of reverence taught us by our mother.

"Go ahead, eat," *Pok* says, eyes glancing at me.

"How about you, *Pok*?" Ra asks.

"You eat, then hurry back."

I bury the spoon in the heap of rice, shoveling it into my mouth. My throat fills quickly, the food a stranger to my body. Next I spoon up the soup, gulping down the warm broth to help wash down the sluggish rice. Then I eat the pumpkin. The blossoms. The soft green shoots. Then the smoked fish with fish sauce, then another spoonful of rice. As quickly as it enters my mouth, it is gone, swallowed. Flavors are fleeting, my body is anxious to receive them.

I slow down long enough to savor the sweetness of pumpkin, the spicy flavor of turmeric and lemongrass. The warmth spreads throughout my body, my hand unwilling to slow. It is as if I'm in an eating contest with myself.

Ra glances at me, then at *Pok*. I notice her calm demeanor, which she used to display when guests visited our home. This was how every Cambodian girl was supposed to behave in front of guests. She should be modest, gentle. The expected behavior was so rigid, so ceremonial, that as children we never ate any meal with guests. So even now, I can see a shyness, a modesty in Ra, although we're only eating in front of *Pok*, a kind stranger.

Hunger doesn't make me modest. I continue to gorge on the food. I feel *Pok*'s eyes watching us—I don't care. I've unlearned Cambodian table manners, all the cultural rules: don't scrape the plate when spooning rice; don't eat too fast in front of guests; watch how others eat, go with the group. Today these things don't apply to me. I've learned too well, adjusting to today's scarcity, living by a proverb I used to hear Cambodian elders say: *Chol sturng tam bought, chol srok tam proteh.* "Follow the river by its winding path, follow the province/state according to its country." One must adapt to one's situation in order to survive. And I'm adjusting to my new environment, a world where formality and politeness are not a necessity—indeed are banned. Instead, cruelty is the law by which the people are ruled, a law designed to break our spirits. In the name of *padewat* (the revolution).

It has been a week since the trip to *Pok*'s warehouse. Even though he works for the Khmer Rouge, *Pok* doesn't have a heart of stone like them. The goodness in him has lifted my spirit.

Ra doesn't come, and I can no longer wait. All my waking hours, I summon up images of the food we ate at *Pok*'s: steamed rice, the pumpkin blossoms, the green shoots, lemongrass, and turmeric root. In my mind, I'm already at *Pok*'s.

The following day I sneak out alone. This time I feel I can walk as fast as Ra. Before I know it, I'm at the riverbank, and not afraid of slipping off the bank or being captured by the Khmer Rouge. Food is my only focus. Hastily, I cross the river, without Ra's help or even a stick. The water reaches my knees, chest, mouth, then my ears! The current spills into my nose. Quickly, I pull my hand from the water. I clip my nose, tilt my head. My legs kick, propelling me. My body floats slightly, my mouth gulps for air. My face is barely above the water, my eyes focusing on my destination. The water recedes slowly to my neck. I swallow air hungrily.

Safe on dry ground, I look at the current and dread my return. But I have to have food.

At the warehouse, *Pok* is surprised, apprehensive. "Did Ara come?"

"No," I answer, my voice vibrating from my shuddering body.

"Wait here," *Pok* commands, his hand pointing to the concrete floor.

Soon he reappears, striding back into the warehouse with food, frowning.

"Hurry, eat. Take the rest of the food with you, be careful."

I dish up the rice, then swallow it down with the broiled fish. I wrap everything in my scarf, then flee.

Back in the river, my gaunt body fights the current and so do my legs, propelling me above the rocks, pushing me forward. Above the water, my right hand holds the food in the scarf, my left hand clips my nose. A short distance ahead, the steep bank awaits. *I'm not going through this again*, I tell myself, relieved to survive this day.

But hunger is powerful, a silent but strong voice inside me. A few days later it orders me to go back to Zone 3. When everyone has gone to work, I stride toward the river.

When I arrive at the riverbank, I'm shocked to see the swelling river. The water is now doubled, and still rising. *I can't cross this!* Yet desperation takes me to the green bridge. As I approach it, I slow down, strolling. Gazing skyward while standing on the bridge, I pretend I'm observing the slanting structures of the bridge, which look like a group of X's interconnected with a flat beam on top. I stand there waiting to see if someone will come and question me as to what I'm doing here. I wait and wait, but I don't hear or sense a soul coming. I turn to look at the shimmering ribbon of water. I'm briefly comforted. My head urges me forward, telling me to go now or never. I hurry across and hop off the bank near the bridge, my butt sliding down the slant ground into the woods, landing by a thicket. As I get up, I hear men's voices and squat down.

Waiting to be captured, I notice that the voices are still in the distance. They're not approaching me. Now curiosity kicks in. I crawl to the next bush. From here, I see three men wearing black uniforms with scarves wrapped around their heads. One sits in a boothlike hut with the butt of a rifle leaning against his shoulder. The other two are outside the booth, facing him.

I pad quietly to *Pok*'s warehouse. When I stick my head inside, *Pok*'s, Sun's, and another man's stares await me. *Pok* strides toward me, his face pale with indignation.

"Who else is coming?" *Pok* demands nervously.

"Only me," I answer softly, lowering my gaze to the floor, then look at Sun and the other man for their reaction. Their faces are masks of apprehension.

"God, you're daring!" *Pok* cries out. He stares at me in disbelief. "How did you get here?"

"Crossed the bridge."

Pok shakes his head, his right hand on his hip. "Aren't you scared of the cadres by the bridge? They will torture you when they catch you! Don't you know? They'll ask me why you are here. They can kill us. Do you understand?" The tone of his voice strikes me.

"Don't ever come back. Don't ever cross the bridge again. Today high-level Khmer Rouge are coming here. It's very dangerous, understand?"

After he calms down, he tells Sun and the other man to take me to a hut. There, we are to be quiet while we eat. No talking, absolutely no sound.

The hut is small, built on stilts with a ladderlike stair in front. Around it are tall trees, casting their shade over the hut. The warehouse is close by, and Sun goes to get food with the other man. Dim light is faintly visible between the slits of the bamboo slabs. I keep looking at it as if my survival depends on it.

Suddenly I detect footsteps climbing the stairs. My head turns toward the door, which softly cracks open. Shadows of hands holding a pot and a large bowl appear. Then another shadow follows. I take a deep breath, relieved to know it's only Sun and the other man.

On the floor before me are silhouettes of a pot of rice and a bowl of soup with dark shadows of vegetables and white chunks of something, perhaps fish. Then a pungent aroma startles me: the tangy, sour smell of steamed-pickled fish combined with freshly sliced cucumbers. My mouth waters, my stomach growls, my fear flees.

In the dark we sit in a circle. Each of us gently spoons up the food and places it in our mouths. I hear only my swallowing. The routine of this secret eating now feeds on fear.

Suddenly *Pok*'s voice erupts. "How are you, comrades?"

"We're so-so," a man replies stoically. "Is the production better?"

My mouth freezes. The shadows of Sun's and the other man's heads turn toward me. But their gazes retreat, turning to the food on the floor. I imagine the cadres storming into the hut, dragging me away, and tying me up. Only after *Pok*'s and the Khmer Rouge's voices trail away do I dare swallow the last bite. Now I understand why the men were distressed to see me. Understanding how my being here can bring trouble to these men, I get up abruptly to go.

"Take some rice with you," Sun urges. He too gets up.

"Wait a moment," the other man says, his voice calm. "Here, we'll wrap up some food."

The men leave to find out when it'll be safe for me to return to my zone. Again, they warn me to be quiet. To wait for them. Alone in the hut, I cry silently. I don't know whether I'm moved by these men's kindness or if I'm simply scared.

Shortly, rapid footsteps shake the hut. I half stand, half squat. "Hurry, get out. Hurry!" A voice whispers urgently.

I freeze.

"Come, follow me. It's okay."

I slip out the door and there is Sun, already stepping off the stairs. I shake as I step down. Once on the ground, Sun pulls me behind a tree. "They're still at the warehouse," he whispers. "When I say go, run. Don't cry if you trip." His eyes ask, *Do you understand?*

"I won't fall," I say, shaking my head, but my tears betray me.

From tree to tree, thicket to thicket, I run with him at his prompting. Then all of a sudden he says, "I'm going back. I can only help you this far. Be careful."

I watch him disappear. I cry and I'm scared. I pray to God and the spirits of *Mak* and *Pa* to protect me. I say the prayer silently, chanting it again and again in my head. As if I am being guided by a spirit, suddenly my fears fade, and my mind focuses on returning safely to my zone. My body feels light, comforted as I hike through the woods and climb the bank onto the bridge, leaving Zone 3 behind.

Safe on the ground of my zone, I turn to look at the grove of trees where the warehouse and hut are. A place where a good memory was born. A memory of kind men and Ra, who brought me to them.

11
A Promise

It is late 1977. For some reason I am sent to a new camp in a stretch of large rice paddies along with a group of children. Like many labor camps, it is as anonymous as the people who work in them. I don't know where we are or what this place is called. From dawn to dusk, I chase birds away from the ripening rice. Now it is midmorning and the sun is shining, and the day is now bearable, warm.

But early in the morning I'm always cold since the shirt I have on is inadequate to shield me from the cool air. The one other shirt I have is at the shack, which I keep for changing into the next day. The morning dew from the grassy elevated pathways coats my bare feet, making the morning almost unbearable.

As the sun shines, I unfold my arms from my armpits like a chick being hatched. Standing up, I fidget, my hands rubbing against each other, my mouth blowing warm air at them. On the distant horizon, amid rice paddies, I see the silhouettes of adults heading out to harvest. It looks as though their heads are floating on the rice stalks.

Just as humans rise to work, so do birds, ready to start their day. Already they are up, flying like black waves. They maneuver over rice paddies as if trying to select the right ones to feast on. As soon as they land, children whose assigned fields are being invaded run toward the birds. Their heads bob between the heads of the rice. They give chase. They shout "Shoo! Shoo!" Their little arms flail in the air.

The birds take off, making fierce chirping sounds as they fly to other rice fields—mine. Then I too run toward them. "Shoo! Shoo!" I shout, joined by a chorus of other children. My hands thrown in the air to scare them.

Laughter erupts in the air as the birds fly from rice paddy to rice paddy. Now it is like a game of land-and-chase. They chirp, we laugh. Beads of sweat roll down my forehead. Our laughter is food for my soul. It has been a long time since I had some. I feel revived—like a little girl again, the thirteen-year-old that I am.

With improved food rations, better than in the village, I think of my family, wishing they were here. Every night I wish fervently that they could enjoy what I've been having: steamed rice and soup with fish and vegetables. I wonder where Ra is now, whether she is still at that camp bordering Zone 3, or whether she has been transferred elsewhere. I wish Avy, Vin, *Pa*, and *Mak* were still alive. *Mak* would have been happy just to have rice and salt. "Having solid rice and salt is like going to heaven," I remember her saying, her eyes filled with longing.

As the night sets in, lying on my earthen bed made of a pile of hay in a small shack, I think of *Mak*. Images of her pale, swollen face at the Choup hospital pop into my head as in a dream. It seems only days ago when Map and I visited her, and now she's gone. Since I feel better, my mind allows me to go back in time to be with her again. Drifting into sleep, I yearn to talk with her, wishing she were here with me.

Mak appears, sitting across from me and Map at the end of an oaken table that resembles *Pa*'s medicine desk at our Phnom Penh home. Below hazy fluorescent lights, I'm spellbound by her presence—her complexion is pretty and healthy, just like it was back in Phnom Penh.

As she gazes at me, I notice the deep sadness in her beautiful face, framed by her neatly combed black hair. I stop feeding Map rice gruel, place the spoon on his plate, and get up from the chair. I pad gently toward her, but before I can say anything, she floats away toward the ceiling. She begs:

"Athy, please take care of your little brother. Feed him food, *koon Mak*. Look after *p'yoon* for *Mak*. . . . *Saniya Mak* [Promise *Mak*]."

"*Mak*, I want—"

"*Saniya Mak*," *Mak* interrupts me before I can finish what I wanted to say. Her face is despondent, and I look at her searchingly.

"I promise . . ." I answer, wanting so much for the deep sorrow in her face to disappear. I want to tell her why I couldn't go take care of her at the Choup hospital. But as soon as I make my promise to her, she vanishes as suddenly as she appeared.

"*Mak*, please come back . . ." I cry, looking for her.

Eyes open, I awake in the darkness. *Where am I?* I ask myself. As I turn my head, the soft sound of the crushing hay beneath my back speaks. Then I know: I'm in a shack, not in my Phnom Penh home with Map or *Mak*.

Mak was real. She talked to me! Mak, did you come to tell me what you couldn't before you died. Oh, Mak, please talk to me again. I'll be waiting.

But she doesn't come; instead, a firm voice awakens me.

"Get up. It's time to work." The shack is rattling.

The familiar shadow of Comrade Thore Meta, my brigade leader, peeks into my shack. When I crawl out of the shack, she disappears. It is early in the morning, still twilight. Another day running along the rice fields, I think tiredly. At least there are no informants to police me. I'm on my own all day with the other children.

Thore Meta, a *neradey*, the Khmer Rouge from the southwestern part of Cambodia, is unlike my former brigade leaders. She has never scolded me when I'm slow to wake up for work. She is lenient and understanding. She is, perhaps, in her early twenties, with a calm face and chubby cheeks. Her eyes are big and dark. Her complexion is white, in striking contrast to her new black uniform, lighter than many *neradey* women's. Hugging her cheeks and earlobes is her naturally curly black hair. She's short, and so is her neck. It looks as if she doesn't have one, as if her head is attached to her shoulders. Though she's not pretty, her kindness makes her more approachable.

Months ago, rumors spread of vicious killings that took place soon after the *neradey* arrived in Daakpo and other villages around Battambang province (in the western part of Cambodia). Their aim was to take over the leadership here and to purge local Khmer Rouge leaders. Even though *Angka* forbids people from talking, word of its orders to execute these leaders spread like the pungent smell of rotten rats. This killing calls to mind a Cambodian saying: *Domrei gnob khom yok chong-ey tao kroob.* "An elephant dies, and one tries to cover it with a flat basket."

That "elephant" was *Ta* Val, people said. He was the top Khmer Rouge leader who oversaw the building of irrigation canals and dams in the western part of Cambodia. He, among others, was captured, placed in a sack, and then run over by a tractor. His crime, the *neradey* charged, was building a dam toward Thailand so that he and his conspirators could escape. Shocked by the news, I wondered why *Ta* Val and others wanted to escape. *What did they fear?* How terrifying it must have been for them in their last moments, as the muffled sound of the roller approached, quivering the earth, then crushing them to death. The *neradey* are brutal, people say, but I'm grateful that Thore Meta doesn't fit that description.

Many rice fields turn golden. The head of the rice weighs down the stalks. Women have been sent here to reap the crop and process the unhusked rice. Their huts sprout near the wooden bridge like mushrooms after a drizzling night. One used to process rice is half a mile from my shack. Behind it, women winnow pounded rice. Their hands tilt rice baskets, one at the back, the other in front. Their fingers spread at the brims, so that the husks fall freely and separately from the white rice.

Inside the hut, other women sift the winnowed rice on a large mat. Diligently, they swirl flat round baskets in circular motions; the grains of rice filter through the tiny holes. Before the evening ration I am hungry, so I linger at the entrance of this hut. Since no one scolds me, little by little I move to squat by the rice piles, then my hand pinches a few grains and shoves them in my mouth. Other children follow, stealing glances at the women. In return, the women flash us warnings as their hands keep busy.

"If you keep it up, you'll get diarrhea," warns a woman in charge who is known as Comrade Murn. She's in her fifties, stocky with dark skin and black hair covered by an old cotton scarf.

I'm relieved to hear a caring warning, and not a scold or a slap. Diarrhea later, but hunger is now. My teeth grind away at this new crop, producing a sweet powdery flavor in my mouth. We take whatever amount Comrade Murn tolerates, shoving it in our pockets or whatever we have, a scarf, or our hands.

As the weather gets hotter, the rice ripens quickly. Bags of pounded rice lean against the outside walls of the hut. The women are twice as busy, working up a sweat as they sift, winnow, and bag piles of processed rice into burlap sacks. Suddenly a woman shoves her sifting basket aside, gets up, then cries, "Oh, I can't hold it anymore! I'll pee in my sarong." She staggers as if her legs are numb from sitting too long.

"Who forbids her from peeing?" says Comrade Murn, chuckling. Her eyes glow, lines form around her dusty temples as her hands sift vigorously. Other women glance at her, their mouths flashing a weak smile.

I stare at the lonely basket sitting on the rice pile and the spot vacated by the woman. On an impulse, I jump into the woman's area, scoop the winnowed rice into the basket, and swirl it. The sifting around me stops. The only thing I hear is the sound of my own sifting basket. I fear Murn will soon scold me.

"Look, look at her! Young like that, yet she knows how to sift rice like an adult," Comrade Murn says in amazement. "And she's not even a farm kid."

Koon la-aw (good child) Comrade Murn calls me, and wonders from whom I learned this skill. I gaze briefly at her, then at everyone. I learned it from watching my mom, I explain.

After *Pa* was executed in Year Piar, I wanted to learn the ways of farm life so I could help *Mak*. I watched her process rice from start to finish. One day I thought I was ready to make use of my observations. I thought I had gotten everything down, so I told *Mak* that I wanted to help her, and she let me. As I sifted the rice, I felt awkward. The rice in the basket didn't go in a circular motion as it did with *Mak*. The basket was bigger than me, *Mak* concluded, and I needed practice. I perspired profusely as I struggled with the weight of the rice and the size of the basket.

Mak beamed and said, "*Koon*, swirl the basket, not your *koot* [butt]. Look at you. Your face is red, your veins bulging. You look like you're going to the lavatory." Her hands reached out to take the basket from me, but I wasn't done learning. I lightly pushed her hands away and resumed my sifting practice. *Mak* laughed at my awkwardness. It had felt good to hear her laughter.

Comrade Murn grins, glancing at me, and so does everyone there. I'm surprised to be the center of attention. I feel a sense of connection with these people. Suddenly I feel as if they're my family, a surrogate family.

I've saved up rice in a bag and salted fish in a tin can, hidden in my shack for Map and Chea in Daakpo. Chea has been staying in Daakpo to look after Map, Ra had told me when we were in the labor camp near Zone 3. Ry is still at the hospital and Than has been sent away, Ra didn't remember where. Sometimes I wish I could just run to Daakpo and take this food to them. I imagine how happy they would be.

I would say to Chea, "Chea, chasing birds away from rice is not hard. Even you would like working as a scarecrow. It's not like building irrigation canals."

Chea would be delighted with me, I imagine, like a proud mother.

The harvest reaches to full speed. Men from various villages will be here, Comrade Murn tells me, to take processed rice to their respective villages. Perhaps someone from Daakpo can take the rice I've saved to my family, she suggests, somehow knowing I've been saving the rice for Map and Chea.

A few days later a caravan of oxcarts arrived by the time I'd finished with the day's work. In the nearby field are skinny cows eating small stacks of hay set in front of them, as if their food is also rationed. Their bodies are covered with sheets of skin, their hipbones protrude like their eyeballs.

Quietly I pad beside the oxcarts. I prowl, peeking beneath each oxcart, where exhausted men are resting. They are sound asleep, arms bent over their foreheads to shield them from the sun. But at one oxcart an old man stands untying a rope from it. Something about him is familiar.

"Excuse me, are you from Daakpo?" I ask in a soft voice. The man turns, his eyebrows creased as if to say, *Who are you?*

"That's right," he says, pausing from untying the rope.

"Are you *Ta* Barang?" My memory speaks. "You used to work in a sugar place in Daakpo, didn't you?"

"How do you know my name?" he asks.

"Do you remember Chea? I'm her younger sister!" I say, surprisingly excited.

A year ago, I tell him, he was kind to Chea and me. At the Daakpo sugar factory where palm sugar is processed for the whole village, he let us scrape white bubbles of sugar formed atop the rim of a huge, heavy pot in which the liquid palm sugar was being reduced to a dark brown, viscous sugar. "Sometimes you gave Chea sugar to bring home. Other times you let her dip yucca roots in the sugar until they were cooked and coated with sugar. Chea said you were the nicest person there."

Ta Barang glances over his shoulder. "In this era," he says, "when you are kind to people, you get punished for it. They took me to reform and replaced me with someone else who is good for *Angka*. Niece, now our country is so different; it's hard to understand." *Ta* Barang sighs, but agrees to take the rice and salted fish to Map and Chea.

A month later, after most of the rice has been harvested, my brigade is sent back to Daakpo. We are told to go back to our families until we are needed again. After a long march, I see a glimpse of my hut. Suddenly two skinny people come running, as if the hut spits them out. It's Chea and Map! Chea dashes in front, scrawny-looking, with Map behind her, his stomach bulging out, a sign of starvation. Carefully, like frail old people, they walk on sticklike legs. Chea manages a smile that conceals pain. Her arms reach out to embrace me.

"When did you get to the village?" she asks, her voice a mixture of excitement and sorrow, tears in her eyes. Map looks at me eagerly, yet his face is tired.

"I just got here, Chea. Hey, Map," I say softly, reaching to touch his head. Having spent countless days thinking of them, I'm jubilant, so grateful to see them. But my excitement is short-lived. Chea's and Map's depleted faces shock me. I have forgotten that their lives have been so different from mine.

In the alcove of our hut in the cool evening, Chea, Map, and I sit, facing each other. Map sits close to Chea like a child wanting to be cuddled by his mother. Chea's fervent, sunken face possesses that motherly quality. I ask her questions, eager to find out if the rice rations have been better in Daakpo since the crops turned out well this year.

"Nothing changes," Chea says dismally. "We're still eating rice gruel, not even enough, mostly water. Every day all *bang* wishes is to have solid rice just for one day. Only for one day. . . . When *bang* asks the cooperative leader why we don't get more rice, he says most of the rice is sent to people in battlefields who build *padewat*."

Tears flood her eyes. "Life is difficult, Athy. One season is just like another. I've been praying for the harvesting season to come so that we can have more rice. But when it comes, the rice ration is still the same, still little. When life continues to be this terrible, Athy, *bang* just wants to die. I . . . ." Chea wipes away her tears. "I just want to close my eyes and die. If I live on, life doesn't have meaning. No meaning at all. Except to live for that day just to have more rice, and that's all."

Chea's tears drip like raindrops. My own burn my eyes. Map looks at her through his tears, then his hand reaches out to her. It is deeply hurtful to see her suffering. Her pain compounds Map's. His four-year-old sunken face looks wounded. Amid all this, I remember what I've been wanting to ask Chea: about the rice and salted fish, my promise to *Mak*.

The thought of it lightens my spirit. "Chea, did *Ta* Barang bring the rice and fish I sent you and Map? Did he?"

She looks at me, then at Map as if trying to find the right words. Calmly she says, "He brought only fish, a little bit of fish."

"How much?" My brow furrows. "I sent a bag of rice, this much rice, and a can of salted fish, this much to the rim." I show her with my hands.

"Athy, he apologized that he ate all the rice and most of the fish," Chea explains. "He was so hungry and he couldn't help himself."

"No! It wasn't for him, Chea—" I wail, unwilling to believe what Chea has just told me. "I saved it for Map. For you. I promised *Mak*, Chea. She came to me. In my dream. She begged me. . . . *Ta* Barang, *ta aakrak* [bad old man]." My head hurts, my chest is stuffed with deep pain. I feel so betrayed.

Chea hugs me tightly. "Athy, don't say that, *p'yoon srey*," she whispers into my ear. "He was hungry—he's only human. If you were him you'd have done the same."

"But it wasn't for him, Chea, not for him. . . ."

12

Though a Virgin,
I'm Called an Old Man

New Internationalist
April 1993
"Return to Year Zero"

> Year Zero was the dawn of an age in which, *in extremis*, there would be no families, no sentiment, no expression of love or grief, no medicines, no hospitals, no schools, no books, no learning, no holidays, no music: only work and death.

The wind howls. Thunder rumbles with low popping sounds, followed by a deafening clap. It trails away in the sky, then it starts all over again. The hut rustles, the panels of the thatched wall flapping. Dense raindrops strike madly against the hut. The monsoons are already here. The summer of 1978 has already flown away. Chea cuddles close to Map and I close to her. On this night, I'm grateful to have the warmth and comfort of my own family. As soon as the beating rain dies down and the wind loses its breath, I fall asleep, snuffed out like a candle. A moment later I'm jolted by a voice. "Get up, go to work," an ugly, blotched-faced informant bellows.

I dread these days. I have to meet other children at the *sahakar*, then the workday begins. As I'm getting out of the hut, I see that the sky is still dark. The night rain freshens the air. The cold breeze makes me shiver. I wish we could go back to sleep, cuddling closely, sharing our warmth.

Chea curses under her breath. Something about *Angka* going to hell. I hope they will, but I'm too tired to be angry at *Angka* now. The sky is cloudy. Along the dike that snakes between vast flooded rice paddies, I walk behind a long line of children and adults, marching off to salvage rice seedlings. By this time of year the rice paddies along the dike would normally be green with thriving seedlings, but now they are all covered with water. Everywhere, as far as the eye can see. It looks as if a giant lake has been created overnight. Only the tips of the seedlings peek out of the water. It looks like there are more heavy rains to come.

The next day is another gloomy day. Wet ground. Overcast sky. The drizzle turns into a pouring rain. The line of children in front of me halts, backs up. The line moves again. Everyone walks around a person who squats on the dike, her head resting on her arms, which are wrapped around her knees. I look at her shivering body, covered with her faded cotton scarf. Her shuddering cry is familiar.

"Chea? Chea?"

The head rises, eyes wet. I embrace her soaking back. She weeps, shuddering. I wail, letting out the pain of helplessness, the loneliness, and the frustration that have been building in me. There is so much suffering to bear that I can't hide it.

"Athy, *bang* is sick and they dragged *bang* out of the hut. I'm very sick. I'm cold; I cannot work, *p'yoon srey bang*. . . ."

Oh, Chea . . . God have mercy. Looking up at the cloudy sky, I'm so overwhelmed by Chea's suffering, and my own. I want to alleviate my sister's suffering, but I'm so utterly helpless it hurts. *Who are they to drag off my sister? How brutal!* The question stirs up a burning anger that I haven't felt for so long. I close my eyes, and I want so much to scream.

"Athy, Athy. Go, *p'yoon srey*. The *chhlops* are coming—" Chea mutters.

Glancing at Chea, I get up and trot away. After a few feet, she is out of sight, blocked by the moving line and the sheet of rain.

The rains die down. The water in the flooded rice fields recedes. Chea has regained her health after two weeks of rest. Her fever is gone. Already she's herself, resilient, friendly like she was back in Phnom Penh.

Our neighbor, a woman, comes to our hut. Chea's face glows as if she is happy to see her. "Good morning. How are you, aunt?" Chea greets her cheerfully in English as if she has been yearning to speak it. I'm surprised, yet delighted to hear Chea talk in English.

The woman recoils, baffled. Chea's lips widen into a grin, "Or, comment ça va, Madame? Trés bien? Oui?"

"You talk like that, I can't understand you," the woman mildly complains, her brow furrowing. "I've brought you some rice. Here." She unties the knot on her scarf, producing a few pounds of processed rice.

"Merci beaucoup, Madame." Chea gently bows, amused.

The woman looks sheepish, gazing at Chea.

Chea explains, translating what she's said. Then she asks the woman how she is doing in Cambodian.

"Well or not, it's so-so nowadays," the woman speaks dismally. "Life is like hell." She whispers. "These days you can't trust anyone, Achea, not even your own children. My children, they're now *Angka*'s kids. They've been turned against me. They don't listen to me, but to *Angka*. You should be careful. Don't speak those languages."

I smile, observing Chea and the woman. I'm proud of Chea, elated by her sparkling greeting. Amused by the baffled look on the woman's face when she first heard Chea speak English. She is a small woman, one of the "new people" who is friendly and seemingly timid.

The next morning the informant who wakes us suddenly appears in front of our hut. His piercing, sinister eyes look accusing. "*Angka* needs to look for books," he declares, inviting himself into our hut. I'm baffled, disbelieving.

Chea waves at me and Map to get out of the hut as the informant ransacks our clothes and blankets. He hops onto the part of the open floor where we cook our food. I hear the sounds of pots and pans colliding. Then he begins digging. Chea looks at me and I at her. Map looks at us searchingly.

The informant leaves; his dirty footprints remain on the slabs of the floor. His wicked eyes glare at us as he carries away a package, our once-hidden past, Chea's personal belongings wrapped in a damp turquoise plastic. In it are a leather briefcase and a handbag. They were *Pa* and *Mak*'s gifts to her for her academic success. The briefcase contains memories of her school years: a spiral math notebook; two Cambodian novels, *Pka Srapone* (Wilted Flower) and *Snaeha Muy* (One Love), written by Chea's friend in college. Primly secured in their slots opposite the books are fancy pens and pencils, souvenirs from her friends. Their pictures, and pictures of her with them, are in a picture album. Beside each wallet-sized photo is a brief friendship note to Chea, decorated with roses, hibiscus, or ivy with blossoms. In the handbag are documents of our births and the titles to our houses in Phnom Penh and Takeo, hidden beneath Chea's colorful traditional satin clothes. In the informant's hands is the tangible evidence of our former lives. *How did he suspect us of having books?* Chea wonders, and I myself can't understand his sudden appearance. Could it be that he was eavesdropping on us when Chea greeted our neighbor yesterday, hiding behind our hut or in the shrubs out front? With the family documents and Chea's books in *Angka*'s hands, we have a lot to lose. Chea keeps her thoughts to herself. She's quiet, preoccupied, as if saying anything at all would get us into deeper trouble. I brace for the repercussions.

At work the following day I worry about losing Chea. I imagine her being taken away to be reformed by the *chhlops* for possessing books, evidence of being educated. At the hut Map is alone, crying. I can see him clearly, sitting, waiting for me to return. His face distressed, heartbroken, just like it was when *Mak* was taken away from him to the Choup hospital.

Returning from work, I brace myself for the worst news. When I arrive at the hut, a bald, gaunt person is squatting in front of the hut with his back facing me.

Chea? No! Tears spill out of my eyes. Chea has shaved her head. She looks so unlike herself, my once-beautiful sister. Her scalp sallow, bony. Her neck thin, dark. From the back, she looks like an old, old person; I can't tell whether she's a woman or a man.

When Chea turns, her eyes meet mine. She looks resolved, gets up and walks over to me. Calmly she says, "Athy, if *bang* looks crazy and ugly enough, the Khmer Rouge might not harm *bang*."

We go through our family pictures, which I've hidden in the roof. To erase *Pa*'s ties to the previous government, I cut out parts of his wallet-sized picture in which he is wearing military police uniforms. What remains is his head, from the neck up. If we should be interrogated, *Pa* never worked for the previous government, Chea says. His former job was in a medical field, and he liked to help people.

The next evening the air is cool. Since it's still light out, Chea and I weed our front yard, where we'd grown corn the previous year. We have two tools, one a knife, the other a small rusty shovel. Suddenly a stern voice behind us shouts "Comrade!"

We turn. It's Srouch, the leader of the informants. Chea rises, facing him.

"*Angka* found books in your hut. What level of education did you have?" he demands.

Chea walks toward him, clutching the knife in her hand. Casually Chea says, "I found those books on a road during the evacuation from Phnom Penh. I didn't get to study much because of the fighting. I know how to read a little. Why? Does comrade want those books? You may have them. I just keep them for wiping myself after I poop." Chea drops the knife on the ground as if her hand has lost its grip. As she slowly moves toward Srouch, she scratches her body—her arms, chest, neck, her bald head—causing Srouch to walk backward.

"That's enough," he says, his brow furrowed. "I only wanted to know if comrade had a lot of education or held any position before."

As soon as the last word leaves his mouth, he flees, disappearing as fast as he appeared. Chea grins at me, and I grin back.

A few weeks later, in the evening, while I weed in the front yard, Chea waters the vegetables in the back of the hut. I can hear voices of girls chatting, laughing, approaching a path behind our hut. They sound carefree. *Strange*, I think. Normally the "new people" would not dare to display this much happiness. When their faces appear out of the woods, I can see why they sound untroubled—they are the "old people." They have it better than us, so they have good reason to be happy. When they near our hut, Chea looks at them, her hands holding the water bucket. "Did comrades just come from working in the woods?" Chea asks nicely. It's her way of greeting some people.

The girls stop talking. One of them, perhaps thirteen years old, studies Chea. Her eyes narrow with contempt, then she shouts, "Crazy old man!" She thrusts a knife at Chea again and again. The others join in. They all chant, "Crazy old man. Crazy, crazy." Together they flail their knives at Chea. They jeer repeatedly. I glare at them until they disappear behind the trees.

Chea stands rooted to the ground, her face filled with humiliation. She looks so hurt. Slowly she puts the bucket down on the ground. As she walks past me, she curses them, "Insolent kids!"

The following night Chea lies beside me; it's only us since Map is with Ry at Peth Preahneth Preah. Close to me she huddles, then she whispers in my ear. "*Bang* wrote a poem last night in *bang's* mind. Listen."

ស្រណោះខ្លួនខ្ញុំ ខ្លួននៅក្រមុំ គេហៅថ៉ាតា
កាលពីសង្គមខ្ញុំខឹងយ៉ាងណា តឡូវនេះណា ធម្មតាទេស្រី
ស្រណោះខ្លួនស្រី អាយុម្ភៃបី គេថាហុកសិប
ធ្មេញមិនទាន់បាក់ សក់នៅខ្មៅក្រិប គេថាហុកសិបព្រោះខ្ញុំត្រួងោ៉ល។
ស្រណោះខ្លួនណាស់ រស់នៅព្រាត់ប្រាស់ វិរសម៉ូម៉ែ
គ្មានទីសង្ឃឹមថានឹងបានថ្មមថែ រួមរស់នៅក្បែររលោកឪពុកអ្នកម្ដាយ។

*I pity *myself*. Though a virgin, I am called an old man.

In the previous society, how furious would I've been. But now it's normal for a woman.

I pity myself as a *woman*. Twenty-three years old,† yet they think I'm sixty.

My teeth still intact, my hair shiny black, they think I'm sixty, for I've
shaved my head.

I pity myself so *much*, living without parents.

There's no hope of caring for them, of living near my beloved mother
and father.

Chea becomes ill with a fever. Her body is hot, refusing to cool
down even with the help of wet cloths placed on her forehead and
stomach. Ra returns from a labor camp in time to help me. Ry and
Map are back from Preahneth Preah. Than remains away at a labor
camp. The others' presence gives me comfort. Now I'm not so scared
to hear Chea mumble deliriously in her sleep, which often wakes
me up in the middle of the night.

Chea is lying on the floor, and her breathing is shallow. After
her fever breaks, she's hungry. But all we have is rice gruel with yam

---

* There are rhymes and rhythms in the original. Unfortunately, these cannot be ren-
dered in the translation.

† Age based on the Zodiac signs, which made her older than she really was. According to the conventional calendar, Chea was only twenty-one.

leaves. The smell of it makes her nauseous. Her body becomes in-creasingly thin. In her soft, yearning voice, she wishes for real food: steamed rice with marinated beef. Pork rice soup. Oranges. Or just warm sweetened milk to take away the bad taste in her mouth. I wish I could go back in time and bring her the kinds of food with which *Mak* indulged us when one of us got sick.

Ra and I sneak out to fish at the West River, flanked by a prairie, two miles from Daakpo. Ra carries mosquito netting, and I hug a metal pan. In the dark sky, the stars pulse. A sliver of the moon lights our way. The crickets chirp, the sad song of our lives. We trot on a path that snakes along new people's huts. The cool ground deadens the sound of our footsteps.

When we arrive at the river, the shadow of the moon reflects in the water. It has been a long time since I was last here. It was when I had to bring cow droppings with the children's brigade to the rice paddies across from the river. Then, Avy was still alive, and so was *Mak*.

Ra suggests that we fish along the leaning tree branches on the other side of the river. This will shield us from the eyes of the in-formants, she thinks. I agree, but dread crossing the decrepit makeshift bridge held up by the stark ruin of pylons sticking out of the water. Attached to the top of these pylons, I remember, are a few horizontal slabs. As always, Ra hurries me along, just as she did when we sneaked out to ask *Pok* for food at Zone 3. I crawl on the bridge behind her. Now I'm not worried about the informants, but about falling into the dark sheet of the river.

Our hands and feet become our eyes. After we cross the bridge, we feel our way into the river. The water is cold. We fish along the bank beside the leaning tree branches. Since the water is shallower near the bank, Ra holds one end of the net toward the center of the river and I fish near the bank. The water comes up to my chest.

Slowly we wade in, with both hands stretching the mosquito net open. The pan floats in front of the net, guided by the arching top of it. Our plan is to scoop the net up beneath the branches. The fish are usually there during the day when it's hot. Under her breath, Ra whispers urgently to me to hand over the pan. After pushing the pan to Ra, I reach out to touch the dark shadow in the center of the net, wondering what we've caught.

"Prawns, lots of prawns!" Ra's excited.

The thought of prawns lifts up my spirit. I can't wait until we finish fishing. Hungry, Ra and I eat some. I grab a few from the pan and shove them in my mouth. They struggle, their tails flick against my tongue. Some are the size of my little finger. Others are bigger.

We hurry back to the hut. As Ra and I walk through the village, the night is quiet. It seems as if we are the only two waking souls. When we arrive at the hut, we try to be quiet. As we are about to place the pan of prawns and the net on the alcove, Chea whispers sternly, "I've been worried to death. What took you so long? I can't sleep. I kept thinking the *chhlops* had killed you, that my younger sisters died because of me." Chea talks fast, her voice growing stronger.

"But Chea, there were lots of prawns," Ra whispers excitedly. "Not knowing when we can fish again, I thought we should fish a lot now. Here, feel the prawns. They almost fill the pan!" Ra pushes the pan toward Chea. "Lots of prawns, hah? Athy and I kept eating while we fished. They're sweet."

"Oh my, still alive!" Chea exclaims. Ry echoes her excitement. Their hands are busy shoving the prawns into their mouths.

In this time of hunger and secrecy, we eat in the dark quietly. Map wakes up and joins us. Together we eat the live prawns, reaching for the pan frequently; it's just like eating steamed peanuts in a movie theater. In my mind, I can see *Mak*'s contented, relieved face as she places the prawns in her mouth. I wish she could be with us.

The luxury of being with my family is short-lived. After two more trips to the river to get prawns, *Angka* reclaims me—it puts me back in a children's brigade located a village away from Daakpo. I stay in a wooden house, a single open room built on stilts with a ladderlike stair, along with fifty other children. Our job is to clear thickets and shrubs in the woods, preparation for the cultivation of yam and yucca root. Despite how hard it is to be separated from my family again, I try to find something positive in this change. I find a little comfort in knowing that Thore Meta, who was lenient and understanding when I worked as a scarecrow, is my brigade leader.

It has been two weeks since I last saw Chea. Working from dawn to dusk exhausts me, leaving me little energy to think of her. But when I do, I miss her so much. Knowing how ill she was when I left, I'm afraid, so afraid, that I'll lose her like I lost *Pa*, *Mak*, Avy, and Vin. Despite the prawns, her fever worsened. Her body temperature continued to rise, and she became more and more delirious. Each day she was slipping away. She needs proper medical care and not simply food. I don't know how we can save her. I think of *Pa* and his medicine desk, the magic that can cure Chea. I want to take her back in time so *Pa* can heal her.

Tonight something is nagging at me. Lying on the floor, I'm wide awake as a voice inside me urges me to go see Chea. The yearning grows stronger, and I sob. Something inside is eating me up. I wail.

"Which comrade is crying?" Thore Meta's voice inquires, her footsteps coming up the stairs.

I get up and sit at the corner of the house, looking at Thore Meta's silhouette.

"Why are you crying, Comrade Thy?" she asks, her voice stern.

"My older sister is very sick. I want to see her. I want to see her before she dies." I break down.

"Go. Go see your sister, then come back. If anyone asks, tell them I let you go," Thore Meta says, her silhouette disappearing into the sheet of darkness.

When I near the hut, a fire is burning in the cooking hole. Yet there's nothing cooking, and the yellow-orange tongues lick the dark space. When I get to the door of the hut, I brace myself.

"Don't let *bang* sin—" My arrival interrupts Chea's faint voice.

"Chea, Athy's here!" Ry announces. Her head turns, and so do Ra's and Map's.

Everyone moves over, making room for me to see Chea. A thin, shriveled body lying on the slabs of the floor. Her breathing is shallow. As I move closer to her, her eyes, deep, sunken, shock me.

"Chea, I'm here," I say softly, wanting her to open her eyes. Suddenly they roll slowly behind the eyelids.

"Athy," Chea whispers. "If *bang* has done anything wrong that hurt you, please forgive *bang*, *p'yoon srey*. I'm sorry. Please don't let *bang* sin." Chea chokes, her body convulsing.

"No, Chea. You've—you've done nothing wrong. You've never done wrong. . . ." I sniff, trying to fight back tears and the pain inside my chest.

"*P'yoon*, all of you, forgive *bang* for the things I've done wrong. Please don't let *bang* sin. . . ." Her eyes close again.

"You have not sinned, Chea," Ra says, her voice tender.

Ry sniffs, her hand reaching out to Chea. "You've done nothing wrong."

"When I die, bury me under the tree in front of our hut. I want to look after all of you. *Mak, Pa yurk* [Our mother and father] died, and there is nobody to take care of you. I want to watch over you. Ra, don't forget, *p'yoon*."

The next day in the woods, I think of nothing but Chea. Her shriveled body. Her pleas for forgiveness. As I stare into space, my hands clear tall grass and bushes. I'm oblivious to the other children working beside me.

"Comrades, it's time for lunch," a man says. It is the drawl of the boys' brigade leader.

The children in my brigade hurry past me to get their rations. But today getting food is a tedious task for me. As I sit under some shade, my hands balancing a plate of dark leafy soup, I hear the voice of the boys' brigade leader inquire, "Does that comrade over there ever smile when she gets yam or rice?"

"I've never seen her smile," a woman says. "She always looks sad. Frowns."

Suddenly Chea's vivid words force their way into my mind again, overshadowing what is here and now. She said, "Come to see *bang* again, Athy. Tomorrow, don't forget." *No, I won't forget*, I whisper to myself, as if wanting Chea to hear me.

As soon as my brigade returns to the commune house, Thore Meta grants me permission to see Chea as if she already knew I would ask her for it. She says, "Go, then come back." Her voice is concerned.

I scamper down the stairs. The breeze is warm, humid. The evening becomes twilight so suddenly. When I near the hut, the fire is burning beneath the hut again. This time it's dimmer. Just as the fire loses its intensity, I find Ra, Ry, and Map lying near Chea. It's quiet. I don't hear Chea's voice as I had last night. I feel I've returned too late. And here I am, wanting to hear Chea talk again, to pick up where she left off yesterday.

"Chea, Chea, it's Athy," I whisper. "I've come to see you, Chea. My brigade leader let me come."

There's no answer. Ra and Ry turn to me, then they weep. Their cries are echoed by Map's. Ry says Chea stopped talking this morning. But she asked me to come back to see her. She must have wanted to tell me something more. She can't stop talking now. She can't.

I sob, gasping for air. Suddenly Chea's hand slowly reaches out to me. I move away, wailing uncontrollably. Her hand drops to the floor. Her throat chokes. Her eyelids quiver, then shut again. This is too much to bear. I leave, running back to the commune.

Through the night I weep. Though the pain is in my heart, my sorrow is shared by the other children in the commune. They cry softly. Their snifflings fill the air.

After work the next day, as I hang my washed pants on the wall of the commune house, my body senses something strange. A sudden emotion surges through my body, then my body is jolted and tears stream out of my eyes. *Chea!* I cry, calling her under my breath. *Chea died. Oh God, please help my sister.*

I hear the sounds of footsteps climbing the stair. I wipe my tears, then before me are the children with whom I share the house. Their faces are a mirror of my sorrow. Soon Thore Meta emerges. I walk up to her, then say, "I want to—" I break down before I can say Chea's name.

"Comrade Thy, your sister came and told me that your older sister has died."

The morning comes. The dawning sunlight filters through the cracks of the house. I just fell asleep, but already I'm awakened by the voice of Thore Meta—it's time to work. Before I can think, everyone gets up and hurries down the stairs, disappearing one by one.

After the noon ration Thore Meta tells me to go home. As she talks, I feel the eyes of other children looking at me. Too weak to say anything back to her, I leave.

When I arrive, *Kong* Houng (*Pa's* father) and a man climb down from the hut, their hands steadying a long wrapped object, Chea. Ra, Ry, and Map are behind them, their red eyes swollen. Once Chea is off the hut, *Kong* Houng and the man secure her with a rope, tying her to a carrying pole. *How sad*, I think, to have Chea disposed of this way. I cry uncontrollably.

As *Kong* Houng and the man dig Chea's grave near palm trees, I look at her corpse. In my mind I speak silent words for me and Chea. I say: *Chea, if I survive, I will study medicine. I want to help people be-*

cause I couldn't help you. If I die in this lifetime, I will learn medicine in my next life.

When night falls, Ra reminds me to go back to the commune house. For a moment I'm not sure what she's talking about. I look at her, my brow furrowed. Only when she repeats the words "commune house" do I remember Thore Meta, who has given me permission to stay with my family tonight and tomorrow.

Lying on the floor, I recall Chea's request. I look at Ra and ask, "Why didn't you bury Chea under the tree?"

"I didn't want to bury her there! I'm scared," Ra says annoyingly.

I can't believe that Ra has denied Chea's last wish, and I remind her of Chea's exact words, Chea's plea for her not to forget. Ry jumps in to rescue Ra, reminding me that Ra is afraid of ghosts. True, she is afraid, and I understand that, but Chea is our sister. She won't scare us. She wanted to watch over us, I reason, but I only scare Ra even more.

Ra hisses at me, "I don't want to talk about it. I want to sleep. I haven't slept since she died."

I awake so suddenly, yet I feel refreshed. It was dark before I fell asleep, but now it's bright and I'm amid layers of clouds. Freely, my body ascends through them, soaring to the next layer, where there's a flat surface like a floor made of clouds. *How strange*, I think, but it looks like the floor of a home, a special home filled with men and women dressed in white clothes. One by one, their arms open to welcome someone. A white carpet magically rolls over the floor. The men and women smile. When I look up to the layer of cloud, a woman descends. It's Chea! Her back faces me. Those people encircle her, then somehow dwindle behind the clouds. "Chea, wait! Wait for me."

"Athy, Athy. Wake up! You had a bad dream," Ry says, and comforts me.

13

Mass Marriage and a Forbidden Love

*J*ust as I'm released from my brigade, Than returns home, too late to say good-bye to Chea. Though he seems shocked to hear about her death, he doesn't look sad. Maybe he's numb like Ry was when Avy died, and he can't shed any tears, or maybe boys have a different way of grieving.

At fifteen, Than has been sent away a lot, more than I can remember. For a while I even forgot that I had an older brother. When he showed up, I was surprised to see him, but also relieved that he's alive.

At thirteen, the nascent adult in me realizes that Cambodia is a nation that houses the living dead. Around me there are starving, overworked, and malnourished people. Death is rampant, as if an epidemic has descended on the villages. Yet *Angka* is nonchalant, doing nothing to stop this plague. For the last three years of my life, since the Khmer Rouge's takeover, I've lost half of my family. *Pa,* Vin, Avy, *Mak*, and Chea. Death is like leaves in the autumn, readily falling from a soft touch of the wind. I wonder who in my family will be the next victim.

As the population dwindles and rumors spread that Vietnamese troops are invading Cambodia, *Angka* awakens. In meetings, the Khmer Rouge stress the need for *chamren pracheachun*, the need to increase the population for *Angka*. Young adults need to be married, they emphasize, and stay in the village to fulfill this goal. Those who stay single will be sent to the front line, to the battlefield.

One bright sunny afternoon Ra returns from a mandatory meeting. Standing by the alcove, she waves urgently at Ry, Than, and me as we weed in front of the hut. Her face looks scared and troubled. As I climb up the alcove, I brace for the worst.

Ra says, "I have to get married. . . . I don't want to go to a labor camp—I don't want to die. . . ."

Married? I'm shocked. All of a sudden everyone seems to retreat into his own silent thoughts. Ry, Than, and I are speechless, our eyes looking at Ra. The color in her face momentarily disappears.

"I don't want to go. I don't want to go," she mutters. "I don't want to die. You have to understand me. I almost died many times."

Ra is agitated. Here, she's going to marry someone, yet she's fearful, and our faces are the mirror of her fright. She tells us that she needs to make a quick decision because *Angka* will soon have a wedding sanctioned for those who want to help increase the population.

"If I'm in the village, there's a better chance for me to survive. I can also help take care of you now that Chea has died."

"To whom are you going to be married?" Ry asks.

"A local man," Ra says dismally, her eyes expressing her dire need of our approval.

"It's up to you," Than says indecisively. Ry murmurs a soft yes. I keep my thoughts to myself.

I remember Ra's last brush with death, and I can understand why she would never want to be sent to a labor camp again. It happened when I was working as a scarecrow while Ra remained in the camp near Zone 3. Ra and her coworkers, out of hunger, had ventured into another zone. They got caught and were accused of being spies for the Vietnamese. They were taken to a crowded, filthy prison where they were interrogated and tortured. But they were lucky. Their brigade leader reported them missing and got them freed.

Two days later, Ra is to be wed. She asks me to come with her to the wedding ceremony, which will take place in Poi-kdurg village. I worry, and am nervous for her. I hope the man she will marry is not mean or abusive.

The sun is bright. We cover our heads with our tattered scarves, dressed in grayish-black uniforms with cotton pants shrunk far above our ankles.

As we scurry barefoot on dusty paths, no words are exchanged between Ra and me. I hope we're not late, for we don't have a watch. We stop at an old barn. By the entrance are two cadres, their necks decked out with red-and-white checked scarves. Hanging from their shoulders are rifles. They stand still, solemn.

Ra and I briefly look toward them as men and women in dark uniforms enter the barn. Finally Ra gets up the courage to ask a woman who is about to enter the barn. The woman tells us that this barn is the site for a wedding.

It's dark inside the barn. I grab Ra's shirt, walking behind her like a blind child. On my right I see dark shadows, patches of heads in rows. I'm overwhelmed by the sight of so many people, perhaps a hundred, sitting quietly. *They are all getting married?*

"Listen for your name," a stern male voice says firmly.

They start calling off names. All I see across the barn are shadows rising, then dwindling behind the sheet of blackness. My eyes return to the comfort of the sunlight filtering through the tiny cracks in the walls as if I need it to stay alive.

"Athy, let's go," Ra calls softly, her hand tapping my shoulder.

I rise, wading behind Ra. Nervous all of a sudden.

At the center of the barn, Ra stands, and I am beside her. Across from us are perhaps six men's silhouettes. *Cadres?* My mind is jolted at the sight of them. *Why are so many of them here?*

Their hands clutch their rifles, one hand at the bottom of the butt and the other on the barrel. They position themselves in the shape of a pyramid. Suddenly a silhouetted body, a man, emerges from my left. He stands beside me. Now I'm between him and Ra.

"Athy, move back. Stand behind me," Ra whispers.

"Comrade Ra and Comrade Na," a male voice erupts.

Before I can hear all that is said, the two cadres in the front turn, face each other, and raise their rifles up.

"The rifles will be the judge when comrades betray each other or break *Angka*'s rules."

My mind freezes shut. The next thing I know, Ra and I arrive at her "husband's " house—a wooden house on stilts with a stair and railings. In the front yard, vines of squash spread over trellises. Large green leaves crowd together, mixing with bright yellow flowers. Near the trellises are rows of yams and hot chili plants. Everything looks like it's well kept. These people's way of life is intact, unlike ours.

In the house, the wooden floor is the color of oak. Smooth. Clean, as if there are no grains of dust on it. The slabs are tightly sandwiched together, well built. It's almost as pretty as *Kong* Houng's house, though much smaller. I study the wooden walls. This room is more spacious than our hut, two times larger.

A woman's voice erupts from the nearby room. "If you want to take, go ahead, take all." The voice sounds hoarse. Old. Irritating.

Footsteps vibrate on the floor. Suddenly Ra's husband, Na, appears holding three pillows in his arms. Na is about Ra's height. Compared to some men in the village, he looks fit with a slightly jutting chin. He looks healthy and strong. He's different from what I had imagined—not ugly or scrawny. He's quiet and seemingly gentle. Now I'm more at ease, not as worried for Ra as I was before.

"Here," he says. His voice is soft, his eyes look at Ra. Ra looks at the pillows, then takes them from him.

Pillows with cases? My eyes widen. I haven't seen pillows since we left Year Piar.

Ra places a pillow by the front door. Then another one near it. The third pillow she drops far away from the one in the middle. It's near the room where the old woman's voice came from.

"That's your pillow." Ra points to the middle one. She lies down sideways, facing away from us, on the pillow by the front door.

I stand there, puzzled, and glance at him. He says nothing. I lie down beside Ra, facing her back.

Ra has me spend several nights sleeping beside her. Most of the time she ignores Na. When he talks to her, she scolds him, angry. He's confused, frustrated.

Ra is mostly at our hut with Than, Ry, Map, and me. Sometimes she brings us food from Na's house. Rice and yams. Though it's not much, I'm glad she does this. It is as if she's trying to take a motherly role now that Chea's gone. But I fear that she will put herself in jeopardy because she has an obligation to *Angka* to be with Na. When she's with us and stays overnight, I'm reminded of the man's stern voice in that dark barn.

"The rifles will be the judge when comrades betray each other or break *Angka*'s rules."

When Ra and I return to Na's house, as we climb the stairs we hear the bellow of a drawling voice. "What kind of a wife are you, never staying home with her husband? Coming and going as you please."

Ra and I turn, and there by the trellises is Na's mother, a short, gray-haired woman, glaring. Ra looks hurt. Resuming the climb, she sighs as if shrugging off the blame. Looking at her back as we climb the stairs, I ponder how changed Ra has become. Angry. Resentful. Even though she is this way, Na has never raised his voice to her. His face shows only frustration, not anger.

Having seen Ra's aversion to Na, I don't think *Angka* will succeed in its goal of increasing the population. A marriage sanctioned in such an evil way will never bear fruit. Even though I'm young, I can't imagine that babies will be produced by these men and women who are made up of bones and sheets of skin, whose physical appearance reminds one of the living dead. Months ago, *Angka* could have spared a baby and its parents. Instead, *Angka* destroyed them.

It was nearly noon, perhaps in November 1975, when my brothers, sisters, *Mak*, and I, among hundreds of other people, arrived at a place near Peth Preahneth Preah. It was a large, open ground studded with tall trees shielding us from the blazing heat of the day. Men, women, and children were gathered to witness a judgment on two people. Their crime, *Angka* said, was loving each other without *Angka*'s permission. Thus they were our enemies. "When *Angka* catches enemies," a leader had announced in the previous mandatory meeting, "*Angka* doesn't keep them, *Angka* destroys them."

One by one, the children, are picked from the crowd and told to stand near the two poles so they can see what *Angka* will do. It sounds as if we are about to see a play, an entertainment.

To the right of the poles are three wooden tables aligned from edge to edge to form one long table. Behind them, sitting on chairs, are Khmer Rouge dressed in black uniforms, perhaps in their forties and fifties, whom I have never seen before. Their necks, as usual, are decked out with red-and-white- and white-and-blue-checked scarves, draped over their shirts. They are well guarded by cadres standing with rifles behind and beside them. The cadres' faces are grave. They stand still, straight like the poles. A few Khmer Rouge at the table whisper among themselves. At that moment I see a stash of spades, hoes, and shovels leaning against a pole planted firmly in the ground.

A one-horse buggy pulls up. Two cadres stride toward it. A blindfolded man, hands tied behind his back, is guided off it. Behind him emerges a blindfolded woman who is helped out of the buggy by another cadre. Her hands, too, are tied behind her back. Her stomach bulges out. Immediately she is tied to the pole near the buggy. Her arms first, then her ankles, with a rope about half the size of my wrist.

A woman in the crowd whispers, alarmed, "God, she's pregnant."

The blindfolded man's arms are also bound to the pole. He's calm, standing straight as his ankles are fastened to the bottom of the pole. Dressed in slacklike pants and a flannel shirt with long sleeves rolled up to his elbows, this man appears intelligent. He's tall. His body build suggests he's one of the "city people." Like him, the pregnant woman looks smart, educated from the way she carries herself. She looks composed. Her collarless blouse with short sleeves reveals her smooth arms. Her once-refined face suggests a once-sheltered life.

Each of the Khmer Rouge rises from the table to speak. Their voices are fierce, full of hatred and anger as they denounce the couple. "These comrades have betrayed *Angka*. They've set a bad example. Therefore they need to be eradicated. *Angka* must wipe out this kind of people."

Abruptly another Khmer Rouge at the table gets up, pulls the chair out of his way, strides to the front of the table, picks up a hoe, and tests its weight. Then he puts it back, lifts up a long, silver-colored spade, and tests its weight. He walks up to the blind-folded man.

"Bend your head now!" he commands, then raises the spade in the air.

The man obeys, lowering his head. The Khmer Rouge strikes the nape of his neck again and again. His body slumps, his knees sag. A muffled sound comes out of his mouth. His lover turns her head. The executioner strikes the man's nape again. His body droops. The executioner scurries over to the pregnant woman. "Bend your head NOW!"

Her head bends. The spade strikes her nape. Her body becomes limp. No sound comes out of her mouth. Only two blows and she's dead. The executioner walks away, his hand wiping the perspiration from his forehead. Suddenly a long choking sound is heard. The woman's stomach moves, struggling. Everyone turns. Someone whispers that the baby is dying.

Oh . . . a cry from the crowd. The executioner runs back and strikes the body repeatedly until the struggle in it stops, still like the pole.

This was a brutal lesson. By now I know the Khmer Rouge's dark side. I fear for Ra for avoiding Na, a defiant act against *Angka*. I am afraid her silent rebellion will carry a heavy price.

14

When Broken Glass Sinks

$\mathcal{I}$t is late 1978, time for the rice harvest and of hope for a better ration. It is also time for *Angka* to reclaim me, putting me back in the children's brigade. Luckily, I am back with brigade leader Thore Meta. At dawn she leads us to the rice field, then brings us back before sunset.

On a cool, clear morning, amid the rolling plains of golden rice flanked by a water reservoir, I harvest rice, stooping down among other children. One hand gathers the stalks and the other cuts them free with the sickle. Suddenly a voice whispers, "Look, two *chhlops* are coming."

I see two informants pad swiftly toward Thore Meta, who is reaping ahead of us. One informant approaches her, then whispers in her ear. She recoils, alarmed. The other informant mouths something. Thore Meta steals glances at us, then toward the distant villages. She talks to a group leader, then quickly scurries away with the informants, wading through the field. They climb into a waiting canoelike boat and begin rowing. I watch her until the boat dwindles to a speck. I wonder if what Chea predicted is happening:

that broken glass is sinking. There have been rumors of the invasion by the Vietnamese into Cambodia.

"Go back to work," the group leader commands softly, her hands waving at us to resume our duty.

"Look, look, three people are coming!" a girl shouts, pointing the sickle at the people crossing the reservoir.

The harvesting stops. Everyone scurries toward the women who have just crossed the reservoir.

"They all run away, they all run away. . . ." one woman mutters, out of breath. The other two, panting, exchange smiles.

"*Mae, mae* [Mom]." A girl runs into a woman's arms.

They embrace, jumping, making dull, muffled sounds in the paddy. For the first time in a long time, I see happiness again. All of us smile at the thought of no more Khmer Rouge. My heart dances in my chest, my mind sings the word "freedom" repeatedly. Years ago, I knew only its pronunciation, but now, at thirteen, I truly understand what it means to have freedom, and to have it taken away from me.

The heavy weight on my soul, my body, suddenly lifts. The scenery around me changes. The golden fields, the clouds, the blue skies are beautiful.

We run to our remaining families, racing each other across the reservoir. We giggle as we splash water at each other. The sound of laughter is soothing; I feel like a child again. The little girl in me returns, and my curiosity soars: *Are they really gone?* I want to know.

From Poik'durng village to Daakpo I run, checking different places to see if there are still signs of the Khmer Rouge. But every place looks abandoned: the children's shelters, the commune houses, and the rice-processing hut in Daakpo. There, empty woven baskets are scattered on the ground. The wooden door on the rice storage building is broken, yanked loose. All the processed rice is gone.

The villages are as quiet as when we were brought here three years ago. Then, there were nine of us. But now there are only five: Ra, twenty; Ry, seventeen; Than, fifteen; me, thirteen; and Map, four. The other four—*Mak*, Chea, Avy, and Vin—are all dead. Like *Pa*. Gone. Forever.

15
A Letter

$\mathcal{T}$he sun shines, and the sky is bright blue. The Khmer Rouge are gone. On a dusty road flows a river of families. People are leaving behind the place that enchained them. Joining them is my family. We are the leftovers the "ghost" doesn't want, *Mak* used to say. On this day, every child, woman, and man looks more relaxed. On their sallow, sunken faces, beaten by the sun, I see hope. Their eyes glow. A few smiles emerge from behind the tired faces. I steal glances at those who are smiling. I wonder if they are experiencing the enormous sense of freedom I feel, as well as the indescribable emotion that bubbles inside me. It's a newly discovered exhilaration.

A stocky woman grins, even while carrying a stick arching from a heavy load. Her bare feet move like the wind, as if propelled by what she's feeling inside. Like many of us, her daughters transport their pots, pans, and food on their heads, and on their shoulders using carrying sticks. When we left Phnom Penh four years ago, the picture was very different. Then, there were cars, motorcycles, and bikes, on which we secured our clothes and foodstuffs, and on which the children could ride. But now everyone walks. Virtually everyone is barefoot, walking on calused, cracked soles.

"Where are you all going?" the stocky woman asks, smiling at me.

"I don't know, *ming* [aunt]," I answer, returning her smile, then I look at Ra for the answer. Instead, I hear my echo.

"I don't know, *ming*," Ra says, flashing an uncertain smile at the woman. "We are following everybody."

"So are we following others. Go wherever there's food." She beams.

In the late afternoon we stop at a village to rest and eat, then replenish our supply. In the fields by the road, we glean rice, whatever was left by harvesters. We join others who are already there, their bags and buckets half or nearly full. And here we are just beginning.

As we work through the field, we spot our aunts stooping and rising as their hands gather leftover heads of rice. They are *Pa*'s young sisters, Aunt Chin and Aunt Leng. Even though we aren't working under the Khmer Rouge, my aunts can't seem to take time to talk. They have to keep busy. Their sunken faces demand the action of their hands. They seem like strangers to me. It takes me a while to realize that they are my relatives. The effects of the Khmer Rouge's abolition of family intimacy slowly seep away from my mind, and a sense of family connection gradually takes their place.

Aunt Chin's brows are furrowed. She motions her head to show us that her children are in the next field. Then she and Aunt Leng ask us where we'll be going after this village. Ra says she doesn't know. Go to Phnom Penh with us, they urge us. And Ra agrees, looking relieved.

But before we have a chance to finish processing the rice we've gleaned, Aunt Leng decides that she, Aunt Chin's family, Aunt Cheng, *Kong* Houng, and Uncle Surg's only surviving son should go ahead and leave first. Her plan is for us to follow them when we're done. Ra asks them to wait as we quicken our rice processing, but Aunt Leng only says they will walk slowly so we can catch up with them on the road. Ra doesn't say anything, her face reddened as she vigorously sifts the rice.

When we set out on the road, we see no trace of our aunts, cousins, or *Kong* Houng. I wish we would somehow run into *Mak*'s remaining sisters and brothers, but there is no trace of them either. It seems that our extended families shot out of their huts as soon as the Khmer Rouge vanished. Again, we are on our own, just the five of us without a destination. We follow others, going wherever we can find food. As the night creeps in, we decide to rest in a village called Korkpongro, taking up residence in the foyer of an abandoned wooden house, as do other traveling families.

Later in the night we sleep side by side. Quickly, I drift into slumber as if someone had cast a spell on me, only to be awakened by the distant voice of gunfire, familiar sounds we all know too well. The dull, hollow explosions of artillery combine with the raucous noise of rifles.

A man's voice bellows in the quiet night. "What was that?"

I spring up, as do my brothers and sisters.

"What happened, what happened?" Ra mutters, alarmed.

People nearby wake. A woman asks the question to which we all wish we know the answer. Who is fighting? The Khmer Rouge? Tonight they won't be surprised, the men say, if the gunfire belongs to them. Only then do I realize we are far from safe.

The next morning everyone in my family resumes our rice gleaning, including four-year-old Map, who helps his elder siblings search for clusters of rice in the hot sun. Scavenging through the already harvested fields, I think of nothing but the golden cluster. When night comes, the gunfire roars in the distance again. It growls louder than the night before, as if the fighting is only a village away. For the next three days it continues, making us feel trapped. Fearful for

our lives, we confide in other families who stay near us. To our relief, they tell us about a prayer gathering and urge us to go.

On a decklike stage covered by a wooden roof, candlelight illu-
minates the wooden floor and a picture of Buddha in the forest.
Sitting behind the candles are old men and women with shaved
heads. These elders could be former nuns or priests. In awe, I'm
surprised and comforted to see candles after all these years. Already
many men, women, and children surround this place, their legs
folded neatly on the sandy ground. Our elders chant prayers to Buddha. Those who know the prayers join in, chanting traditional words
in Pali. The palms of their hands are pressed together and raised to
their chins. It is a humble spiritual gathering that fits this fearful
night.

Even with the nightly prayers, our souls cannot be comforted.
The sound of war is powerful. We have to leave Korkpongro. Many
families move on, even though there's still rice to glean. Having col-
lected some food, we decide our safety takes precedence.

We arrive at the next village, Chhnoel, before nightfall. Here,
there are people camping along the shoulder of the road, by the
huts and cottages, and beneath the coconut, mango, and palm trees.
Their shelters are in place, made of blankets, sarongs, and tarps.
Everyone looks weary, especially Map. I know he is hungry, but he
doesn't cry for food as we search for a place to camp in a dry rice
paddy.

The next day, warned by the neighboring women that rice is hard
to find, requiring a lot of walking, we decide to have Map stay in
the tent or play outside with the other children. As we leave with
the women, Map cries, his eyes following us. After a few days have
gone by, Map is better at coping with our daylong absences, and
plays with other children.

Living near our tent is *bang* Meng's remaining family. She and Ra
worked together in the same labor camps. She, her aunt, young sis-

ters, and a baby brother also used to live in Daakpo. She is about twenty, Ra's age, short and thin with straight black hair down to her chin. Her eyes and light complexion suggest she's part Chinese. By her composure, she appears intelligent. She reminds me of Chea. In only a few days, our families have become close. We have both lost parents and are learning to depend on ourselves.

Rice is becoming scarce. It's been a week since we arrived here. Today we barely glean enough for a day's meal. When we get back, news awaits us—a letter from the Khmer Rouge telling us to leave Chhnoel.

A couple were given the letter and told to warn everyone. In it, the woman says, they warn us to leave this village. If they should find us here, no one will be spared. They will kill everyone, including a baby in a hammock.

"Oh, I don't think they'll come," a man says, his hand brushing aside the fear. "They probably think the Vietnamese soldiers are here and are afraid to come. They just want to threaten us. Don't worry."

The following day we go to glean rice again, leaving Map at the tent. Since rice is hard to find, Ra and I go north with a group of women while Ry and Than head south with others.

Ra and I work quickly, trying to get as much as possible of the little rice left. In the distance my ears pick up faint dull, hollow sounds. I pause.

"Ra, the sounds of gunfire. Can you hear it?" I shout.

"Yes, *ming*, the sounds of gunfire! Coming from there," Ra cries, pointing. She signals to the women near us to come.

"Oh, it's far away," a woman says, brushing aside our anxiety. "I'm staying a bit longer." She returns to her stack.

My heart hammers. I want to leave. The gunfire becomes louder. I turn to Ra for a decision, but she looks at the other women.

"I'm staying a bit longer, too," one woman decides, then the rest agree, including my own sister.

Another hollow boom sounds closer than before. "Ra, let's go!" I scream at her. "Can't you hear it? It's getting louder and louder!"

"Everyone is still—" Before Ra finishes, the woman next to us takes off.

She cries, "I'm going, I'm not staying, my children—"

Ra grabs the rice bag and the basket, and off she runs. Again, I'm behind her, along with the other women.

The resonant booms approach closer and closer to Chhnoel. When one explodes nearby, all of us cry. In my mind I scold the women, and I'm angry at Ra for not listening to me.

Across the rice paddies near Chhnoel, children, women, and men are running for their lives, like red ants whose hole has been destroyed. Mothers with babies, one arm pinning them against their bodies while the other holds on to the bundles of belongings riding on their heads. Some yank their children's hands. Others carry foodstuffs on sticks. Their children trot behind, shuffled in the crowd. At that instant I'm reminded of Map and yell to Ra.

Amid the flow of humans, she flashes a distressed glance at me. When we get to our tent, Map is not there. Than and Ry are not there either. Most of the tents are disassembled, vanished. Ra shouts at me to find him while she packs.

The crowd flows around me as I peer at every kid I see. They are all crying, just like me. Suddenly I spot a boy screaming, looking in the direction from which Ra and I came. On a mounted path between rice paddies, he is stomping hysterically with his hands flying in the air. I run, my hands parting people away from me as my eyes try to keep track of him. When I get closer, I recognize his clothes. It is Map!

"Map, Map. I'm here, over here." I raise my hand, waving.

He runs to me, his hand wiping away his tears. I grip his other hand. He glares at me. "I waited a long time," he barks. "Why didn't you come sooner?" He shoots another angry look at me, his long eyelashes rise, then fall.

I'm so relieved and thankful to find Map and to see his furious little face scolding me that for a moment I'm oblivious to the gunfire.

Ra is distraught. She shouts for me to carry a load, what looks like bags of rice, pots, and pans, all tied up to be carried on a stick. She lifts her load onto her shoulder, then drops it back down. She picks up a mat, all rolled up and almost twice Map's height, and hands it to him. Now we run, heading toward a small makeshift bridge built over a ditch. The crowd backs up. A hollow boom thunders. Everyone cries hysterically. Ra steps down into the ditch and then up on the other side. I follow. Map is behind, struggling. The weight of the mat slows him down, pulling him backward. Ra is up ahead, a dwindling figure in the crowd. I'm waiting for Map. "Come on, hurry," I mutter to myself, frightened for Map and myself.

When an artillery explodes, followed by the raucous pop of rifles, everyone moves forward. I run across one dry cracked paddy to the next, climbing the mounted path. "Map, hurry, hurry," I shout, wanting Map to step up his pace. When I turn to look for him, he is far behind, a paddy away, standing still. He is crying, his hands holding the mat that is taller than he is. I wave for him to come. He shakes his head. I drop my load and run to him, he drops the mat and walks toward Chhnoel. I wail, screaming, "No, don't go back—"

Map vanishes among people and trees. Standing still, I wait for him to return, but I see only other children and their families. I place my load on my shoulder and run forward.

"RA, RA, STOP!" I yell. She turns. I pause, crying.

"Where is Map?" she asks, her eyes alarmed.

"Run only for your own sake," I bawl. "You didn't help me look after Map. Now he's gone, running backward."

"Backward where?"

"Toward the Khmer Rouge!" I yell, then point to the trees and fleeing people.

Ra puts down her load, runs, then stands by a mounted path. "*Ming, poo* [uncle], have you seen my brother?" Ra asks, her hands reaching out to the men and women, but no one looks at her.

"Hey, Ra, your brother is coming!" a woman shouts at Ra.

Ra's eyes search, then her legs leap over the path.

The woman trots by me with two girls. I ask her, "*Ming*, is my brother coming?"

The woman nods. Now I remember who she is—her tent was close to ours in Chhnoel.

Suddenly Ra and Map appear without the mat. Ra pulls Map up the path. When Map nears us, I scold him. "Crazy kid, running backward! Don't you know you'll get shot!"

"The mat's too heavy, my legs hurt," Map snaps. "You didn't wait for me. You let me run by myself!"

Together we trot, catching up with the woman and her daughters. Then we are ahead of them again. When we're near Kandal village, about two miles from Chhnoel, the woman calls out to Ra.

"Hey, *neag*, let's rest a little," she begs, out of breath.

We stop near a ditch a few steps ahead.

"We'll rest with you, *ming*," Ra says, panting.

Frustrated, the woman shouts at her daughters, "Throw something away. It's too heavy, hurry, hurry."

Ra looks at her load, pulls out a pot, a cutting block, and a bag of salt, then she cries. "Thy, I can't throw these away. We need—"

Boom! An artillery shell lands nearby. We jump into the ditch, then Ra sticks her head out. "*Ming*, over here!"

When the firing subsides, we climb out of the ditch. To avoid any attack by the Khmer Rouge from the Kandal village, we move to a grove of trees away from it. Here, resting on the ground among the trees, we are by ourselves. Two families. The woman, her daughters, Ra, Map, and me. Now that I've caught my breath, I can feel my body aching. My mind slips, giving in to exhaustion. My head nods, I'm dozing off. I try to open my eyes, and try to listen to Ra and the woman as they talk about their fears.

Soon, though, someone emerges from the trees. We stand up, ready to run.

"It's Meng . . . only Ameng." Ra runs to her, and I follow.

"Ara, Ara—my siblings, oh, my aunt, my aunt," *bang* Meng stammers incoherently. "Ara, they're all dead. Dead. The Khmer Rouge killed my family."

Bang Meng pants. Her body trembles, wobbling. Her hands grip the carrying stick that balances two big trunks on her shoulder. Ra grabs the carrying stick from her.

Free from the load, *bang* Meng cries in a long, shrieking voice and stammers about the death of her family. Suddenly her legs sag, then she pulls herself back up. At that second a wave of flies recoils, bouncing off her blood-soaked blouse, then is drawn back to her.

When she calms down, she tells us what happened, tears spilling out of her eyes. "We were tired and afraid of getting hit by bullets and bombs, so we stopped. We hid in a paddy with four other families behind this path. Suddenly a man wearing black, a Khmer Rouge, approached. He walked up to a boy, a sick, swollen boy, hiding near the road. Oh, Ara, *ming*, it's awful. . . ." *Bang* Meng breaks down, shaking.

"He begged, raised his hands to his forehead. He said, '*Poo*, don't kill me, please don't kill me—'

"That Khmer Rouge said to the boy, 'I won't kill you,' but as he said that, he pulled a pistol and shot the boy in the head, right in the head. When I saw that, I knew we were next," *bang* Meng continues. "As he strode toward us, my brother, sisters, aunt, the girls from this family, everyone, and this old grandma, all *sampea-*

*hed** him. They implored him, saying, '*Poo, khmuy,*† chow,‡ don't kill me, don't kill us.' When he was close, I shut my eyes. I covered my face with a scarf and hat. I lay down on the ground near the feet of my aunt, sisters, and brother. Suddenly I heard shots, loud shots. Oh God, everyone fell on me. Warm blood seeped onto me, my clothes. Then I felt a foot on my chest, then I thought he'd shot me. . . ."

Later, *bang* Meng heard footsteps coming. She feared that the same Khmer Rouge had returned to kill her. As she cried, trembling in horror, the footsteps stopped near her. Then the hat covering her head blew away. She shivered, wailing, her hands over her face. "Don't be afraid of me," a man's voice said. "I'm not going to harm you. I'm a good soldier, a *PARA*¶ soldier."

He said that when he noticed *bang* Meng's body was still breathing, he felt compelled to save her. Having explained himself, he advised *bang* Meng to leave Chhnoel, and so here she is with us, alone without her family.

Having heard *bang* Meng's story, we all decide to move farther away from Chhnoel and Kandal. We join a group of people in an area with hay-colored grass. A few older men and women talk, the rest stare at the grass or into space. We camp there overnight.

The next morning *bang* Meng ventures to Chhnoel with other people who lost their families. Tears well in her eyes as she describes the stench and the heap of corpses removed to a field to be burned. "Ara, my baby brother is gone," she sobs. "He's pale, bloodless. Lifeless. . . ." She asks Ra to go with her to see her family's corpses before

---

* A gesture of respect involving pressing the palms of the hands together, then raising them to the chest or chin.
† Nephew or niece.
‡ Grandchild.
¶ The Khmer People's National Liberation Front was an anti-Communist resistance group that fought against the Khmer Rouge. It was led by Son Sann, a distinguished prime minister from the Prince Sihanouk era.

they are burned. In this time of loss, Ra can't refuse a friend. Struggling to decide what is the right thing to do, Ra takes Map and me along for fear of separation if the Khmer Rouge should attack again.

When we arrive at Chhnoel, the presence of the Khmer Rouge still lingers. Clothes in disarray, tarps, blankets, pots, and pants are strewn near coconut and palm trees. I dread coming back here. As we approach an alley behind a group of houses, a warm breeze carries a terrible odor. Before I can ask about it, we are looking at a black ashen ground, half the size of a rice paddy.

"Oh no, they've already burned my relatives," *bang* Meng cries, shocked, her hand covering her mouth.

She hurries over to the charred body parts. Ra scurries after her. Holding Map's hand, I'm rooted to the ground. I cringe as *bang* Meng and Ra survey the dark ashes and partially burned remnants. The stench repulses me, but the ghostly silence moves me to take Map over to Ra and *bang* Meng. Now we too are staring at the charred remains.

"Ara, this was where my siblings and aunt were. Look." *Bang* Meng walks up to a blackened piece of a small chest. "Maybe it's a part of my young brother. It's small."

Glancing at the scorched chest with its rib cage still intact, I pull Map away. My eyes take refuge in the trees in a faraway field. I shield Map's face with my hand, my stomach churning.

As we're leaving, walking back along the main road of Chhnoel, *bang* Meng tells us stories she heard on her first day upon returning here. Pointing to a group of palm trees, she says that the *PARA* soldiers found the body of a murdered woman sprawled beside that of her newborn with its legs torn apart. She says babies were killed by the sharp sawing edges of a palm branch. A woman with edema was shot in the head in a house. I wish *bang* Meng had not told us these stories. I pray that Ry and Than didn't return here to look for us. I pray they are still alive somewhere.

16
The Exodus

Our arrival in Sala Krao village is met by a commotion. We, along with fifteen families who seek safe haven, merge with a procession of men and women who glare angrily at three men with their hands tied behind their backs. Escorting them are two men in civilian clothes and two Vietnamese soldiers in dark lemon-green uniforms and helmets. The soldiers are among the few we've seen so far, though we've been told more are stationed on the far right off the road.

"They're Khmer Rouge," a man in the crowd exclaims. "They dressed up like civilians so they can infiltrate this village."

My mind shuts off, refusing to take in any more news. The man's voice drones on. The sharp throbbing pain of a badly decaying, infected wisdom tooth returns. The swelling of the gum flares up at a bad time. The pain saps the little energy I have left to get to Sala Krao. Luckily, on the road among displaced families, we spot Than, Ry, and Phally, Aunt Leng's former servant who worked for her back in Phnom Penh. When the Khmer Rouge attacked Chhnoel, they managed to run farther south, then followed other families until we were reunited. Than and Ry help me carry our foodstuffs, a heavy load that was slowing me down. Even now, carrying nothing, I have a difficult time walking.

"Athy, lie down here." Ry taps me on my shoulder, her hand points to a cloth spread on the ground near the exposed roots of a tree.

My body savors the rest, welcoming the awaiting cloth.

The sound of a hollow boom. A loud, bright fire bursts. The ground shakes. I feel hot. "*Mak*, help me—" I hear myself scream in a long-drawn-out plea.

"Get in the water, get in the water. Hurry."

"*Mak*, help me. . . ." At that moment I think I'm dead, but I feel my body being dragged along and it's getting wet. The muddy water seeps into my mouth and ears. I struggle, trying to get up. A voice commands, "Don't stand up, Athy!" I feel a tug on my shoulder. I open my eyes and Ry is beside me. *We're in the pond!* I don't understand. . . .

Suddenly a baby cries, and only then do I realize that we're being attacked by the Khmer Rouge again. It's night, a moonlit night. Shadows of heads scatter above the water. The baby's older sister, perhaps three, cries as well. Her mother whispers, "Don't cry. If the Khmer Rouge hear you, they'll kill us. Stop." The little girl stifles her tears, gazing at her mother. Her father moves slowly in the water to be near her.

Another weapon is fired from a distance, sending a loud noise into the night. By now I know what kind of a weapon this is—a bazooka with a cylindrical rocket. In seconds it strikes a branch on the very tree under which we had settled, setting the leaves briefly on fire. Suddenly a loud boom erupts from the Vietnamese soldiers' side, sending us screaming for cover. "About time. I thought they were all dead!" a man says in relief.

The firing from the Khmer Rouge stops. Then it starts up again, but stops after two consecutive firings from the Vietnamese's artillery. After the third one, the night becomes quiet. I'm relieved, thankful that the Vietnamese soldiers are here tonight to oppose the Khmer Rouge.

In the morning I'm awakened by voices. A short, thin Vietnamese soldier in a dark lemon-green uniform and helmet is striding along the road with a briefcaselike bag in his hand. With him are two girls, perhaps ages eight and ten. They come over and squat among us. The girls stand beside him; the younger one surveys our group. As the soldier speaks in Vietnamese, the older girl looks at him, listening. Then she translates for us. "He wants to take a look at everyone to see if you are hurt."

The soldier removes tiny fragments of shrapnel embedded in our backs, faces, and arms. Tonight a silver-haired man whom Than has befriended offers to let us stay under his wooden house as long as we want. It's safer to be here, he says. We address him respectfully as *om*, great-uncle. If the Khmer Rouge attack again, the trees and the road will shield us from a direct hit. The house is built on stilts with a spacious balcony all around. In the front there are stairs made of cement and wooden steps and a platform. We are relieved to have this place to stay in.

Two soldiers come to visit us the next evening. These soldiers could be brothers; they are the same height, about five feet five, with thick black hair and tan, refined skin. They look healthy, strong, and cute, especially when they smile. Their eyes briefly study Ra when she gets up to sit in the cooking area. At twenty, hardship hasn't robbed Ra of her beauty. Her slender figure, light complexion, and chin-length hair make her attractive, prettier than any woman I've seen. Of all of us, she's the healthiest one.

One of the soldiers picks up a metal container and asks me in broken Cambodian, "What is this called?"

I slowly tell him the one-syllable word for container. He tries to say it, but he doesn't say it right. Grinning, he repeats the word. I shake my head. He tries it again. Still, he gets it wrong. When I say the word faster, I hear the wrong echo coming back at me. It's like saying the word "cow" and hearing the word "cook" echoed back.

Tranh is his name. He speaks less Cambodian than the other one, Minh, who constantly steals glances at Ra. After learning a little Cambodian, Minh and Tranh tell us about Vietnam, about their lives there. About dancing. About music. Suddenly Tranh dashes away, disappearing on the road.

He'll be back, Minh tells us, smiling.

Soon Tranh appears with another soldier, grinning sheepishly. Minh gets up from his squatting position, hands the metal bucket to the soldier, then says something to him in Vietnamese. Standing face-to-face, less than a feet apart, Minh and Tranh beam, then nod at the soldier.

On cue, the soldier begins to drum on the sides of the bucket, creating a soft, chiming upbeat sound. His mouth moves, followed by pretty lyrics in Vietnamese. Before I know it, Minh's and Tranh's bodies sway gracefully, arching forward and backward like two bamboo rods swaying in unison to the rhythm of the wind. Their hands dance, swinging in circular motions. They smile, laughing. I'm amused.

An endless line of people marches on the road snaking in front of *om*'s house. Standing on the shoulders of the road, we watch men, women, and elderly people walking barefoot. Some clutch babies in their arms. Most transport bundles of pots and pans, and personal belongings on carrying sticks or their heads. A few own old bikes on which they transport blankets and foodstuffs. Young children are tugged along, their hands gripped either by their mothers or older siblings.

Om asks a thin man about his destination. "We don't want to live in Cambodia anymore," he says decisively. "Life here is too difficult. We don't know where we're going, we just want to leave this country."

From morning to afternoon for the next three days, Sala Krao is the gateway for an exodus. Their destination, we later find out, is a camp on the border between Cambodia and Thailand.

Ry, Phally, and I befriend a local woman named Art. We call her Aunt Art, a slender and friendly woman with beautiful dark eyes, perhaps in her early thirties. She has a baby girl. Inside her small wooden home, located half a mile from *om*'s, there are fishing baskets, pots, pans, sifting baskets, and waffle irons hanging on nails embedded in the walls. *Waffle irons!*

Upon returning to *om*'s house, I check his millstone, which is used for grinding soaked rice into batter, among other things. Later in the evening I discuss with Ra, Ry, and Than my idea of making waffles to trade in the village for processed rice. The main customers would be the travelers who pass by Sala Krao, I tell them. People travel, they get hungry, and they buy food. My goal is to live on the rice profit so we don't have to farm. Ra says it's embarrassing to sell when none of the local people sell anything. Than doesn't think people will buy my waffles, and thinks I'll be wasting the rice I invest in the waffle making.

Unlike Ra and Than, Ry thinks I should try. With support from her, I soak about four pounds of rice to make batter for tomorrow. At dawn I get up, wash the soaked rice and the millstone, then grind the rice into batter. After an hour I'm done, then I mix the batter with a dark golden palm sugar, a pinch of salt, and water. With eggs and coconut milk, I think, the waffles would have been as delicious as the ones we had back in Phnom Penh, but as it is, they're still good.

On the shoulder of the road, beneath the shade of tall trees, I pick a spot, an intersection where many people cross. Setting a pot of the batter down on the ground, I dig a hole, then set three stones on its edge to support the iron.

Ry brings me firewood, Aunt Art's waffle iron, a platter, a fork, and a piece of ember from *om*'s house to start the fire. Map brings me an empty bucket and an empty twelve-ounce milk can. Before long I begin making waffles.

Ry, Map, and I myself are my first customers. We eat the first two waffles since they were stuck to the iron, all crumbled up. I shove a piece in my mouth. Map eagerly picks up pieces and eats as soon as I give him the go-ahead. Ry smacks her lips, thinking.

"Athy, it's not that sweet." She gazes at me, still thinking gravely.

"I know," I say, grinning, glad to finally hear her comment. I didn't want to use a lot of sugar in case we didn't trade and ended up eating our own product.

Ry smiles and says, "This kid," shaking her head. "I'll go back and get some more sugar."

"That's why I asked you to help," I say, laughing.

Gradually, children from Sala Krao come to watch us. They stand gazing hungrily as I peel one waffle after another.

Ry tells them, "*A-oon*, go get rice. Tell your moms that you want to eat waffles." She smiles sheepishly and waves at them to go. She laughs for having said it.

"One can of rice," I add, picking up the tin can from the empty bucket and showing it to them, "and you'll get two of these." I point to the waffles on the platter. Ry nudges me, giggling. Map smiles quizzically.

The batter is gone faster than I'd ever imagined. Carrying a good load of rice in the bucket, our investment and profit, I joke with Ry about our day's work. Ry teases me, repeating some of our customers' comments. I assume the roles of both the customers and myself, speaking as if I'm in a play. Map grins, gazing up at us, his silly sisters, as we giggle like schoolgirls again.

With our little waffle stand comes a makeshift market. On the shoulders of the road lined by shade trees, people from Sala Krao and other villages join in the trading. They bring papayas, coconuts, squashes, live fish, and woven baskets, anything usable, to trade for processed rice. Several other people set up competing waffle stands, so we turn to making and selling noodles.

The market expands further, spilling out from the shoulders of the road into a large wooden-covered building. In two months, with the influx of travelers, suddenly food, everything, is also traded for small pieces of twenty-four-karat gold cut from necklace chains, bracelets, and ring bands, a lighter currency than processed rice.

I'm surprised to see that people still have fine jewelry. Looking back, I remember the time when the leader from Daakpo told us to give up our jewelry to *Angka*. He said it was bad for us to possess material connected with the "American imperialists," and now it helps people to buy meals.

As with the waffles, other people begin to make noodles, competing with us for customers. Soon we feel the effects of this competition and can barely sell our food.

Ra, Than, Ry, and I discuss our future survival, a way to earn our living. After talking to some travelers from Kompong Cham, Ra, Than, and Phally decide to go with them to the border to buy goods from the Thai merchants to bring back and sell in Sala Krao.

One day, after they've left, Ry and I decide to take a break, especially since we haven't sold many noodles in the previous days. Having the burden of trading off my shoulders, I play jump rope under the trees in front of *om*'s house.

Later a girl my age, thirteen, comes and asks if she can play. Gladly, I say of course. We play rock-paper-scissors. I win, so I get to jump first. As I jump, I can't stop smiling. It feels as if I'm at recess after a long morning in class. When it's time for the other girl to jump, I'm excited just to watch her.

The girl's mother calls her away. While I continue to jump rope by myself, she comes back. Excitedly, she says that she and her mom are going to buy food near Thailand and bring it back here. She asks if I want to go. I wonder how long it will take to get to the market near Thailand.

Her mom says, "Oh, it won't take that long, and before you know it, you'll be back here. A kid like you can carry four boxes of instant noodles and you will make a lot of profit. Do you want to go? I'm taking Srey with me."

"Yes," I say excitedly. I imagine myself carrying four boxes of noodles on my back. Already my mind travels to this market. In a split second I'm back in Sala Krao. *Easy*, I imagine, just like the woman said.

I tell Ry that I'll be back in two days. Sensing my excitement, Ry smiles as she splits half of the gold we've earned from selling food. In a hurry, I leave with Srey and her mom, and I don't get to tell Map where I'm going.

Our journey is much longer than Srey's mother told me it would be. We walk through villages and fields. Thirst and fatigue overwhelm me. Srey's mother says we must keep on walking and warns me to hide my gold somewhere on my clothes where it won't be easy to find in case we meet with robbers.

We come to a large lake filled with tall, grasslike plants called kak that grow three to four feet above the blackish water. I don't want to go in. Having come this far, Srey's mother warns me that she's not going to turn back. If I go back by myself, she says, I'll get lost. If I go ahead, I can buy the noodles and make a profit.

Srey and her mom are waiting impatiently by the lake. Trying to weigh my options, I watch a group of adults crossing the lake. Among them I spot Phally, heading toward me. Looking distressed and shocked to see me, she places her hand on my shoulder. She tells me how she and the group she was with were attacked and robbed. When the gunfire erupted, everybody ran, and she doesn't know where Ra and Than are.

I know going ahead to the border is dangerous. But I decide against going back with Phally. At least Srey's mother has gone on this journey before. Phally doesn't know the way, since this is her first time. I say a few words to Phally to relay to Ry and Map, and then follow Srey and her mother into the cold lake, which is now as dark as the night.

We continue on the path, escorted by *PARA* soldiers for a brief while, and then take refuge for the night at the edge of a forest. The next day we come to a clearing where several other people are scampering. Srey's mom warns us that we must run across it quickly. "This is where robbers can see us, and people get shot at. If you hear gunfire and shouting, don't stop. If you fall, get up and run. When I say 'go,' start running. You hear?"

When she gives the signal, we run, trotting on the sharp edges of cracked ground. I pray to *Pa, Mak,* and my ancestors to protect me. We all make it safely across. Later, we have another obstacle in our way—land mines. We are told to follow in the footsteps of the person in front of us as we cross a grassy field. With luck and help from a higher power, and thanks to everyone's calmness and meticulousness, we make it across the field safely.

Srey's mom surveys our new surroundings, then excitedly says, "We're almost there, almost to the New Camp."

17

The New Camp

*I*t is May 1979. We arrive at the outskirts of the New Camp late in the afternoon. The sunlight is less intense, giving us a break from the heat. Before us, in the midst of a forest, stand doorless golden-grassed shacks built closely together like mushrooms sprouting from beneath the trees.

Srey's mom takes me to the shelter of *om*'s daughter, who has come to stay in the camp with her husband. When we arrive at the camouflage-colored tent, Srey's mom calls out, her hand shaking the cloth wall. In a few minutes *om*'s daughter, whom I call *bang*, crawls out of the tent. She's tall and slender with curly black hair falling to her chin. Her complexion is as light as mine.

"Have you seen her sister and brother around? They left Sala Krao two days ago," Srey's mom says to her.

"No, my husband and I haven't seen them," *bang* says, knitting her forehead. "We've been trading with the Thai and haven't seen them there either."

Srey's mom asks if I may stay with them until I find Than and Ra. The couple agrees and assures Srey's mom that I'm welcome.

Exhausted, I let them discuss matters among themselves. I squat down as their voices drone on. The next thing I know, *bang* is guiding me through her tent to a space she's made for me to sleep, separated from her and her husband's area.

Bang asks if I want some food to eat. I shake my head, then lie down on the welcoming blanket spread on the earthen floor.

A voice hums. Something gently pops. I spring up, sitting in a dark space filled with heat. When I fumble my way out of the space through a wall of layered of blankets, I come to the area where *bang* and her husband sleep—but they've gone.

Near the half-open cloth entrance to the tent, the sunlight filters in, shining on a covered plate of steamed rice with a piece of fresh broiled fish near a small bowl of golden sweet-and-sour sauce with sliced white onion, minced garlic, fresh shredded red chili, and ground peanuts. My mouth waters. I breathe the air greedily.

Having had no food except water for nearly two days, I swallow down everything in a flash. The rice, fish, and sauce are so delicious. The tasty sauce, which I'm pleasantly surprised to have, takes me back to my homes in Phnom Penh and Takeo. I wish I were eating this kind of food with my parents and siblings again. But that is no longer possible, and I am here alone without a brother or sister.

One day stretches to four. Still I haven't found Ra and Than as I comb the camp, wandering past shelters and various food stands selling deep-fried bananas, yams, soup with steamed rice, vegetables, and fresh meat—an alluring makeshift market that is more bustling than I could ever have imagined possible. As I head back to *bang*'s tent, giving up on today's search, a voice calls out my name urgently.

I stop, then turn back, looking for the voice among so many roaming people. Finally, on my left near a thicket, I spot a hand waving by a row of huts. I study the woman, who now waves at me with both hands. I walk over to her, and she asks, "Do you remember me?"

Her name is Sitha, a small-built, short-haired woman, perhaps in her mid-thirties. Her voice is gentle, polite. She reminds me that we met at Korkpongro, a village where we first heard the Khmer Rouge's guns soon after leaving Daakpo. She says I would remember her father. She points to her hut, to a wise-looking, friendly man whom I now recall. I remember how much I prayed when we were in Korkpongro. Perhaps those prayers were heard, and here we are, meeting again. To my pleasant disbelief, she has seen Ra and Than, and gladly offers to take me to where they're staying.

As we approach a golden-grassed shack situated near a mound with two tall trees, Aunt Sitha points to it and says that it is where Ra and Than are. Smiling, she bids me good-bye, leaving me excited about my reunion with my sister and brother. I imagine their surprise at seeing me, their little sister, standing in front of them. When I arrive in front of the doorless hut, I see a woman in a bright blue blouse and a flowered skirt sitting on a mat with her back toward me, engrossed in something she's making. *That's not their hut*, I think disappointedly.

I hurry toward where Aunt Sitha and I parted, hoping to catch her and tell her she was wrong, but she's gone.

Returning to the hut, I decide to ask the woman if she knows Ra and Than.

"Excuse me."

The woman turns around.

"Ra! Oh, it's you." I laugh, surprised and happy to find that she is my sister after all.

Beaming as she gets up from the mat, Ra asks, "Whom did you come with?" When did you get here?"

Ignoring her questions, I eye her from head to toe. Her healthy, glowing skin. Her eyes. They're happy, vibrant. Finally I find the words to describe how different she looks since I last saw her a week ago. "Ra," I say, smiling exuberantly, "you have spirit, you have meat [gained weight]. You have good skin. You look like *koon chen* [someone of Chinese descent]."

Ra grins broadly, her hands reaching out to me, speechless at my bluntness.

I sit on the mat beside Ra and she tells me that Than's out trying to buy merchandise from Thai merchants to trade with travelers on their way to Cambodia.

"Isn't he scared?" I knit my eyebrows. "I've heard that it's dangerous. Thai soldiers arrest Cambodians and torture them, beating them up. Is that true, Ra?"

"Well, there are Thai soldiers patrolling, I've heard. But you have to know when to go to trade with the Thai merchants," Ra explains, not so sure herself. Suddenly her face shines with excitement. "Athy, over here, if you have Thai money or gold, you can buy lots of things. They have everything. Pineapples, chickens, beef, ice, everything. All you could ever want to eat." Ra grins comically. "All you need is money."

"No wonder you have meat on you."

So relieved and exhilarated, I chuckle with Ra. Since the Khmer Rouge's takeover, I have not laughed this hard with my sisters or brothers. But today we laugh until my cheeks and belly hurt. My face becomes warm, my soul at ease.

Afterward I go to *bang* and her husband and tell them the news. They are relieved that I've found Ra. When I return to the shack, there's Than, smiling, happy to see me. And squatting by the entrance to the shack, there is the man whom Ra has told me about, from Kompong Cham province. Dark skin, medium build, with long, defined eyebrows. His name is Vantha, his nickname Preag. He had traveled through Sala Krao with a few men and a woman from Kompong Cham. Everyone else, Ra says, has gone back except him.

Considering how uncomfortable Ra is around men, I'm surprised that Vantha is allowed to stay here. If *Mak* and *Pa* were alive, they would not have approved of this living arrangement. But then, who is to say that one should follow the old cultural rules when the circumstances are so changed? What I'm most concerned about is how to survive in this camp. When Than and *bang* Vantha go to trade with the Thai, I talk to Ra about selling food, knowing I would never jeopardize my life by going into Thailand to trade.

She rejects the idea and suggests that I give the gold I've brought to *bang* Vantha. She explains that we can live off the profits from *bang* Vantha and Than's trading. Looking into her eyes, I realize there's no point in arguing with her. For the moment I accept Ra's suggestion and hope that I too can depend on Than and *bang* Vantha, a stranger, with my gold.

Than and *bang* Vantha embark on a new business. After our meal, Than and *bang* Vantha seek out customers and bring them to our shack. They are middlemen, exchanging gold for Thai money, then we exchange this money at a higher rate with travelers who buy goods to take back to their respective provinces.

My role is to inspect the authenticity of the gold and weigh it, using our little brass scale. I'm good, Ra and Than tell *bang* Vantha, at distinguishing the twenty-four-karat gold from the fake jewelry or the nongold sheets. I've learned from the other traders as well as from my own observations the appropriate heaviness and color of the gold.

When in doubt, I've learned to place the jewelry or the so-called gold piece on the embers in a cooking pit or set it on fire with lighter fuel. If it's real gold, the color remains the same, bright gold. If not, it turns black. So far, I haven't been swindled.

Rumor has it that we'll be moved into a camp inside Thailand. Ry and Map are still in Sala Krao. If we are moved, we'll be separated forever, we fear.

A few days later, I'm relieved to hear Than's offer to go back to Sala Krao to bring Map and Ry here. If they start moving people out before he returns, Than emphasizes, Ra and I are not to leave.

While Than is gone, Ra confides to me that she and *bang* Vantha have decided to get married when we are moved to the new camp. She says, "If I don't marry him, don't love him, he said, he'll go back to Kompong Cham to his parents. If he's gone, who's going to take care of us? Cambodian elders would say it's good to have a man to support the family. I want you to be with me when we get married."

At night Than arrives with Map on his shoulders, a human bundle whose hands are draped over Than's head, about to slip off at any time. Than lifts him up and puts him down on the mat near Ra and me. Map is quiet. No word, nothing, comes out of his mouth. He sits still, his eyes sad, exhausted.

Getting up from the mat, I peer along the alley in front of the shack, but there's no Ry. "I left her," Than fumes. "She walks slowly and carries nothing. Walks a little bit, stops. Walks a little bit, stops. Rest, rest, rest. . . . Since we were near here, I didn't want to wait for her."

"So where is she?" I ask.

"I don't know! She wanted to rest, so I left her. I carried Map because he couldn't walk, and he got heavier and heavier. I'm also tired, but I kept on going, but *she* kept wanting to rest. . . ."

Worried, Ra says, "She doesn't know her way around here. You should have waited for her."

Sitting down on the mat, Than is quiet. His head rests on his arms atop his knees.

"Athy, tomorrow go look for her. Look around the entrance to the camp and you should find her." Than speaks tiredly, his voice now composed, concerned.

When the light streaks the morning sky, I spring up from the mat. Ry is the first thing on my mind. I trot and run, hoping Ry hasn't gotten up and begun to look for us.

Along the grassy path flanked by clumps of trees, I search for Ry. I check once, twice, three times, walking far out of the camp, yet I can't find her. The fourth time, on my last attempt, I still don't see a trace of her. I cry.

Standing against a makeshift fence of freshly cut logs encircling a large open field of stumps and thickets, I watch young, skinny men in civilian clothes who are leaping over the stumps, each making a stabbing-shooting gesture with a piece of wood. One stumbles and plunges to the ground. Laughter erupts from the other side of the fence. When I turn to look, I see a group of children giggling among a few chuckling adult spectators.

Amused, I smile, laughing with the other children. As more men fall, they guffaw at their own clumsiness. Suddenly two cold hands tightly cover my eyes. Startled, I turn sideways and hear giggling. I reach up to pry the hands open, but they grip my face harder.

"Who is it? Who is it?" I demand, irritated.

No answer.

I swing my hands to hit whomever it is, and the person moves, jerking my head back. Angry, I pry at the hands again and they come loose. When I look behind me, I see Ry, laughing comically.

She chuckles, pointing at me. "I've been standing behind you, and you didn't even know that I was here. You kept laughing." Ry imitates my laughter, very amused.

We hurry back to our shack, and Ry updates me on where she slept and what she had for dinner last night. She says she bought herself dinner with the gold she's brought, and found a family who let her sleep in their hut. What a free spirit she is! And there I was in our shack, worried about her. Now I'm at ease, very grateful that she's come home—a home that is defined not by the camp where we live, or the shelter that covers us, but rather by those in our family who are left alive.

Our shack is more crowded with the addition of Ry and Map, but I wouldn't have it any other way. I remember a saying in a song, "It's more bearable to have a crowded home than a crowded heart."

Ra has told Ry, Than, and Map that she will marry *bang* Vantha, and that seems to be okay with them. We all feel it is her decision to make.

One evening Ra and *bang* Vantha go strolling in the camp and come back with a little girl about six years of age. She's thin, about Map's height, her face hid behind streaks of black dirt, her nose runny, her hair short like a boy's. Her shirt and pants are ragged.

Sitting down on the mat between Ra and *bang* Vantha, the little girl sniffs, then wipes her nose with the back of her hand. *Bang* Vantha glances at her proudly.

"Ara and I want to adopt her as our daughter. She's an orphan. What should we name her?"

Ra thinks, studying the girl. "Name her Savorng, because she is articulate and talks like *sarika*."* Ra seems proud of herself for having chosen the name.

Bang Vantha agrees and thinks Savorng is a smart child. He says that they saw her in an alley near the market, where she was addressing passersby with this mature young voice. She would say, "Uncle, aunt, please help me. Please give me money and I'll wish you and your family long life and good health."

Map becomes teary and moves closer to Ra. Savorng does the same, declaring, "She's my mom!" Her hands peel Map's hands from Ra's folded legs.

Map cries, looking helpless, neglected. *Bang* Vantha laughs, amused. Ra finally turns her attention to Map, placing her arms around him. He sobs endlessly, and cries harder when some of his

---

* Similar to *avorng*, a nickname for a type of black bird with white and yellow markings on its head which could be trained to talk.

clothes are given to Savorng after her bath. He runs over to her and tries to pull her shirt off.

"No, it's mine!" Savorng pulls away, glaring at Map.

The move into a Thai camp never materializes, but a warning of a Khmer Rouge attack suddenly surfaces in the camp. We gather in the alley in front of our shack. Tomorrow, it is said, at about ten o'clock in the morning, the Khmer Rouge will attack the camp. Their goal is to seize the camp from the *PARA* soldiers, and we will be caught in the combat zone, a man reports dismally. Before returning to our separate homes, some elderly women suggest that we should get up early to cook food. If we are forced to flee again, they reason, at least we should have a full stomach.

We get up early and prepare a wonderful meal. Steaming food has been dished out on the mat. Seven plates of rice. Two bowls of soup with pineapple chunks, catfish, lotus shoots, tomatoes, mint, green onion, and browned minced garlic. Among the soup bowls lie a plate of fresh broiled fish with sliced cucumbers and two small bowls of sweet-and-sour sauce.

I eat a few bites, but I am too anxious to finish, and go outside. I go around the shack to the back corner and hike up the mound, then climb up one of the two tall trees. I climb up higher, far above the shack. If I turn, I can see in all directions.

Peering toward the woods to my right, I glimpse something unusual—white-and-red-checked scarves amid tall greenish trees. Men in black. One carries a rocket-propelled grenade. Others carry rifles, bazookas.

I yell to my family, "I saw the Khmer Rouge. I saw the Khmer Rouge. They have guns. One is holding a "banana bud"* gun.

---

* Referring to the grenade that is inserted into the barrel, which is similar in shape to a banana bud.

They're wearing black clothes. It is the Khmer Rouge, I'm sure, it's the Khmer Rouge."

Ry comes running toward the mound, peering toward the woods where I've pointed. Our neighbors emerge from their shacks and congregate by our shelter.

While I'm still in the tree, artillery explodes behind our shack. Gunfire roars, showering the camp. I freeze, clutching the tree trunk with all my might. Ra, Map, everyone darts to the trench and water holes. Ry is on the mound, sobbing.

"Ry, help me!" I scream long and hard. Flat against the mound, she waves at me to come down, but I shake my head, tears streaming down. I'm afraid the flying bullets will hit me.

"*Ry!* . . . " I lean my face against the tree.

"*Athy!* Get down," Ry shouts in a long-drawn-out voice.

I gaze at her crying face and shake my head. Suddenly more explosions erupt, one right after the other, producing shattering noises that rattle the trees and our shack. *I have to get down, I have to get down. But I'll get shot.* I cry, frustrated.

Ry gazes up, waving again. I focus on her face, then slide down, landing beside her, hugging the mound. My hands and the soles of my feet throb from sliding down the tree, but soon the pain is overshadowed by the raucous, endless noise of gunfire.

"*Mak, Pa,* God of the Earth, please protect us, please protect us. . . ." Ry prays hysterically. She grabs loose dirt and throws it over her head repeatedly.

Propelled by Ry's hysteria, I begin to pray as she does. I call upon the spirits of *Mak, Pa,* and the God of the Earth, then powder my head and face with dirt and at the same time try to breathe.

Ry and I move behind the mound, in the opposite direction of the area where I spotted the Khmer Rouge. There lies a shallow-breathing man whose head is caked with blood and whose uniform is like that of the *PARA* soldiers.

Ry moves closer to him. "Uncle, where did you get hit? Can I help you?" Her voice is warm and gentle.

Slowly, the pale man speaks. "I'm hit in the temple. I'm thirsty, but maybe I'm okay. There's a woman hiding by me, right there." He points. "She is bleeding a lot, she got hurt in the stomach."

I follow his hand, and there she is, pale, lying in a pool of blood. Realizing we could be next, I suggest to Ry that we move to lower ground to hide. She agrees, and when an artillery shell explodes nearby, Ry crawls swiftly, disappearing into a water hole near our shack, leaving me panicked.

On my stomach, I pull myself to the wall of the shack, hoping the fierce popping sounds of rifles will let up so I can join my family in the trench. Suddenly another artillery shell explodes. In a flash of horror, I thrust my body through the wall of the shack, crawling across it and down to the trench.

"God in heaven, please help us, help us. Save us from evil, from the bombs and bullets. Help our children . . ." shouts a woman in prayer as she lies on her stomach, the palms of her hands pressed together.

A Thai merchant whom I've seen before hides beneath a cave-like groove in the trench. Compulsively, he claws the earth that houses shards of broken glass, his hands soaked with bright red blood mixed with dirt.

"*Samdech Aov* [Father of Princes], please help me. Help us, help us, *Samdech Aov* . . ." an old woman prays, her palms pressed against her forehead.

Samdech Aov? I'm distracted from my silent prayers by this mention of the person to whom she's praying: Prince Sihanouk. *He's a man, maybe once a king, but not a god.* I stare at her in disbelief, and for a moment my mind tunes out the cries and the surrounding noises.

The shelling and firing stop. We sit up and look at one another, relieved, yet we're not sure what to do. But soon some of us share our own fears, describing our close escapes. A woman, our neighbor, rambles, gesturing with her hands. "I didn't know what happened, but suddenly the shelling scared me to death so that my spirit almost left me. But when I saw Ra crawling, I followed her. I kept my head close to the ground. . . ."

Ra's anxious face wants to tell her story. Everyone else's is a mirror of the person who is sharing his or her story. Suddenly everyone's head turns toward the woods where I spotted the Khmer Rouge. I'm startled to see men marching toward us, wearing black uniforms with checked scarves around their necks. Fastened to their shoulders are rifles, bazookas, and rocket-propelled grenades; their waists are decorated with rounds of ammunition.

Walking by, they study us. I watch them, bracing for the moment when they will shoot us. Everyone else begs for their lives. I don't. I'm too petrified.

"We are not going to kill you!" a tall Khmer Rouge declares sternly.

"Thanks, *loks*, very much, thanks, *loks*, very much . . ." a neighboring woman says in tears, her hands pressed together, which she raises to her forehead many times.

Shortly after they disappear into the community of shelters, gunfire starts up again. Everyone cries as before. The Khmer Rouge are clashing with the *PARA* soldiers somewhere in the camp. Everyone climbs out of the trench, runs, and hunches down alongside the trench into the woods. For a second I don't know where my sisters and brothers are. All I know is that I am running for my life. Suddenly a bullet whizzes by; I jolt forward, avoiding it, and when I look ahead, there's Ry, holding Map's hand, and Ra with Savorng. I pray to the spirits of *Mak* and *Pa* to protect me.

In a grove of trees, we rest. Other families do the same. On the second day Than, *bang* Vantha, and other men venture through the forest near Thailand. When they come back, they are excited. They say they've seen "Americans." And these Americans told them that we will be picked up and taken inside Thailand.

A few days later, before we can even see anything, the sound of a truck shifting gears approaches. It emerges from tall trees along the road in a cloud of dust. Then another truck, and another. A total of three trucks, bow-roofed and covered with thick cloth. Everybody moves near the trucks. Women and children are helped into a truck in front of us. Men climb into it on their own. Quickly, the truck is filled. Fortunately, we are in it.

Leaning against the tailgate, I gaze at the disappearing landscape on the side of the Cambodian border through a cloud of dust. Then it hits me—I'm leaving my homeland. I silently bid good-bye to the spirits of my family. *Good-bye, Mak. Good-bye, Pa . . . Chea. . . . We have to go. . . .*

18

Khao I Dang Camp

The truck caravan has been traveling on unpaved, dusty roads studded with trees and open fields, turning from one winding road to another. Then the trucks pull into a charred field with a dark, ashen ground containing blackened stumps as small as my thumb and as big as my wrist. They look like burned matchsticks.

The trucks pull out, driving away one after the other. A man informs us that the trucks are going back to get the rest of the people, and that food and water will be brought to us.

There is no shade to be found, so we stand barefoot on the hot ground, and my feet become darkened by the ash. Little children cry for water and none of us have any. Map and Savorng, too, are thirsty and hungry, their faces sad and sour, their brows knitted. More Cambodians are brought in those trucks, and later in the evening food and water are finally brought to us. At night we sleep on the ground, the sky our roof.

The next day the trucks bring us bamboo rods, thatches, and strings. Every man, woman, and child helps out in the building of huts, handling tasks ranging from carrying bamboo rods to bringing strings to the Cambodian men who are doing the construction work. Within days long-thatched huts with ten compartments for ten families are erected side by side, separated by an alley. To each one, a leader is assigned to represent the families, ensuring that they receive food and water rations. This camp is called Khao I Dang,* surrounded by a barbed wire fence near which a few Thai soldiers patrol. They make me feel safe from the Khmer Rouge.

We are given colorful plastic plates, bowls, water buckets, and blankets. These are our blessings, and I count them. Yet I wish for the day when we won't have to ration food or water, when we can each just help ourselves to the steamed rice or soup and not have to worry that we might have taken too much.

A few weeks after our arrival, Thai merchants come to the fence, hovering by it, away from where the soldiers are patrolling. We're hungry, and they bring cooked corn on the cob, eggs, and vegetables to sell to us. Word spreads from one hut to the other. At night boys and men run to the fence to trade, which results in one death— a boy is shot by the soldiers.

In a month, instead of people running to the fence to trade, Thai merchants bring their goods inside the camp. After midnight the shuffling of feet and the whispering of anxious voices echo along the alleys on both sides of our hut. They have to keep their activities secret from the Thai soldiers.

Every night there's trading, then the chase along the alleys, followed by the search of people's huts. Through it all, whether we are involved in the trading or not, we get harassed. But the people who suffer most are those Cambodian buyers who get caught, whom the soldiers kick and beat with the butt of their rifles. Eventually a

---

* Toward the end of 1979, in response to the international outcry, the Thai government allowed the United Nations High Commissioner for Refugees to open holding centers inside Thailand. Khao I Dang opened in November and within two months had swelled to a city of 120,000. "Khao I Dang was for a while the largest Cambodian city in the world," noted Timothy Carney, an official with the American Embassy in Bangkok (U.S. Committee for Refugees, "Cambodian Refugees in Thailand: The Limits of Asylum").

makeshift market springs up during the daytime, filled with noodles, vegetables, and even beautiful blouses and sarongs.

Today our hut is filled with the sweet fragrance of curry spices cooked with freshly squeezed coconut milk, beef, onions, string beans, and yams. In a green plastic strainer on an empty water bucket are bundles of noodles arranged in a spiral formation, which are to be eaten with the beef curry, bean sprouts, and mint. Fifteen guests, mostly Ra's and *bang* Vantha's friends, are all crowded into our hut. With their legs folded, some sit on the mats spread on the earthen ground near Ra and *bang* Vantha. Others stand by the door.

Savorng, Map, Ry, Than, and I sit on the bamboo deck on which we sleep, watching Ra and *bang* Vantha being married by an old man, perhaps a former Buddhist priest. In the far corner of the bamboo deck is an offering Ra makes to the spirits of *Mak, Pa,* Chea, Avy, Vin, Tha, and our ancestors. Two bowls of curry. Two bowls of noodles. Two waters, and burning incense secured in a small tin can of rice. This offering is an invitation to the deceased to attend the wedding, and at the same time signifies that a favor is being asked of them to bring happiness and health, and whatever else Ra has prayed for.

"May Ara and Vantha have a happy marriage and lots of children," *bang* Vantha's closest friend, Uncle Lee, wishes. Everyone laughs.

Ra, twenty-two, smiles sheepishly. Her face is smooth, refined. Her hairstyle elegant with upswept curls, she looks like a Chinese movie star in her cream lace blouse from Phnom Penh, which she managed to keep safe during the Khmer Rouge time.

Uncle Lee smiles fervently, gazing at Ra and then at *bang* Vantha. He has been to our hut and has gotten to know our family, and we've gotten to know his, and he kept telling *bang* Vantha to marry Ra. Many times he warned *bang* Vantha in front of us, "If you don't marry her, I'll marry her myself. I'm not joking. What are you waiting for? She's a good woman and from a good family."

Bang Vantha and Ra sold their twenty-four-karat gold necklace and bought this food for their wedding celebration. Uncle Lee's mom helped us purchase the meat, vegetables, and noodles as well as do the cooking.

When night falls and everyone is in bed, a soft, gentle voice whispers a song. A song of excitement, lust, and regret. It is Ra's voice, coming from a room she made by hanging blankets on a separate deck opposite the place where Ry, Than, Savorng, Map, and I sleep.

អូយ . . . វើរើប . . . ស្រីបរអស់អារម្មណ៍ ភ័យឪងណាខ្ញុំ
អូយរាត្រីទឹកឃ្មុំ ខ្ញុំបំស្ពាយខ្លួន
ហ៊ី . . . សែនស្ពាយៗ រូបកាយក្រមុំ ដូចផ្កាក្រពុំ
ឥឡូវប្ញុំក្រេបហើយ ក្រេបហើយៗគេហើរចោល
បើគេចោលខ្ញុំមែន ចិត្តឈឺយអួលណែន មានតែទឹកផ្នែកទេ
ឱនេះហើយស្នេហ៍ ទើបតែបានស្គាល់រាត្រីទិមួយ
សូមមេត្តាករុណាខ្ញុំផង បងឈឺយៗបងក្រមុំមានតែម្តង
គ្មានទេពីរដងបងឈឺយ។

Ooy . . . Excited. All my feelings aroused, nervous
On this honey night I regret my body
Hm . . . Regret, regret, a body that is like a blossoming flower
Now the bee has taken the sweetness, then he flies away
If he really leaves me, my heart will hurt
And there will be only tears
So, this is love, that I've known for the first night
Please be kind, kind to me
Honey, honey, a virgin would only be once,
Not twice.

We arrived in Khao I Dang three months ago, in November 1979. Now a private classroom has been set up to teach us English. I have to find a way to pay the monthly fee, which is 150 bahts.* It is a lot of money for me since I don't have any salary, or any allowance except food rations. I decide to use the remaining gold I brought from Sala Krao and hadn't turned over to *bang* Vantha. I will trade this gold for my education, I tell myself. I'm going to sell it, and it's better that I keep the matter to myself.

Ra is alarmed that she has stopped menstruating. Lately she has been very ill, and so she stops going to the English class. Our women neighbors tell her that she's pregnant. When a woman is pregnant, they say, she usually has morning sickness. She throws up, feels ill, and has wild cravings for certain foods like pickled green mangoes or tamarinds.

When you don't get the things you want to eat, our next-door neighbor says, it is like a pain nagging at you. And Ra has these symptoms of a pregnant woman. Eagerly, she tells our neighbors what she craves, and the women laugh. Ry and I join them, and Ra smiles weakly.

Soon everyone is talking about a movie that will be shown. It's about Christianity, our neighbor says, and Jesus Christ. I'd heard about Jesus Christ before from Chea when she learned about him back in Phnom Penh and had sung songs to Ry, Ra, and me. Now I want to know about him. How is he different from Buddha? When the day comes, I go with my family to an open field where there are already many people standing in front of a big screen secured on a mound.

After the movie starts, it begins to rain. First it drizzles, then it pours. A few people have umbrellas, but most of us stand, getting soaked in the rain. Men use their shirts to shield them from the raindrops. Most of the shivering children and adults leave, including my brothers and sisters. I shudder, chattering, hugging myself,

* At the then current exchange rate, 150 bahts equaled $7.50.

crying as Jesus Christ's hands and feet are being hammered to the cross. Though I don't understand all that is being said, I'm deeply sad and feel connected to the movie, to Jesus Christ, and to the sorrow of those men and women who miss him.

I think of *Pa* and his execution.

Ra comes from the market, smiling exuberantly as she sets down the groceries she has bought. Her stomach is round, protruding like a small watermelon under her blouse. Ry and I are eager to find out what's on her mind. What is making her this happy and silly?

Ra smiles, rubbing her hands together to display her excitement, then walks away to the cooking area. Tired of being in suspense, I demand excitedly, "Ra! What is it? What are you smiling about?"

"Do you want to know who I saw in the market today?"

"Who?" Ry and I speak at the same time.

"I saw Aunt Eng [*Pa's* cousin]. When I saw her, I thought, *Who is that? I've seen her before.* Then I knew. Do you want to know what she told me?"

"What?" I ask.

Aunt Eng, Ra says, has found out that Uncle Seng, who left Cambodia two days before the Khmer Rouge's takeover, is now living in America. She has written a letter to a friend of hers who lives in California, asking her if she knows him. Apparently, her friend wrote back and said that she indeed knows of a Leng Seng, who lives in Oregon. Aunt Eng has asked him to sponsor her family in America, and now he's working on the paperwork from there. And we, Ra is eager to add, can also go to America.

I jump up and down like I'm on a spring. I smile, taking in this wonderful, unbelievable news hungrily. After all these years of loss and hardship, I reflect, we receive this news—Uncle Seng, *Pa's* only brother, is alive, and he will bring us to America. *Oh, God, thank you.* I jump, humming and laughing.

After two months of studying English, I have to give it up. Ra has been having cravings. Some nights she tells me and Ry that she cries, wishing she could have these foods. Since she doesn't have any money left from the sale of her gold necklace, she often saunters in the market just to look at the food she wants, wishing she had money to buy it.

I can't stand seeing Ra's sad face and decide to give her all the money I have left from selling my gold. Ra's eyes glow when I hand her the money. She holds the money close to her heart and smiles. Ry gazes at me, surprised, happy. Later we all go to the market and buy whatever Ra is hungry for, and she is the happiest pregnant woman I've ever seen.

One sunny day Savorng, Map, and I are waiting in line for our water rations. Two girls, one about my age and the other about Savorng's, walk up to us and call Savorng "Peang." The younger one touches Savorng's hand and smiles. Savorng pulls back, striding toward me. The girl asks Savorng where she's living. Savorng squints, staring at the two girls in bewilderment, then looks at me with a frown on her face, as if asking me to help her.

Curious, I ask them how they know Savorng. The older girl tells me a story about Savorng's family. Back in a village in Cambodia, after Savorng's parents died, a Khmer Rouge family took her in and raised her. When the Vietnamese soldiers invaded Cambodia months ago, this family fled to the jungle, leaving Savorng behind. Later, as the other families in the village were leaving for the New Camp, she followed them and came to live with an old woman in the camp, who asked her to beg for money and food, and it was then that Ra and *bang* Vantha met her and brought her to our shack.

Now Savorng is okay, I tell the girls. She lives with my family and we have renamed her. The girls are happy to see her and hear that she's doing well. Savorng steal glances at them, then her eyes return to the gravel ground.

As we wait for the water to be distributed, I think about Savorng's life. About her dead parents, and the Khmer Rouge family who took her in and raised her. It is interesting how fate has brought her to us, who are also orphans. I'm sad to learn of her story, but relieved that she's with us, and hope that perhaps she'll get to go to America, too.

Khao I Dang quickly expands. New huts have been built to accommodate the influx of people being brought in. Lately, rumors spread among us that a lot of people are leaving Cambodia and are now living on the border. I am sad that Cambodia has become a hollow shell with fewer people in it, even though I understand the need to abandon our homeland as war and oppression have been in our lives far too long.

Some people, who either can't wait to be brought into Khao I Dang or who will never have a chance to come here because of their arrival status on the border, have paid other Cambodians to smuggle them in. One of them is Uncle Aat, *bang* Vantha's cousin from Kompong Cham province. For each Cambodian smuggled in, a fee must be paid to the Thai soldiers who patrol the camp.

To supplement our meager food rations, Than, at sixteen, decides to go with some older men to the frontier and smuggle people in. Later he operates on his own, since he knows the way to the New Camp and has learned enough Thai to communicate with the soldiers. When he is gone longer than he told us he would be, I worry. I can see him being shot, and having his money taken from him. When he returns, I'm relieved, gazing at him with admiration for his bravery and his help in acquiring more food for our family. Later, when Uncle Aat and *bang* Vantha go with him, I sleep better.

My efforts to learn English don't stop when I can no longer pay my former teacher. I study English on my own. I review the translations of words from the *Essential English Book I* I bought and my notebook. I practice combining words to form sentences, speaking out loud to myself.

I find another way to learn English as well. Wandering around the camp, I once overheard English words spoken through a window overlooking an alley. I followed the voice and saw four men standing in the middle of a long hut, copying something into their notebooks. Standing on my tiptoes, I peered between the men's shoulders into the class and saw English letters and vowels written on the blackboard.

Though I am ahead of the class, I've been coming just to listen to the English words spoken by the teacher. I've learned to rise early to secure a spot by the window so I can see the blackboard, as others have also discovered this place. Mostly men, along with a few women, come crowding behind us. Looking over our shoulders, they copy notes from our notebooks, and those who are behind them copy from theirs. With each passing day, more people come, plugging up the whole alley. The famished crowd of Cambodian students spill out into the adjacent alley almost as far as a quarter of a mile, copying notes under the hot sun.

The presence of the other women makes me feel a little more at ease, less concerned about what Ra, Than, or *bang* Vantha might say to me if they found out that I've been standing among men. Together we bend the rules of our own culture. It's not appropriate for a woman to be among men, Cambodian elders would say, and some of my relatives would likely echo this view. But I would defend myself and say, I'm here to educate myself. If people are concerned about the inappropriateness of the situation, then they can give me money and I'll sit in class and be proper.

After weeks of corresponding with Uncle Seng in Portland, Oregon, sending him information about our birthdays and birthplaces, we have been notified that we must move to another camp, called Sakeo II. The people who get to go are Aunt Eng and her family, *bang* Vantha, Ra, Ry, Than, Map, me, and Savorng, who is listed as our sister. All except Uncle Aat, *bang* Vantha's cousin. He came to the camp after our seven names had been sent to Uncle Seng for sponsorship. Still, *bang* Vantha wants Uncle Aat to go to America instead of Savorng, but Ra says we can't leave Savorng here because she's a child, only six or seven years old. Uncle Aat, on the other hand, is an adult, she reasons, and he can fend for himself. Later, like other families, he can apply to go to America or another country like France, Canada, or Australia. Uncle Aat looks sad, disappointed, but he seems to understand Ra's dilemma, having to choose between him and Savorng, whom she and *bang* Vantha have welcomed into our family.

Uncle Aat has been nice to us; he has shared food with us and given me money to spend. He speaks politely to us, unlike *bang* Vantha, who acting aloof toward us ever since he began spending time around his so-called "cool friends." *Bang* Vantha has changed. Now he is more belligerent, especially toward Than, particularly since Than began earning money from his smuggling. *Bang* Vantha often puts Than down or berates him for no reason. Than ignores him, but later he tells him to back off and to act like an adult, as an older brother in-law should act.

One night *bang* Vantha came home and told Ra in front of us that his friends had said that "friends are hard to find, but a wife is easy to get." He agreed, he said. He smirked, proud of himself. He avoids walking beside Ra now that she's pregnant. Ra keeps her thoughts to herself.

In the evening he provokes fights between Savorng and Map so he can watch. He makes them clutch the bamboo rods at the roof of the hut and tells Savorng to kick Map hard. Ra can't seem to stop him, and we can't say a thing because he is like a dictator ruling our family. In the end, Map and Savorng hurt each other and they both cry. Usually Map gets hurt the most since he can't swing fast because of his protruding stomach, a lingering trace of malnourishment left from the Khmer Rouge time. Savorng ends up kicking him in the stomach. They continue fighting until *bang* Vantha thinks they've had a good fight. When they cry and *bang* Vantha smirks, I wish Ra had married Uncle Lee. She would have been better off with him, for he adores her and our family. But now it's too late. She is pregnant and will give birth soon. And here we are about to be moved to Sakeo II Camp, a place I am leery about. I've heard it houses a lot of former Khmer Rouge. And here we are in buses waiting to be taken there.

My fears quicken as the bus picks up speed and the trees and landscape on the road pass by. I cry as my fears turn to sadness. With each passing moment, I'm taken farther away from Cambodia. I miss *Pa* and *Mak*, Chea. . . . I turn to look for Ra and Ry behind me. They too, cry. Many people do, their red eyes expressing their silent fears. Soon an English song eases our sorrow. A Thai man sitting by the driver reaches out to a portable stereo and presses one of the buttons. Suddenly a song comes on and the bus fills with sensational music:

> Oh oh yeah yeah I love you more than I can say
> I love you twice as much as tomorrow. . . .

Smiling through my tears, I gaily tell Ra and Ry that I understand these words. They smile, looking proud. I turn back, wiping away my tears and enjoying the song.

19
Sakeo II Camp

$\mathcal{I}$t is July 1980, and here we are in a new camp. Sakeo II Camp is smaller than Khao I Dang, but it is cleaner and nicer. Doorless shelters, called quads, are built in groups of four, all facing each other with a large open space in front. Along an unpaved road lie rows of quads, made of wood and thick gray sheets with wooden floors. Also on this road, which snakes through the camp, are a large two-story wooden building that says "Public Health Center" and, across from it, quads where people can send letters or applications to the American, Australian, French, and Canadian embassies requesting permission for resettlement.

A family of seven, we share the quad with another family. As at Khao I Dang, we receive food and water rations. Many times the rations are better than what we got there. However, it's still not enough for all of us.

Refugees here are no different from those I saw in Khao I Dang. They wear flowered blouses and sarongs or pants. I haven't seen anyone wearing black uniforms like those of the Khmer Rouge, so I am not as scared as I was before coming here.

I walk along the main road to the market, approaching the Thai soldiers' barracks. Suddenly a Thai song comes over the loudspeakers. Ahead of me, I see a few soldiers stop and stand straight, their rifles lowered. The butts of the rifles touch the ground. Other Cambodian refugees have noticed them, so they too stop. I do the same.

While the song is being played, an old man limps past me, his eyes staring at the ground. The old man keeps on tottering along. As soon as the song is finished, one of the soldiers darts after the old man, raises his rifle, and strikes him on the back. The man drops facedown, struggling. When he fumbles to get up, the soldier roars in his face, speaking in Thai. Then the soldier drags him to the barracks, disappearing behind the metal gate. The old man looks perplexed, frightened. Horror-stricken, every Cambodian refugee stands rooted to the road, watching helplessly.

Later the barracks becomes a place where it is common to hear people squealing in pain. One day a man's voice screams in agony. Suddenly a tall man with brown hair leaps over the fence and quickly takes snapshots. The Thai soldiers run up to him and corner him. One snatches the camera from him, pulling the film out of it, and shoves it at his chest. The photographer walks backward as the soldiers snort at him in Thai.

A few weeks later, I witness a torture within my own family. A friend comes running over to Ry and me, telling us that *bang* Vantha has beaten Than up, and Than is chasing after him with a hatchet.

On the main road, Ry and I proceed, looking for Than. Ahead of us is *bang* Vantha, sauntering. When we reach him, Ry asks him what happened, and he says, "I hit Than a little bit, and he chased after me with a hatchet, so I told my friend to tell the soldiers to arrest him. Now the soldiers are beating him. Go help him."

Through the metal gate, Ry and I peer, wondering where they have taken Than. We shake the gate, crying. Soon a soldier lets us in, and lying on the ground is Than. His face is swollen, soaked with blood and dirt. His body rolls as the two soldiers kick him and beat him with the butts of their rifles.

Ry screams, and I wail for every blow they strike at Than. We press the palms of our hands together, begging them to stop, but they keep on beating Than, then pour water on him, and when he groans they beat him again and again.

"Please stop torturing my brother. Stop!" I yell, moving in closer to the soldiers. "He's only a kid. Please stop hurting my brother. . . ."

All of the soldiers there watch, including a man in civilian clothes. They look on as Ry and I plead for mercy. Ry's fists pound the ground as if the pain she sees being inflicted upon Than is too great to bear. Turning away from the sight of Than being beaten, I implore the oldest soldier, who is sitting on a chair, to stop the beating. He looks away, his face cold. Finally they stop, and we take him home.

Ry, Than, Map, and I move in with Aunt Eng and her husband and two daughters. We sleep inside the quad and her family sleeps in the alcove in the front. Savorng remains with Ra and *bang* Vantha. Ra doesn't say much about what happened. It seems that *bang* Vantha has again succeeded in convincing her that the fight wasn't his fault but Than's. Perhaps she is too devoted to him, or has succumbed to her role as the submissive wife. But whichever it is, her inability to resolve the situation, along with *bang* Vantha's immaturity and rudeness toward us, has caused our family to drift apart. We hardly see her or Savorng anymore.

A few private English classes have just opened. I attend all of them, then quit each class as soon as the teacher reminds everyone to bring money to pay the class fee.

Later my dilemma is solved. A public school called Sras Srang opens in the camp. It is situated in a big open space on the outskirts of the camp near the woods. Built on pilings with stairs and a landing, the school has five classrooms for grade six to nine. English is taught as well as math, Cambodian composition, and physical education.

It has been six years since I attended a formal school. Now, at fifteen, I enroll in the seventh grade, two grades higher than when I lived in Phnom Penh. Today in class I survey my classmates, perhaps fifty of them. We sit on the wooden floor that still gives off the fragrance of freshly cut wood. Boys sit among themselves, and the girls sit with girls, and I'm with them, folding my legs near the door of the classroom with a notebook, pen, and pencil in front of me.

Like me, Than, seventeen, who recovered from the soldiers' abuse, also enrolls in the seventh grade, but in a different class from mine, and he has a different teacher. Ry, on the other hand, attends an eighth/ninth-level class, which is down the hall from mine. Later she plans to take a teaching course, she says—her goal is to become a teacher, teaching children Cambodian.

Ra had a baby girl on September 30, 1980, a week ago. One afternoon she and Savorng bring the baby, Syla, to our quad. When Ry, Than, and I come home from school, they are sitting in the alcove where we cook our food. With them are Map, Aunt Eng, and her daughters.

Syla is tiny, dark-skinned with thick black hair. Her eyes are shut, lips suckling, her hands formed into fists. Savorng cradles her, and she sleeps peacefully. We all look at her, and talk about her, and not much else.

Nowadays going to school is like a hunger. Every night I anxiously look forward to returning to school the next morning. After school I diligently study math and English. As soon as I get back to the quad, I do my schoolwork, going over my notes and what will be taught the next day.

One day my teacher, whom I call *Lok Kruu* (*Lok* means "sir," and *Kruu* means "teacher"), hands back our math test. Knowing I did all the problems correctly, I am eager to get my test back. When I get it, I see the red mark indicating a score of nineteen out of twenty. I check a multiplication problem marked wrong and realize that my answer is correct.

I show *Lok Kruu*, who changes my grade. Happy, I smile as I return to my seat. I show my test to a classmate who sits behind me. She says it's good that I got everything right. She, on the other hand, made a few mistakes. She asks if she could borrow my test. I hear giggles behind me; Sida hands me back my test, then goes to *Lok Kruu* with her test in her hand. She comes back, smirking. She says to me, "Thy, I've gotten more points, too. Twenty out of twenty!"

Shocked, I'm speechless. How can she be proud of cheating, having copied my answers to get more points! But soon I'm even more appalled. Two girls sitting behind me, as well as a few boys, go to *Lok Kruu* after Sida showed them her test.

Lok Kruu's face reddens as they come up to him. I watch, taking deep breaths. He tells them to go back to their seats, then darts out of the classroom. When he returns, he says nothing, sitting at his desk, composed.

Loud footsteps stride down the hall. Soon the principal, who is in his early forties, appears. I want to get up and tell him what has transpired. I want to point to Sida and those who copied the answers from my test.

As soon as the principal steps into the classroom, he demands, "Who instigated the cheating? Who did it first?" his hand on his hip.

I stand up to explain. "I—"

"You!" The principal attacks me, his index finger stabs at me repeatedly. "Why did you instigate the cheating? What kind of a student, a girl, are you? Cheat. . . ."

Shocked, I peer at him, rooted to the floor. My face becomes hot.

Ever since I was a little girl I was taught to respect my elders, but how can I respect this man? I was oppressed by the Khmer Rouge, who took away my freedom, but *no one has the right to treat me this way now!* I glare back at him as he continues to fume.

My hand on my hip, mirroring the principal's stance, I tell him, "If you don't know the truth, don't accuse me of inciting the cheating. If you're stupid, don't act like you know." Words tumble out of my mouth, words that I could never imagine using when addressing an adult. My hand is raised, my index finger pointing back at him. "You are an adult, act like one. If not, no one will respect you, even though you're the principal."

The principal barks, pointing, calling me an insolent girl. Composed, I tell him to behave and to listen to himself, speaking like an adult telling a hysterical child to calm down. *Lok Kruu* scurries over to the principal, then firmly says, "That student didn't instigate the cheating."

The principal recoils, his eyes searching *Lok Kruu's*, as if he is trying to digest what *Lok Kruu* has just said. Suddenly I feel as if I'm in a corridor of silence. The principal leaves as quickly as he entered.

On the wall of the post office I read news and advertisements about missing families. Perhaps some long-lost relatives might be looking for us. I then scan the lists of names of people who have mail from relatives. Soon I see my own name.

I open the letter, and it says: "Dear Granddaughter Thy, Grandpa has arrived in Khao I Dang and is staying with your friend Sonith's father at the temple. . . . Your aunts, Chin and Leng, and their families are still in Phnom Penh. Later they will also come to Khao I Dang. . . . As for your mother's side of the family, your aunts and uncles and their families are also living in Phnom Penh. . . ."

I can't believe that Grandpa has found me after all this time since he, Aunt Chin, Aunt Leng, and their families left us at the village before Korkpongro. It was about a year ago today. Now we are reunited through a letter.

A few weeks later, I receive another letter from Khao I Dang. Accompanying it is a picture of Aunt Chin and her children, and Aunt Leng with her second husband as well as Cousin Navy, who is the only survivor in her family of seven. Everyone was brought safely into Khao I Dang. I'm so grateful. Only years later can we laugh together about the perils of their journey. Knowing how risky it was to come to Khao I Dang, they hid their jewels of gold and gems in their bottoms. But when they grew exhausted from the long, tiring journey, no one seemed to remember about their treasures. Aunt Leng's husband, on the way to the New Camp, had to defecate behind a bush, and it was there he left behind the hidden gems. A similar thing happened with Aunt Chin's daughter.

The other stories were thoroughly grim. The vicious killings in Year Piar came full circle in the end. The remaining relatives of the people who were executed returned for retribution soon after the liberation. In a rice paddy they went up to those people who were involved in the execution of their families. There, with knives, they killed those people, butchering them.

Years of cruelty had thus been answered in kind, yet I took no satisfaction in learning about this. I'm sad that these remaining relatives who survived the Khmer Rouge were reduced to the Khmer Rouge's level. Such revenge will change nothing, I think. It doesn't bring back the dead. But I'm relieved that none of my relatives were involved in this revenge. I'm grateful that I didn't have to witness this killing.

Considering how unhappy I've been at Sras Srang school since the incident with the principal, I elect to quit. Now I have a new experience to embark upon. Ry and I have enrolled in a training program for physical education instructors. One thing that is comforting is that I can learn English on my own, and soon Ry suggests, I will go to America and shall have the opportunity to study many things. In this program, we'll get paid a monthly salary of 150 bahts. We are to be trained as teachers, yet we get paid.

Ry says I am to tell the recruiter that I am nineteen because you have to be at least eighteen to enroll. She says that they'll believe me since I'm taller than many Cambodian women of eighteen. At the Department of Physical Education and Recreation, a number of girls and women, perhaps twenty, have signed up to be trained as instructors. Sitting at the benchlike tables, we study the rules of volleyball, which are described in a four-page handout. After going over them for two mornings, we begin the actual training of volleyball, and the chair of the department informs us we will get our uniforms, which brings a smile to our faces. I can't wait to get into mine.

At first we are terrible at the game. As we practice, we all get better. I love the game and become one of the best players. The women's volleyball games draw not only an audience of refugees but also some Western foreigners and a few Thai soldiers who carry rifles. After one game, Rey—one of the players who didn't play the last game—nudges me. She says that she has noticed the Thai soldiers watching me, and that they speak among themselves as if they are interested in me. I turn, glancing at them; they are still standing by the volleyball court looking our way. A pang of fear overwhelms me. I become jittery, recalling stories of rape.

Two of the three soldiers come to the volleyball court again. They seem to be fixated on me, some of the girls say, but I'm not scared because the crowd surrounds us, and I walk home with everyone when we finish.

On the third day in the midafternoon, as I am walking by my-self near the post office to my quad, I hear quickened footsteps be-hind me. Then suddenly a voice says, "*Sawatdee khup* [Hello]!"

I turn, startled. A soldier's gaze meets mine. He's one of the sol-diers who has been watching me! He carries a rifle on his shoulder, trotting toward me. Realizing who it is, I run without looking back.

When I get to the quad, there's no one home except *Om* Soy. Once I calm down, I tell her what happened. She warns me to be careful.

It has been about two months since I joined volleyball training. I have found a new meaning to life in a refugee camp, where I can enjoy myself even though I'm confined to this place, physically barred from the outside world. On the volleyball court, I'm free, energized. With freedom, I bloom, becoming competitive, fun, and silly. Life has gradually begun to return to normal, and now this— having to fear the soldiers.

Another late afternoon, I'm talking with *Om* Soy as she cooks. All of a sudden there is a look of concern in her eyes, which stray to view something behind me. Perplexed, I turn, and there is the soldier who has been following me. He is standing right behind me. His eyes look into mine. In a heartbeat I leap into the quad, fright-ened, while *Om* speaks Thai with him.

"Athy! Athy!" *Om* Soy's hoarse voice calls. "Come on out. Come out. He's gone."

Om Soy explains. "That soldier has been wanting to marry you. He has been in love with you since he first saw you. But I told him that you already have a fiancé in America who is waiting to marry you. Well, you don't have one, I made it up so he'll leave you alone. He looked sad, then said good-bye to me."

At fifteen, I'm in a state of disbelief, repulsed by the idea of mar-riage, especially to a Thai soldier since I've witnessed Thai soldiers' brutality toward refugees, including Than. But deep down I feel bad for him for falling in love with me. Yet I can't return his interest in me, rather I'm afraid of him. I worry.

Later I write a letter to Uncle Seng, and *Om* Soy urges me to tell him to get my family out of the camp as soon as possible. It seems as if she can read my mind.

I tear a piece of paper from my notebook and I begin to write:

Dear Uncle:

My brothers, sisters, and I have been staying in refugee camps for a long time. We've been at Sakeo II Camp for a while. Before, I thought living in refugee camps was safer than living under the Pol Pot regime, but the truth is, it's not that safe. I have heard stories of Thai soldiers raping Cambodian girls who look for fire-wood in the woods. Now I have problems. A Thai soldier has been following me. Today he came to my quad. I'm scared of him, Uncle. Please sponsor us out of here soon. We don't have any more parents, please help us. We can rely only on you because you're the only uncle that can help us now. Please get us out of Thailand soon.

From your niece, Chanrithy Him

On the afternoon on January 27, 1981, all the trainees gather at the Physical Education and Recreation Department for our graduation before our two hundred or so guests arrive. Already, in the department's large space under a covered roof, tables and chairs are neatly arranged. In the far corner across from the main office, a small stage is crowded with drums, guitars, and microphones.

But what is really exciting is how pretty all the girls look. Ry wears a white long-sleeved blouse with a long dark green skirt. Our friend Arom also has on a long-sleeved blouse of soft light green with a dark green skirt. Her older sister Anny is dressed in a beautiful yellow blouse with a bow draping down in front. As for me, I'm decked out in a bright red short-sleeved velveteen blouse and a long skirt with a sequence of four lines of colors—bright blue, neon green, light orange, and hot pink—alternating throughout the fabric.

A special meal has been prepared and some of the tables and chairs are removed to make room for dancing. The band plays music that I heard long ago in Phnom Penh. It warms my heart, yet it makes me homesick. But soon my emotion changes. I'm thrilled to see many people get up to dance a Cambodian folk dance. Men clap their hands and put them to their chins—they ask the women to dance. I have a wonderful evening, the most fun I have had since the Khmer Rouge regime.

A few days after the graduation, I recruit children and teach them volleyball. The little boys and girls enjoy playing. They laugh, giggling, so happy. It is invigorating to be among them. But I hear about an opening at the Public Health Center. Since Khao I Dang I have been hoping to work as a medical interpreter. A friend tells me the center is looking for volunteers to help educate refugees about tuberculosis and preventive measures. If I'm interested, he says, I need to appear at eight o'clock in the morning in front of the center. I tell him that I'll be there.

The car picks everyone up in front of the center, then drops different groups off at various sections of the camp. Going from quad to quad, I work with two Cambodian men and Janice, an American registered nurse. My main task is to inform families about the symptoms of TB and preventive measures. When Janice administers TB skin tests to baby boys and girls, I caress their cheeks, hoping to distract them from the poke of the needle.

The work is important to me. But it won't last long because my family will soon be transferred to Mairut Camp. Part of the process of coming to America involves going through transit camps. Aunt Eng's family has just been transferred to another camp. Already I begin to miss my friends.

Our bus stops behind another bus amid a green landscape where tall grass and distant coconut trees stand majestically, swaying in the soft breeze. *So this is Mairut,* I think to myself. It's pretty. The air smells different. Fresh, as if we were near a body of water. We are led to large quads about two and half times the size of the ones in Sakeo II Camp. Like the ones in Sakeo II Camp, these are built facing each other in groups of four. In front of them is a huge open space where flowerlike plants grow in little square gardens. Our assigned spot, a doorless compartment in the center of the quad, is spacious, and it has long fluorescent lightbulbs! Electricity! What a treat!

It is awkward to be living again with Ra, *bang* Vantha, baby Syla, and Savorng. We haven't talked to *bang* Vantha since the incident when the soldiers tortured Than. Now we share the same living space, and it's uncomfortable to just talk to Ra and Savorng or play with Syla. When Ry, Than, and I are around *bang* Vantha, we each pretend the other doesn't exist.

On the outskirts of Mairut Camp, Ry and I go exploring with our friends Arom and Anny, who have also been transferred. When we come to a watchtower, I decide to climb it. Looking between the branches of tall trees, I see a body of blue and green water with waves rippling in the distance. As I near the top, I see a few people looking out, away. I hurry in their direction, and I can't believe what I am seeing. *It is an ocean!** A vast blue body of water along which stand coconut trees. I shout to Ry, Arom, and Anny to come up. This is my first time seeing an ocean. I'm grateful to be alive.

Later we get to go to the ocean. The beaches fill with people. Some rest below the coconut trees. Others, like Than and us, have water fights, soaking each other with our splashing.

Many people, perhaps a hundred, crowd offices that hire refugees for various paying jobs, such as interpreter or teacher. For two days

---

* The Gulf of Thailand.

I've been without luck. At least I find that there will be a public school offering English classes. The classroom is made of thatch and bamboo rods. In it, there are seven long benchlike desks, one row on the left, one row on the right. The girls sit on the left. The boys choose the right side of the classroom near the desk of our English teacher, who is one of the refugees. We study grammar as well as practice conversation.

It is May 1981. My family is transferred to another camp after two months in Mairut. It is a long ride on the bus from Mairut to Pananikom Holding Center. The gate of the camp opens as our bus approaches. The weather is hot, humid. Map and Savorng frown. They are thirsty for water. Baby Syla cries, fussing.

With seven other families, we are led through quads that look like the ones in Sakeo II Camp. We walk through a barbed wire gate connected to a barbed wire fence encircling four empty quads. The ground in the middle is eroded and muddy. This place is at a remove from the main population of refugees. We are told that they have no other quads for us to stay in except these—a place where Thai soldiers used to imprison Vietnamese refugees.

I remain in the quad for two weeks until we are transferred to another camp, called Lompini. Everyone else goes to a makeshift market. Ry and Than take Map and Savorng to see it and urge me to come along. But I don't want to. I'm afraid of the Thai soldiers, who continue to patrol and threaten us.

To keep myself occupied, I study English. I go over my note-books, reviewing grammar. When I get tired of memorizing various tenses, I read the *Essential English Book I*, my mind temporarily lost in the dialogues between characters.

Here I am safe, but boredom overwhelms me. The first week, when everyone goes to the market, I feel lonely. I feel as though I am a prisoner. When the second week comes, Ry and Than bring me tapes of Cambodian songs that we used to listen to back in Phnom Penh.

Every day I listen to the tapes. Romantic songs sung by the late superstar singers Sinsee Samuth and Ros Sarey Sothea fill the quad. I remember how much I liked to watch the Cambodian classical dancers perform in Phnom Penh when *Pa* took us to performances, and how much I wanted to learn these dances. I remember *Pa*'s passion for them.

For *Pa*, someday I will learn to perform those classical dances. I would dance gracefully to the music of bells and drums. Like the dancers I saw in Phnom Penh, I would gently step forward, my curved fingers sweeping the air, as I approached the audience. When I finish they would clap, and I would be proud of myself for having performed well—for *Pa*.

We are moved to another transit camp on June 8, 1981. A Thai civilian leads us through a concrete alley past shelters and clotheslines. We are to stay in a concrete-shed-like shelter with moldy floors and walls. A cool breeze is blowing, bringing the stench of urine as if we were surrounded by toilets.

Lying on a plastic tarp spread over the concrete floor, I wait for Than and Ry to bring back our food rations. When they get back, they explain that the Thai people who distribute food had to check our group picture, taken by the immigration authorities in Sakeo II Camp, and match it with their documents. Then they looked at Ry's and Than's faces to be sure. Those who came without pictures were refused food.

Map, Savorng, and I gather around a small pot of soup and a container of rice. Than dishes out rice. Ry ladles the soup into a bowl. All of a sudden Ry lets go of the soup pot. "Worms in the soup!" she cries, recoiling. Than takes it in stride, scooping the worms out of the soup. I know we've had to eat worse than this before, but that was under the Khmer Rouge.

Luckily, after being here for only a week, we pass the physical examinations. We are given permission to leave Thailand, to head to the next refugee camp in the Philippines.

20

Philippine
Refugee Processing Center

On the night of June 20, 1981, we arrive at the airport in the Philippines. The trip here from Thailand seemed like an eternity. Now the idea of lying on a bed sounds luxurious, but we need to take a bus to the camp.

The next morning when I open my eyes, sunlight filters through the window into the room where Than, Ry, Map, and I sleep. I sit, thinking, *Where is Ra . . . bang Vantha, Syla, and Savorng?* Then I remember, they are sleeping downstairs.

I get up, then pad softly down the stairs so I won't wake anyone up. Curious about this camp, I run along the concrete walkway and I look at my surroundings. I gaze at the wooden two-story apartment buildings on my right and left. They are long structures divided into individual units. Each family, it seems, has been given a unit, like ours, with an upstairs and a downstairs. After admiring these buildings, I look to my right and there it is, in the distance, a majestic hillside with thriving green trees, grass, and a huge white cross. I'm mesmerized by everything. The apartment buildings. The greenery of the hillside. The concrete walkways that snake between the apartments. The beautiful landscape of grass, shrubs, and flowers near the walkways and along paved roads. I like the spacious yard in front of each building. I marvel, taking in the beauty of this camp, and I'm grateful.

Ry and I are washing dishes behind our apartment when suddenly a sweet, gentle voice interrupts our talk. "My friends, how are you?" a voice asks with a distinct accent.

We turn, and there is a small dark-skinned Filipino woman behind us, smiling. "My friends, do you want to trade rice for vegetables?" She shows us baskets of limes and other fresh vegetables. I glance at the vegetables, but quickly I look into her bright, friendly eyes. Her tone and welcoming spirit astound me. We have never met, yet she calls us "my friends." Her words and spirit say "welcome." I think of the camps in Thailand we've been in and how we were treated there. In those camps we were always the culprits. The soldiers were always ready to jump on us during trading. But their own people, the merchants, always got away. I'm appreciative of this Filipino woman. She makes me feel at home.

Soon after we arrive, we are told that people ages sixteen to fifty-five have to study English as a second language (ESL) and cultural orientation (CO) for three months before our departure for America. In the intensive ESL class, we will study about clothing, housing, employment, the post office, and transportation. For the CO class, we'll study general subjects such as sponsorship, communication, lifestyles, and sanitation. Though I look forward to learning these subjects, I can't help feeling overwhelmed by the number of subjects we have to master in such a short time. But the education here is free, and I need to do some catching up before going to America. I am looking forward to attending these classes.

In the ESL class, we have both Cambodian and Vietnamese students. Our teacher is a Filipino lady. When she enters the classroom, she glances at us and frowns. I wonder if she is mean like some of my teachers back in Cambodia, who pulled boys' sideburns and hit the palms of our hands with a long bamboo stick. As she puts her woven bag down by her desk, she faces the class. Her red-painted lips widen into a smile. I feel relieved. Now I'm ready to learn anything that will prepare me for America.

Our first lesson is learning how to greet someone in English, how to shake hands. When it's time to practice, our teacher asks a girl sitting beside me to get up. She is to shake hands with a Cambodian man in our class. The girl shakes her head, her face flushed. The teacher asks another girl, and she too shakes her head. She looks embarrassed just to be called upon, let alone to be shaking hands with a man.

"Come on, you guys, get up and shake hands with those men. Look, they are not bad-looking. In fact, they're handsome," says our teacher, making the men smile.

No one gets up. Our teacher asks a Cambodian man and a Vietnamese man to come to the front of the class. They introduce themselves, then shake hands. The teacher stares at us and says, "You see, it's not hard to come up and shake hands. Watch me. My name is Marie. How do you do?" She shakes hands with a Vietnamese student. "Here, I'm still shaking hands with him and I'm not going to have a baby. Don't worry. You're not going to have a baby by shaking hands. Now, come on and practice."

I'm annoyed by her comments. She should have been informed of our culture, and known that our way of greeting people is to press the palms of our hands together, then raise them to our chins. Even I, who am brave under many circumstances, am embarrassed by the idea of hand shaking. We need time to adjust.

As Marie urges us to volunteer, I begin to have courage.

She asks a Vietnamese student named Minh to stand in front of the class. Smiling, she says, "Would someone come up and shake hands with Minh. He's handsome." The class laughs. Minh smiles, his eyes becoming smaller as he gazes in the girls' direction.

I stand up. The teacher smiles. She croons, "Come on, Chanrithy. You can do it! Okay, introduce yourself first, then shake hands."

No problem, I think, smiling to myself. I walk up to Minh, then I say, "My name is Chanrithy. How do you do?"

The girls giggle behind me, making Minh smile.

"Hello, my name is Minh," he says, glancing at the girls. "How do you do?" He looks at them again.

I reach out to shake his hand. He steps forward to shake mine, but as soon as his hand nears mine, I pull it away. I dash back to my seat, then laughter erupts.

Beaming, I look at my teacher, whose hand covers her face and whose body quivers with suppressed laughter. The men on my right guffaw. Minh's face is as red as the face of a hen who is trying to lay her eggs. A Cambodian man behind him nudges him, and he smiles sheepishly.

"Oh, Chanrithy. Why didn't you shake Minh's hand?" the teacher asks sympathetically.

I reply, smiling. "I will next time." *It serves him right for smirking at the girls earlier.* I look at Minh. His face is still red.

A week after our arrival, we were told to see the immigration officers. *Bang* Vantha walked in the opposite direction of their offices. Sitting on chairs at the immigration office with other families, we wait for him to come. Ry and Than blame Ra for not berating *bang* Vantha for his behavior. Ra says, he'll come. He's an idiot, she admits, to play around on a day like today. We keep looking at the doors, but there is no sign of him. As soon as his name is called, we all stand up, frowning at each other. Suddenly his smirking face appears at one of the doors. This is not the first time he has played with our emotions. He seems to take pleasure in making us mad.

After the meeting with immigration, *bang* Vantha says that he has changed his mind. He doesn't want us to be with Uncle Seng. Instead of going to Portland, Oregon, he says he is happy to relocate. He will go anywhere the immigration authorities send us, and we will have to go also.

He smirks. Ra ignores him, holding Syla in her arms. Ry's angry, her face red. Than keeps his thoughts to himself. Savorng and Map frown at *bang* Vantha. Many Cambodian refugees desperately want to go to a country like the United States, sending letters and applications for resettlement to the embassies of America, France, Australia, Canada, and any other country who might be willing to take them. They worry about their fates and pray that they will be remembered, yet my own brother-in-law is ungrateful for his own good luck.

My friend Sothea takes me to Phase I, a medical clinic that provides medical care to refugees. It looks just like a clinic in Phnom Penh, and is surrounded by lush flowers and plants. There are concrete sidewalks. Paved roads. It's been a long time since I saw such a place.

Inside the building Sothea gives me a tour, showing me examination rooms with chairs, posters, and equipment I've never seen before. The front desk, where patients are received, has a long, smooth counter with a few nice chairs behind it. There are even telephones. Never before have I seen a place for refugees that is so—so modern, so well established. And the pharmacy is also nice. It has shelves along the walls with boxes and bottles of medicine neatly arranged, the variety of labels and names of medicine catch my eye. Suddenly a shadow of a memory comes to mind. I'm taken back in time to Phnom Penh, to *Pa*'s medicine desk. The times when he took care of me when I was sick with asthma.

Sothea introduces me to some of the staff: Dr. Sophon, a Cambodian from Canada; Mary Bliss, an American registered nurse, and Dr. Tran, a former medical doctor from Vietnam. Surprisingly, I find myself shaking hands with them naturally. All of a sudden I feel like an adult, so mature.

Sothea is going to America and needs someone to take her place as a medical interpreter. She asks if I am interested in the job. I am more than interested, I tell her! She laughs, tickled by my excitement.

Now one of my dreams is about to be realized. In Khao I Dang, I wanted so much to speak English. I wanted so badly to be a medical interpreter. Sometimes I daydreamed while I studied English. I envisioned myself translating for patients, working with doctors and nurses. It would be rewarding to help my fellow refugees who have gone through so much. Now this dream is coming true. Perhaps my other dreams will come true also, when I go to America. I remember what I promised during Chea's burial: *Chea, if I survive, I will study medicine. I want to help people because I couldn't help you. If I die in this lifetime, I will learn medicine in my next life.*

Than complains that no one has thought of teaching Map Cambodian. Than thinks Map, seven, should learn Cambodian because it's his own language. He will teach Map, he says, since we don't have *Mak* or *Pa* to take that role anymore. I'm proud of him for thinking of Map. I listen to him and glance at him teaching Map as I study medical terminologies from the Cambodian medical manual Sothea gave me. I watch Than scribble something in a notebook. It's fascinating to see my older brother take this responsibility upon himself.

Than recites the Cambodian alphabet, then he tells Map to say it after him. After a few times, Than has Map repeat it on his own.

Map looks bored, uninterested. Map tells Than that he wants to go out and play. Than says he has to study Cambodian and scolds Map to repeat after him. Map mumbles what Than said. Than asks him to recite the alphabet on his own. Map can only remember a few letters. That makes Than mad, so Than hits him on the shoulder.

Map cries. Than raises his hand to hit Map again. Map cringes. Map looks at me for help, but I don't want to say anything because Than is eighteen, older than I am. He wouldn't listen to me because I never thought of teaching Map and he has.

Sobbing, Map repeats after Than again. Than tells him to recite the alphabet on his own. Map says a few characters, then he stops, his eyes braced for more slaps. Than hits him on his shoulder, then says, "Why can't you remember? It's not that hard. You're stupid." Than glares at Map.

"He's not stupid!" I tell Than. My voice comes out louder than I intended. "He's just starting to learn, and you want him to know everything. What kind of a teacher are you?"

"Don't tell me what to do," Than snaps at me. "I want to teach him. If nobody teaches him, how is he going to learn?"

"You're not teaching him, you're torturing him." I'm amazed at how the words fly out of my mouth.

Ry appears at the top of the stairs, and I don't hesitate to tell her what has transpired. I tell her what I think of Than, of the way he teaches Map and disciplines him. Map gets up and walks over to Ry. Than glares at me. He says that I am good at criticizing but don't help to teach Map. For a moment I don't know what to say because it's true that I haven't taught Map anything.

Then I remember what the Cambodian elders used to say, "A good teacher has to have patience in order to teach students." From watching Than I know he doesn't have patience, and he is not a good teacher. Instead, he is an overbearing brother. Appalled by what Than has done, Ry, twenty, tells Than not to worry about

Map now. He's only seven, she says. Since then Than has not taught Map.

Than is angry that I raised my voice to him. But how could I not raise my voice when he treats Map that way? Than expects me to act like a proper Cambodian girl. But I can no longer look the other way if I feel someone is being hurt.

The following evening, lying on my back with the medical manual sitting on my chest, I can't stop chuckling. I'm so tickled and embarrassed at the same time. My stomach begins to hurt. My cheeks are getting tired. Tears spill out of my eyes.

"What are you laughing about?" Ry asks, grinning.

"Oh, nothing." I say, laughing.

"If it's nothing, why are you still laughing?"

I chuckle harder, shaking my head. Ry stands close to me, smiling, demanding to know. Finally I say, "Okay!" I tell her that I've been studying medical terminologies for my job at Phase I. She looks at me as if to say, What is so funny about that? I tell her that studying and memorizing the terms are not funny, but that I'm tickled because I'll be embarrassed when I have to translate for men and women who have medical problems that relate to their reproductive systems, their private parts. "How am I going to translate for older patients if I'm so embarrassed to say these terms? I'm young, Ry," I plead. I recite the terms that will be hard for me to translate. Ry laughs. She says perhaps over time, I'll be less embarrassed. But I tell her that I'll be mortified as I translate these words.

She smiles comically and says, "Well, you're the one who wanted to volunteer in the medical field."

"I know! I'll just have to be professional and hope I won't burst out laughing."

I'm happy to volunteer at Phase I. When I'm there, I look forward to helping patients. I work like an eager salesperson. Through the rectangular barred window of the pharmacy, I watch for the customers: Cambodians, Cambodian-Chinese, Vietnamese, and Chinese. As soon as I see them coming, I dash out to the front-desk area, inquiring as to their needs. If I'm not sure they're Cambodians, I ask, "May I help you?" If they are Vietnamese, I let Dr. Tran know. With the Cambodians, I inquire about their medical problems, gathering information before they see whoever is on duty.

After translating, I help fill the patients' prescriptions. I get good at reading the scribbling from Mary, Dr. Sophon, or Dr. Tran. When we are not busy, I stay in a pharmacy. I look out the window or read the labels on the medicine vials, boxes, and bottles, wondering about the ingredients in each medicine, and how they help patients feel better.

Sometimes I take my badge off my blouse and look at it admiringly. It has a small picture of me smiling which I cut out of a bigger picture taken at the party after I finished ESL. At sixteen, I'm proud of myself. I look at the badge again and again, so happy about the work I'm doing.

I sit on a stool in the pharmacy waiting for the Vietnamese patients whom Dr. Tran has just seen. A few young Vietnamese men approach the barred window of the pharmacy. They talk among themselves, smiling. Each gives me his prescription, peering at me earnestly. I pick one prescription. I read the name of the medicine. I search for it on the shelf. As I wrap up the white tablets, I hear the words "beautiful" and "I love you" spoken by one of them. As I hand the patient his medicine packet, my gaze rests on his sheepish, smitten face. I take refuge in another prescription, looking for the name of the medicine. When I'm done helping everyone, the smitten patient says to me "I love you" in Vietnamese. Though I understand the words, I simply give him a friendly smile, pretending I'm not aware of anything out of the ordinary. Suddenly he steps toward the window and says "I love you" in English. I don't know how to react to that, so it is easy just to say nothing. His friends laugh softly, then say something to him in Vietnamese.

Strange yet fascinating to notice men being attracted to me. Maybe *Om* Soy is right. That even though I'm young, I look mature beyond my years. Thus people take me for a woman, not a girl, a teenager. I don't want to be rude to anyone, but I don't have any guidance on how to deal with men at this unsettled time.

Phlor Torrejos, my CO teacher, takes the whole class to a beautiful stream three miles from the camp. She is Filipino, short and a little chubby with straight black hair that comes to her chin. Her bangs drape down above her eyebrows. Her face is always ready to smile. She's kind and personable. For this trip, she has brought food for the entire class. I admire her for sharing her personal life with us, telling us how she has persevered through hardships. Now she's a senior writer/editor for the Communication Foundation for Asia.

In class, she says if we fail to accomplish our goals the first time, we have to try again. Many times it takes more than one attempt. She says it's kind of like falling and getting up. If we fall, we have to get up. Sometimes we fall more than once, and we have to get up more than once. Sometimes getting up is hard, but we must do it, no matter how long it takes—we have to be strong, she says.

After a long hike, we take a rest on large rocks beneath the trees. When we are having lunch in the shade, I look at Phlor, grateful. She wants so much for us to succeed in our new lives in America. I think about the life that awaits me in America. I wonder how many times I will have to get up from falls when I'm there.

But I know myself—I will get up if I should fall. I always have. My mind relaxes. My ears tune in to the voices of my classmates, hiking along the stream. The sound of water running between rocks is soothing. With her eyes closed, Phlor rests peacefully in the shade.

Her clothes are still wet from swimming in a clear pond. Lying on a flat rock near her and other women classmates, I feel the precious solitude of the Morong Bataan. I feel as if I'm connected to the calm, still earth. I feel as if today is a dream. The cool breeze touches my face. My arms. My soul. It has been a long time since I felt a sense of inner peace. Being in this camp has made that possible, for we've been given enough food to eat. We have running water. Electricity. We have school. We have clean, pretty apartments to live in. I don't have to worry about the Filipino soldiers. I feel protected. I feel safe. I feel loved, accepted by the local people who work in the camp. I am finally free of life-threatening situations.

Ratha tells me that a doctor needs a translator. I hurry down the hall and check one examination room, but no one is there. I walk to the adjacent one, and the door is ajar. I hear a voice trying to speak Cambodian. I take a peek. Suddenly a set of big, dark eyes stare back at me. *A new doctor?* I ask myself. I've never seen him before. He wears a stethoscope around his neck. He looks Filipino and is cute—young with shiny black hair and dark eyes with long eyelashes.

Getting caught peeking, I need time to recoup. I take a deep breath, regain my composure, then knock on the door.

"Yes?"

I introduce myself, telling him my name and who I am. He stands up and says, "I'm Dr. Tanedo, Achilles Tanedo." He reaches out to shake my hand. I shake his hand, and I'm not even embarrassed. Not a bit. Marie would have been proud of me.

I translate for the patient, but mention to the doctor that I haven't seen him here before. He says that he works mostly at the hospital. *A hospital?* I didn't know that this camp had a hospital. But I don't ask for further clarification. All I want is to establish a rapport, and it isn't hard to do so. I acquire the information from the patient regarding her illness. In about ten minutes, Dr. Tanedo writes her a prescription, and my mind is already at the pharmacy, trying to locate her medicine on the shelves.

Ry is excited, calling my name as if memorizing it. "Athy, Athy, I've got a letter, I've got a letter. We're going to be with Uncle Seng."

I look at her, overwhelmed by her exuberance. I'm between excitement and confusion. Ry catches her breath, calming down to explain. She says, "Do you remember I told you about my friend helping me write a letter? About *bang* Vantha saying he wanted us to go anywhere?" She pauses as if letting me digest what she has just said.

I reach for the letter in her hand, remembering what she is talking about. She asked a friend to write a letter on our behalf so that we could go to Uncle Seng in Portland and not be randomly placed, as *bang* Vantha has threatened. I open the thin letter and read the response: "Please tell these kids that the P.A. listed Mr. Leng Seng as a possible sponsor and did not say 'anywhere.' [signed] TP." I gape, eyes widened. A burst of joy tumbles out of my mouth—I scream.

We didn't have many patients today, yet I'm tired, and hungry. I slowly walk toward home. The day is still bright. Some families sit outside in front of their apartments. Then a person, a woman wearing a long skirt, darts out of an apartment, my apartment. She runs as if she is in a race with herself, heading toward me. *Ry?*

Smiling, I pause, watching her run. I'm amused—my older sister runs like an excited little girl. Her face beams radiantly. She is jubilant. Ry grabs my shoulders, she shakes me, she croons: "We're going to America, we're going to America—"

"Really?"

Ry nods, then hops, and so do I. We don't care how foolish we look in front of our neighbors. We are oblivious, absorbed in ourselves. As we calm down, I ask her if she heard our family name and our BT number (a number assigned to each family) called over the loudspeakers. She nods repeatedly.

Facing the sky, I close my eyes and smile. Suddenly I'm in a whole new world, a world that gives me hope and makes me float. Every part of my body savors these exalted, indescribable feelings. My feet lift me up. I dance on the concrete sidewalk. Ry watches me, grinning. . . . Today I just want to shine, to celebrate.

I look forward to our new life, yet I'm nervous, scared. Everything seems hopeful, yet abstract. The unknown scares me. It doesn't help thinking of American or Cambodian girls my age who have parents. In America I won't have *Mak* or *Pa*. I feel uncertain, unstable because my life has been so different. I wish I could plan it, laying it out like a calendar.

It's only six more days until we leave for America. I make a mental list of friends to whom I want to bid good-bye. For the past few days, I've been thinking about this sweet old woman, a patient who has problems with her eyesight and legs. She can't see or walk well. When I translate for her, she calls me "daughter" in a gentle tone of voice. I address her as *Om*, great-aunt, since she is, perhaps, older than *Mak*. When she saw Mary Bliss, she complained of a numb sensation in her legs. Since I haven't seen her for a few weeks and she has missed her follow-up appointment, I have to visit her.

It's about seven o'clock in the evening. I arrive at her apartment and peek inside. There she is sitting. Her legs folded on a mat, her face dark but pale. She looks up. She says, "Oh, there you are. Good. You've come. Come on in. You can sit anywhere you'd like. Sit down, sit down. I'll get some cakes." She gets up with difficulty, her legs seem heavy.

On the wall of her apartment is a poster of Buddha sitting on the lotus blossom beneath a tree in a beautiful, colorful forest. In front of him are angels in golden clothes, their legs folded, the palms of their hands pressed together reverently. Below the poster is a can of burned incense and four candles that have melted down to half their original length.

Om staggers toward me. Her mouth widens to form a weak smile. She hands me a bag of steamed cakes, made of sweetened sticky flour and beans wrapped in banana leaf, which she sells in the makeshift market in the camp.

At Phase I, when I last saw her, she had urged me to look for her in the market or to go to her home so she could give me cakes. She kept thanking me and God after I translated for her and filled her prescription, then brought it to her and helped her out the door. Today I've brought her a package of medicine which she would have gotten if she had gone to her follow-up appointment.

"Here, daughter," *Om* says. "Take these cakes to your family. Thank you so much for bringing me medicine. *Om* is sad because *Om* can't walk well. My husband is old. He's always at the temple. We don't have children, so nobody gets the medicine for *Om*. *Om* doesn't know who to ask. It's difficult."

Understanding her circumstances, I tell her that I've been thinking about her, wondering if she's all right. *Om* presses her palms together, raises them to her forehead, then faces the poster of Buddha and says, "*Sa thook, sa thook.* May God in heaven take care of you. Daughter, you're so thoughtful, thinking of *Om*."

After visiting with her for an hour, I'm tired. She seems very lonely, and shares with me her problems in Cambodia and in the refugee camps both here and in Thailand. When I begin to get up and say good night, she says, "Why hurry, daughter? Stay a little bit longer. Here, have some more cakes. Stay until my husband comes, then he can do fortune-telling for you, find out about your life in America. You don't have any kids to worry about, visit with *Om* a little longer."

When her husband comes, she gets up with difficulty, introducing me to him. I've been waiting for him to do fortune-telling, she tells him. When he has his back to her, she places fifteen pesos in the chalicelike container.

Her husband hands her an oaken stack of bound sheets, which she then hands to me. I look at it, then I remember. It's called a *kompee*, a Buddhist sacred treatise that I saw at a temple in Phnom Penh. *Om* hands me a stick of incense. She tells me to wish in my mind, then raise the *kompee* to my forehead and insert the tip of the incense somewhere in the *kompee*. As soon as I insert it, she tells me to open to the spot where the tip of the incense lies. She says, "Now read and find out what fortune waits for you in America."

I read the fancy print in Cambodian, my mind half asleep. It says something about going to hell. Suddenly *Om* stops me from reading further. Both of her hands clap mine to close the *kompee*. She says I didn't concentrate hard enough when I wished for good fortune. "Let her try one more time," she says to her husband. Before he says anything, she tells me to concentrate and wish for a great fortune. Her hands wrap around mine and lift them to my forehead, then she says, "Now concentrate. Wish for a good fortune."

I wish for good fate, good fortune. God, please help me in America, I say tiredly in my mind. Somehow I find myself pouring my soul into my wishing. I hold the *kompee* up longer so *Om* thinks I am wishing hard, concentrating hard. I just want to see her happy. I hope I have some luck tonight and the incense lands on a good page.

That's enough, *Om* says lovingly. She tells me to turn to the page and read, coaching me like I am a little girl. I read from the page and it says that I will have a good fate, and that a *sathey*, a wealthy person, will find me and support me in every way. Before I finish reading, *Om* interrupts, "You see, daughter? When you focus your mind, you get a good fortune. *Om* believes that daughter will have good luck in America as the words say in the *kompee*."

I've packed everything I own: a few clothes, notebooks, pens, the *Essential English Book I*, tattered family photos I'd hidden, a medical dictionary Sothea gave me, and a small packet of medicine for anyone who might get sick on the plane. In the packet I put my ID from Phase I in case we are questioned about the medicine. I tell Ry that I've packed everything, then I run down the stairs and yell out to her that I need to go to Phase I. I need to say good-bye to my friends.

On the concrete sidewalk, I trot. Tears burn at the back of my eyes when I think about leaving PRPC today. I hope they're there. I don't want to leave without saying good-bye. I've told everyone else at Phase I that I'm going to America. Streams of tears course down my cheeks.

"Chanrithy, Chanrithy," a voice sounds behind me.

I turn. My eyes search for the voice. An American woman runs toward me. *Mary Bliss?* She smiles and quickens her stride, leaping over the flower bed near the sidewalk.

Smiling, I say, "Mary, I'm going to America today! I've been wanting to say good-bye to you."

"That's what I heard from the people at the clinic. That's why I came to find you, so I could say good-bye." She gazes at me, her arms embracing me.

She hands me her address in Washington, D.C., and tells me to write her so she can write me a letter of recommendation for a job in America. Looking into my teary eyes, she apologizes that she couldn't say good-bye to me sooner because she was out of the country in Thailand. Knowing I'm pressed for time, she says her good-byes and wishes me good luck in my new life in America.

I wipe away my tears and hurry into the clinic. I go up to the front desk to find out if Dr. Tanedo will be at the clinic, but he's only working at the hospital today. A lump forms in my throat. When the nurse at the desk hears I'm leaving, she calls Dr. Tanedo at the hospital, who says he will find me when I go to my mandatory physical exam before departure.

I smile, thank her, then rush out the door. I can't help smiling radiantly. I've been teased about Dr. Tanedo, but I don't care. I do have a crush on him, but he's been kind to me.

When I arrive home, Dr. Tanedo is already there. "Hi, Dr. Tanedo. Thank you for coming to say good-bye to me," I exclaim, smiling brightly yet embarrassed to have him look at me.

He returns the smile and tells me that he came as soon as he heard I was leaving the camp. He's so kind to take the time to come. I feel awkward, embarrassed again. I lower my eyes, then realize I need to introduce Ry, Ra, and Than. He reaches out to shake their hands. He's so formal, professional.

"Chanrithy, what are you going to do in America?" Dr. Tanedo asks gently.

"I'd like to go to school, maybe study medicine. Perhaps it's too late for me to go back to school. I'm sixteen already. I haven't gone to a formal school for seven years, since the fall of Cambodia." I look down at the ground, pitying myself that my childhood passed by during the Khmer Rouge regime and in refugee camps. I feel so behind. I'm scared. America, the country I've been waiting to go to, now scares me.

"Chanrithy, you're still young, only sixteen. You can go to school. . . ." Dr. Tanedo looks at me sympathetically. He searches for my lowered eyes, then says, "In America, you can study whatever you want."

His gentle, hopeful voice gives me courage. I level my gaze and look at him. In my heart I want to say, *Really? I can study whatever I want? Then I'll learn many things. . . .*

His eyes tell me I can. I feel at ease, comforted. He is the first person with whom I have shared my hopes and fears. Now I feel a weight has been lifted, and I'm grateful.

"Athy, people are going to the physical examination!" Ry points to the front yard. Families clutch their belongings and children, trotting toward a group of large tents where the physical examination will be.

I look at Dr. Tanedo. I don't want to say good-bye. He offers to carry my duffel bag and reaches out to pick it up. We all hurry to the tents.

We arrive at a tent. Soon *bang* Vantha's name is called. Anxiously, *bang* Vantha rushes into the tent, and Ra, with Syla in her hands, also steps in, her eyes signaling to us to follow. We go in. A Filipino woman orders *bang* Vantha to take his clothes off in front of us all. He rightly refuses. Then the woman orders us all out.

Walking out of the tent, I give this woman a stare, angry at her need to belittle us. Dr. Tanedo asks what happened, and when I explain, he suggests that we give him our documents.

From tent to tent Dr. Tanedo goes, talking to Filipino medical workers in his own language. All we have to do is stand near him. The workers glance at us, then turn their attention to Dr. Tanedo. Ry grins off and on, stealing glances at me, then at Dr. Tanedo. Finally words tumble out of her mouth.

"Not bad, Athy. You have a doctor friend to help us." She grins again. When I smile, she giggles. Ra, too, smiles. Savorng and Map seem to understand, so they join in. *Bang* Vantha flashes a weak grin.

Soon Dr. Tanedo returns to me and says that we are all set. He leads us toward a line of buses along the paved road. On the sidewalk near the buses, clumps of families stand by their belongings, their faces red, eyes swollen. A young girl weeps by a sad-looking man. Glancing at her face, I too break down. Ry wipes her eyes.

Cradling sleeping Syla in her arms, Ra blinks her tears away. Most of the women cry, but the men just look sad. People bid their good-byes and remind each other not to forget to write.

The sounds of ragged sobbing resonate. Families' names are being called. People get on the buses. Suddenly mine is called. I want to tell Dr. Tanedo that I'll miss him. But when I look at him, all I can do is cry. People look at me, and I just cry. No words come out of my mouth. My tongue is stuck.

"Athy, hurry." Ry waves at me by the entrance to the bus. Map and Savorng throw me a frowning glance. Embracing Syla in her arms, Ra, too, hurries me. She stands by *bang* Vantha as they crowd onto the steps of the bus. Than is already on the bus.

Overwhelmed by it all, I dash to the bus. When I'm on it, waiting to be seated behind Ry and Map, I realize I've forgotten to say good-bye to Dr. Tanedo one last time. I look out the window, and he stands there watching me. I want to get off, but people are coming up onto the bus.

"Athy, Athy!" a voice calls. Urgent taps shake the window near me. When I turn, through my tears I see my friend Sereya's sobbing face. I move close to the window. Sereya's face breaks into a smile. "I tried to run as fast as I could to get here before you were gone. Oh, Athy, I'm going to miss you."

I scold her not to cry because she is only making me cry even more. But she doesn't listen. She wails, and I cup my face in my hands.

"Chanrithy?" A gentle voice speaks. I turn toward the voice, and already Dr. Tanedo is sitting beside me.

"Oh, Dr. Tanedo!" I sigh, happy, yet sad at the same time.

"I'll ride with you until we get close to the hospital, then I'll get off there."

"Thank you," I say softly, my left hand wiping my eyes. I feel a gentle hand squeeze my right hand. I look at Dr. Tanedo, and he whispers to me not to cry. I want to say I can't, but I can only shake my head.

"Athy, you're leaving us. You're leaving us. Nobody's going to make us laugh anymore when you're gone," says Sereya, reminiscing. I choke, laughing, shaking my head.

Oblivious to everyone on the bus but Dr. Tanedo, I tell Sereya that amid this sadness, she must remind me of all the laughter I've brought to her and our friends. What a friend you are! I tease her. She giggles, amused at herself.

Feeling silly for laughing through my tears, I explain to Dr. Tanedo. He looks at me and gives me a sad smile, then his hand holds mine tightly. I'm comforted. But as the bus starts up, Sereya wails, tapping on the window again. "Good-bye, Athy. Good-bye," she yells.

The bus takes off. Sereya trots along. The bus accelerates, Sereya wails. I cover my face, sobbing.

"Chanrithy. Chanrithy, don't cry," whispers Dr. Tanedo. His hand rubs mine again and again.

The bus stops. Dr. Tanedo gets up, gazing at me, and wishes me good-bye and good luck.

The night welcomes us at the airport. The city lights dimly shine in the dark sky. Clutching a bag of food in one hand and a duffel bag in another, I breathe in the cool breeze. I scurry along beside Map, Savorng, and Ry. Than is ahead of us. *Bang* Vantha is in front of him. Ra trudges behind him, hugging Syla to her chest. I'm with my family, yet my mind is still at the camp. I miss my friends, more than at any other time in my life.

But as the plane takes us up into the sky, I feel at ease. I'm riding to freedom, carried in the belly of a bird. *We've made it,* I think to myself. We are crossing the ocean, above the world that has enchained us. We're alive.

I think about what awaits me in America. I imagine Uncle Seng looking at the picture of us we sent him, remembering the faces of his older brother's remaining children, whom he has not seen for six years, since the day he stepped out of the gate of our home.

In my duffel bag, there are other pictures, tattered photographs I managed to keep safe during the Khmer Rouge time, moving them from the roof of one hut to the next. They travel with me to America, along with the indelible memories of Cambodia's tragic years; of *Pa* and *Mak*; of Chea, Avy, and Vin, of twenty-eight members of my extended family and countless others who perished. With me, they are safely transported to America, a trip only made possible by Uncle Seng. He is the bridge leading me, Ra, Ry, Than, Map, Savorng, Syla, and *bang* Vantha to freedom. We are like the dust of history being blown away, and Uncle Seng is like the hand that blocks the wind. We are leaving behind Cambodia, ground under the wheel of the Khmer Rouge, and flying to America. There, we will face other challenges, other risks, in a new place in which we will have to redefine ourselves, a kind of reincarnation for us all.